# A HEART FOR AFRICA

## MOIRA COOKE

A Bright Pen Book

Text Copyright © Moira Cooke 2011

Cover design by James Fitt ©

All rights reserved. No part of this publication may be reproduced, stored in a retrieval system, or transmitted in any form or by any means, electronic, mechanical, photocopy, recording or otherwise, without prior written permission of the copyright owner. Nor can it be circulated in any form of binding or cover other than that in which it is published and without similar condition including this condition being imposed on a subsequent purchaser.

British Library Cataloguing Publication Data.
A catalogue record for this book is available from the British Library

ISBN 978-07552-1329-0

Authors OnLine Ltd
19 The Cinques
Gamlingay, Sandy
Bedfordshire SG19 3NU
England

This book is also available in e-book format, details of which are available at
www.authorsonline.co.uk

# DEDICATION

THIS BOOK IS DEDICATED TO

## TRESFORD MWAME . . .

The first starfish rescued and thrown back into the ocean

And to members of . . .

## THE WEDNESDAY HOUSE GROUP . . .

Who helped toss him back in the water!

**NOTE:** All accounts in this book relate solely to the activities of:
THE TANWORTH STARFISH FUND REG. NO. 1101416
They do not relate to any other charities, registered or otherwise, of a
similar name, whether operating in Zambia or elsewhere.

# ACKNOWLEDGEMENTS

My grateful thanks go to the following people for their help and support either in the writing of this book or in the work of **STARFISH**:

To my husband **BOB** for sharing all the thrills and spills of Zambia, and also for his help with proof-reading the text and providing photos.

To my daughter, **ALISON**, for her endless advice on all things Zambian, and for putting up with our presence as well as our long absences in Kitwe and Choma.

To our dear friends **MR MWAPE MBAI** and **MR WILSON CHAMA** for their help on so many of our projects and without whose loyalty, help and support, NOTHING would ever have been achieved!

To all our partner organisations including:
**ALICK NYIRENDA** (former ED) and staff of **CHEP** (Kitwe) and in particular **EVELYN LUMBA, ISAAC MUMBA, NKAZWE MUSUNGAILA, KAI DIMINGO** and **DAMSON CHUNGA**.
**FAITH LYENA** (Director) and **QUISTIN CHALWE** of the **FAITH ORPHANAGE FOUNDATION** and in particular to the orphans and carers of the **CHILUMBA COMMUNITY**.
To **PASTOR JOSEPH MWEWA** (deceased), staff and pupils of **SALEM CENTRE FOR STREET KIDS**, Kitwe

To the following communities who granted us the privilege of adding something to their lives:
The **KAPUTULA** community and staff and pupils of **KAPUTULA COMMUNITY SCHOOL**
**MILDEN CHOONGA** and the **SIMOOYA** community
**CLIVE AND ELMA WIXLEY** for their unbounden hospitality
**CHOMA DHO** including **MR SIMASIKU** and **MR BANDA**
**PASTOR MWEETWA, MR AND MRS KAUSENI**, Deacons,

Deaconesses and congregation of **KAFUBU BAPTIST CHURCH**
**CANON ZULU** and parishioners of **ST MICHAELS KITWE** and **ST ANDREWS CHIBULUMA**
The head teachers, staff and pupils of **MUSONDA COMMUNITY SCHOOL, IPUSUKILO COMMUNITY SCHOOL, KAMAKONDE COMMUNITY SCHOOL, TWATASHA COMMUNITY SCHOOL**

To all the many colourful characters who people the pages of the book and who will live long in our memories including: **TRESFORD, MR BANDA (Musonda), PASTOR BWALIA, ALEX, DYNASS, NKAZWE MUSUNGAILA, MR CHIPOTYO, AUGUSTINE MUMBA, SID, GEORGE, FREDERICK PHIRI, MILDEN, EVELYN, MR CHALWE . . .**

To all our loyal supporters in UK, who, though they may never have been to Zambia, have assisted in changing the lives of so many for ever.
In particular **REV TIM HARMER** and those who served on the **EXECUTIVE COMMITTEE** of the **TANWORTH STARFISH FUND** Members of the **WEDNESDAY HOUSE GROUP** of **ST MARY MAGDALENE, TANWORTH IN ARDEN**, who formed the decision making body, and who devoted so many hours of love, fellowship and loyal support.
The congregation of **HOCKLEY HEATH BAPTIST CHURCH**, and in particular church secretary **DERRICK HANCOCK**, for their spectacular fund-raising.

All the named and unnamed **INDIVIDUALS AND ORGANISATIONS** who have donated to Starfish or who have helped in any way to raise funds.
All individuals as well as local churches, schools and groups in the **HALESWORTH** area who have so readily taken on board the work of Starfish and made its continuance possible in a new area.

And finally . . . **THE STARFISH STORY** as told on numerous occasions is attributed to **Loren Eiseley**.

# CONTENTS

# INTRODUCTION: A BIT OF A LAUGH!

Early in 1968 my husband Bob and I chanced upon an old college friend. . .

"I'm off to Kenya in a couple of months!" Our old friend slapped Bob enthusiastically on the back. "Why don't you give it a go, it'll be a laugh!"

"Just imagine, Africa!" drooled Bob later that same evening and I knew a seed was set to germinate which could change our lives forever.

Thus smitten by the same bug, Bob submitted an application to the Ministry of Overseas Development. In due course he was invited for interview on the understanding that similarly qualified wives would also automatically be offered a job.

The bad news was, there were no vacancies for Geography cum History graduates in Kenya. The good news however was . . . they were crying out for them in Zambia. We dug out the Atlas and located Zambia, a country which, up until then, we'd barely heard of.

"Look, it's bang in the middle of southern Africa!" exclaimed Bob gleefully. "From there we'd be able to visit Rhodesia, Malawi, South Africa, the Congo, Mozambique, Kenya, Tanzania . . ." He reeled off countries as if he was reading from an exotic travel shopping list.

So Zambia it was!

We spent three years there from January 1969 until August 1971. In January 1972 we moved southwards to settle in Rhodesia, Zimbabwe as it later became. We remained there until August 1976. Our son was born in 1970 in Mufulira in Zambia and our daughter in 1972 in Salisbury, now Harare, in Rhodesia. From that point on, our hearts as well as their passports were indelibly stamped with their countries of birth.

In 1976 the Zimbabwean 'struggle for independence' escalated out of all proportion. Travel became impossible. Our lives as well as those of our children were no longer safe. Faced with the prospect of keeping guns in the house or else waking up one morning to find ourselves slaughtered on the front lawn, we conceded that for us, the Africa dream sadly was over.

As we sat in the plane on the tarmac at Salisbury airport, grim faced yet determined not to cry for the sake of our children, Bob said through gritted teeth, "If I *ever* come back to Africa, I will *never* leave it a second time!"

To which I retorted, "Well I am *never, ever* coming back to Africa!"

Such oaths can create impossible conflict. Yet it wasn't difficult for either of us to keep our side. Though we travelled extensively, we never returned to Africa either on holiday or to live during a twenty-six year period.

But 'never' doesn't figure in God's vocabulary. And, we had bargained without our determined daughter who, in 2002, announced she was returning to Zambia on a VSO placement.

"Zambia?" we echoed incredulously. "But that's in . . ."

"Africa, right, and I shall expect you both to visit!"

She subsequently married a Zambian and had two children who, by birth, are one-quarter Zulu and one-quarter Matabele, thus further cementing our relationship with Africa. Our life, as well as that of her family is, for better or for worse, wedded to that of Africa as a whole and of Zambia in particular. Zambia has become our 'second home.'

This book attempts to show how we returned to and rediscovered our 'heart for Africa'. It runs parallel to and compliments my first book, 'Bwanakula Thandi . . . the story of the building of Kaputula School.' It re-introduces many of the characters from the first book and also introduces a host of new ones. However, while 'Bwanakula Thandi' restricted itself solely to the building of Kaputula School, this book deals with our work in community schools and on other Starfish projects there.

While it is true no other project created quite the heartaches and tears of the Kaputula project, it does not mean the others were any less eventful nor lacking in excitement and adventure. And yes, it does return to Kaputula also.

"Africa will be a laugh!" claimed our friend. Well, yes, for us Africa has produced many laughs. But it has also produced many tears as we attempted to discover our calling to help people there. Above all it has produced a treasure chest of memories to share with others.

Happy Reading!

# CHAPTER ONE: ZAMBIAN BY CONCEPTION . . .
## *Thursday December 12<sup>th</sup>, 2002*

Lusaka International Airport at 6.30am. The sky is cloudy and overcast. It's even trying to rain. Well, this is the rainy season, though maybe not rainy seasons as we remember them.

Thirty years ago, living in Zambia, we rose each day to a brilliantly blue sky. Gradually white cotton wool puffs of clouds would appear over the horizon, eventually forming themselves into huge billowing banks of anvil shaped clouds. Finally, unable to contain themselves any longer, they would disgorge their contents onto the hapless and frequently umbrella-less population below.

We never did work out why, in a thunderstorm, Africans remove their shoes and carry them on their heads. The rainy season may well, due to climatic change, have altered its pattern, but I wouldn't mind betting Africans still take off their shoes in a rainstorm and carry them on their heads.

This morning the Lusaka sky looks as grey and drear as any UK rainy day sky. It is even quite cool as we exit the airport terminal to find our daughter waiting to greet us. We pinch ourselves. Is this really the Africa we have not set foot in for twenty-six years, indeed the continent I swore never to set foot on ever again? Or is it merely a dream from which we will rudely awaken to discover this isn't really our daughter working here as a volunteer but some stranger who merely . . .

Standing behind our daughter is a young Zambian just itching to be noticed. Certainly he is a stranger, though the welcome grin splitting his face would indicate he also is expecting us. Is he a boyfriend? A colleague from work? Or simply someone to help carry the luggage?

Ali smiles and kisses us saying, "Welcome to Zambia!" Then turning to her companion announces, "This is Alex."

So, no clues here for two bemused parents. Then because Ali kisses us, Alex kisses us too. I've never kissed an African before, but I suppose in the new Zambia, there's a first time for everything. Certainly kissing Africans wasn't at all the done thing thirty years ago when we lived firstly in Zambia, then later in Rhodesia.

But this isn't the Zambia of thirty years ago; this is the Zambia of here and now. Things have moved on. Maybe white people kissing Zambians is now the norm. Certainly to show any reluctance might not be very well received.

Later that afternoon we meet Ali's work colleagues. She has come out to Zambia as a VSO in order to set up an HIV Aids resource centre in the capital Lusaka. Eventually the information and resource materials stored there will be made available to the whole of Zambia. In Zambia one in five people is HIV+. Until a person develops full blown Aids, there is no way of telling just by looking at them whether that person has the disease or not. Could kissing Zambians carry a certain risk after all?

Ali's colleagues are predominantly Zambian. Almost all are large, fat, cheerful black women dressed in a gaudy array of materials. They are either very wealthy or very healthy or both. In Zambia, where size matters, fatness is a sure indicator not only of a person's health but of their wealth and social status also. Telling someone they are fat is considered a compliment, though it's one I could certainly do without.

The women chorus as one, "Welcome to Zambia!"

We tell them, "It's welcome back to Zambia! We used to live here thirty years ago. In fact our son was born in Mufulira while Alison was born in Harare." I only just remember in time to say Harare and not Salisbury, as the capital of Rhodesia was then known. The name Salisbury perhaps smacks of a dim and distant colonial era best forgotten in the new Zambia.

"So Alison, you are not born in Zambia?" teases one of Alison's colleagues.

"Ah, but she was conceived here," I let slip in a moment of misguided inspiration.

Which revelation produces hoots of laughter and much hand clapping from the assembled women. "So Alison, you are a true Zambian after all!"

"Only just!" I hasten to clarify. I was a mere two months pregnant way back in 1971 when we completed our three year teaching contract in Zambia and moved down to settle in Rhodesia. But why spoil the ladies' pleasure with technicalities. The fact that Alison is Zambian by conception so raises her standing amongst her work colleagues, that everyone loses sight of her true colonial heritage.

That evening Ali, assisted by Alex, prepares dinner. There is still no clue as to his real role. Is he the cook-boy perhaps? *Whoops, yet another politically incorrect word to be avoided at all costs nowadays!*

"Would you like to pick some mangoes for your breakfast?" Ali calls from the kitchen.

Now I really am confused, bowled over by the twin forces of rapidly mounting culture shock combined with sleep deprivation following a ten hours night flight to get here. It is 7pm and pitch darkness reigns outside in the tropical night. Does my daughter seriously intend me to venture outside and shin up a tree in order to pick mangoes for breakfast?

Certainly there is a mango tree outside to the rear of the flats where she is housed. Earlier today some Zambian children were attempting to knock off the ripening mangoes using a long pole. In Africa some things never change. It reminded me of an occasion many moons ago in Mufulira when Bob caught a man in our front garden bag in hand helping himself to ripened guavas from the guava tree.

Selecting his words somewhat more carefully than the man grabbing guavas willy-nilly from our tree, Bob asked what he thought he was doing.

"Oh Baas," the hapless thief replied, "I would not have picked them if I had known you were there!" His air of assumed innocence suggested that it was Bob's sudden appearance on the scene, and not his own complicity, which compounded his crime!

But I am not after all expected to shin up a mango tree in pitch darkness, risking life and limb or the wrath of spitting cobras or whatever else populates mango trees after dark. Instead two young Zambian lads about twelve years old and muffled to the eyeballs against the cold or recognition or both, have appeared at the back door selling mangoes, avocadoes and mealies.

"Did you grow them yourselves?" I ask naively.

"Er, no . . . we just have them." Two pairs of black eyes regard us cagily. while two pairs of spindly black legs are poised ready to scarper should we show any sign of taking matters further.

Perhaps it's better not to ask too many questions. Certainly these two know where to sell their illicit produce . . . to unsuspecting 'mzungus' willing to pay not to have to shin up mango trees in the dark.

In exchange for our unwitting complicity, these two will eat tonight. Not the mangoes, avocadoes or mealies they have with them, because we buy their entire supply. Stolen or otherwise, we'll try not to let it spoil our enjoyment of produce costing a fraction of UK prices. In twenty-first century Zambia, it clearly pays not to ask too many questions.

"Everyone has to get by somehow," shrugs Ali. "Even twelve year old boys . . ."

Over breakfast we attempt to get to know Alex better. Alex is a street kid. Apparently Zambia now has a problem with street kids. There are dozens of them, he tells us, begging on the streets of Lusaka, selling things on street corners, even riding the trains between Lusaka and the Copperbelt.

What is more, Alex considers himself one of the lucky ones. He has received financial help from a friend of Ali's in order to set himself up in business buying things cheaply such as watches and cigarette lighters in Botswana and South Africa, then selling them at a profit back in Zambia. The thought that he may also have resorted to stealing crosses my mind, but then why should he confess that anyways?

"How did you become a street kid?" we ask.

Alex shakes his head dejectedly as if the memory proves painful. "It was because I had a very hard time growing up in Mongu." Mongu is a sandy outpost located about as far west as you can go in Zambia without erring into Angola, which is maybe not such a wise idea.

"It was like this, when my mother died, my father was not willing to bring us children up on his own, so that is why he was looking around for a second wife." More head shaking. "Ah, my stepmother, she was not a good woman. She already had children of her own and naturally she was favouring her own children above the children of my father."

"In what way?"

Alex shrugs non-committally. "You know how it is," he says. "They are getting the lion's share of the food, the best place to sleep in the sleeping hut, while my father's children, all we are getting is, 'Do this, do that!' It was as if we were becoming her servants."

"Are you saying she starved you?"

But Alex is unwilling or unable to go that far. "For me it became impossible to go on living in my father's house so I was sent to live with my uncle. Aieeeh!" Alex's pupils roll heavenwards revealing the whites of his eyes in stark contrast to the smooth black skin. "The beatings, they were terrible, till I was black and blue all over and I can hardly walk."

By now Alex's story has developed a familiar ring, that of Snow White or Cinderella, or indeed that of many modern day dysfunctional families anywhere in the world. His definition of a 'wicked stepmother', or indeed a 'wicked uncle', seems rather vague. There are few specifics. Certainly he seems to have been deprived of essential care such as food, clothing and

6

education, though beating their children is not as frowned on in Zambia as here.

"So you came to Lusaka?"

"Yes," he regains his composure. "Indeed I ran away to Lusaka where I was living on the streets until a friend of Alison found me."

"So how did you survive, that is before Alison's friend came to your rescue?"

Another vague shrug, "By my wits," he says with a disarming grin and a flash of white teeth. "When I had money I bought and sold some things to make more money. Sometimes I guarded the 'mzungus' cars at Manda Hills shopping centre. When all else failed sometimes I had to beg for food."

"And now?"

"Now Alison's friend is helping me . . . and Alison," he adds as an afterthought, the help being from her meagre VSO's allowance.

"So you're doing okay now?" we can't help asking.

Alex looks not so sure. What is okay? His understanding of okay seems as vague as his concept of the wicked stepmother and the wicked uncle of fairy tales. He gets up and leaves the breakfast table in order to get himself more coffee.

Bob and I glance at each other. "Do we give him something?" I murmur.

Now Bob shrugs. "Search me."

"But what would we give him? Cash?"

Bob shakes his head emphatically.

"Food then?"

"I think he's getting enough of that here already!" Bob nods towards what remains of the breakfast mangoes.

"Do we offer to help him with his business then?"

"Search me! Besides, I'm not sure he's our responsibility."

"So whose is he?"

We sit in profound silence pondering just whose responsibility Alex is. In the end we offer him nothing. No money, no food, no help. Mainly because we're not sure what we're dealing with.

When we lived here before, Zambia never had a street kid problem. Why should it have one now? Why, on the continent which invented the extended family, should Alex or any other child take to scratching, begging or stealing for a living on the streets? We are confused and out of our depths.

No, we are not so naïve as to suppose that in thirty years things have not changed in Zambia. Nevertheless we never anticipated coming face to face with the dilemma of what to do with a street kid barely twenty-four hours after arrival.

But heck, we've only come here for a holiday, a sentimental trip down memory lane. What has Alex and his ilk to do with that? What can Zambia and its attendant problems possibly have to do with us? In barely three weeks' time we'll be out of here, on a plane back to the UK leaving Zambia and its problems for others to sort out. Certainly not for us, definitely not for us!

## CHAPTER TWO: A QUESTION OF GRACE AND HOW TO THINK POSITIVELY . . . *Friday December 13<sup>th</sup>, 2002*

Today is Friday the thirteenth, our second full day back in Zambia. It is also an important day because we are to meet for the first time a young man named Tresford Mwame.

Tresford is a part time gardener at the offices where Ali works. He is also HIV+, but unable to afford the cost of antiretroviral drugs necessary to manage the disease. Following an appeal from Ali to the Wednesday House Group, which currently meets at our house in Tanworth in Arden, members of the house group have agreed to fund Tresford's treatment at a cost of £55 per month. In 2002 private treatment is the only reliable form of Aids treatment available in Zambia. Without it Tresford would die.

So the important moment has arrived to meet Tresford. He is a nervous young man with a sniff and twitch, very thin but with a ready grin, which stretches almost from ear to ear. We also meet a young woman named Chilufya who also works for the organisation. Tresford has already taken the momentous step of testing and admitting he is HIV+. However, although Chilufya is stick thin, indicating she may also be positive, she has so far refused to be tested.

In Zambia, HIV Aids is a major problem. It is compounded by the stigmatisation of those known to be suffering from the disease. As long as a person doesn't submit to the test, then in their eyes they continue to be negative. The moment a person tests positive, they face rejection from friends, family and employers alike. In particular, young unmarried women may be cast out onto the streets by their families. Chilufya is gaunt to the point where her trousers hang on empty limbs. Though still pretty, her eyes are heavily shaded by drooping eyelids, while her hair is almost non-existent. How long can she survive without knowing whether she needs treatment?

"Ah, you are good people paying for my treatment," Tresford grips our hands between his own clammy palms. Tresford also suffers from malaria, TB and has frequent lung and chest infections as well as sores and ulcers on his body. "One day I will be big and strong once more."

This is hard to imagine given both he and Chilufya resemble walking skeletons. Yet such thoughts remain unspoken. Instead we say as brightly as we can, "That would be good."

"In fact I am so delighted that you are paying for my treatment, I would like to take you to Kalingalinga to meet my parents."

"Er . . .um . . ." I turn to Bob for inspiration. *An escape route preferably. Surely Tresford is joking?*

Kalingalinga is an African compound and as such largely uncharted and scary ground. When we lived here before, African compounds were for Africans and considered off-limits except for a small minority of workers such as police, nuns, priests and their ilk. 'Mzungus' on the other hand lived in neat tree-lined suburbs. Besides, we are currently driving around in an expensive 4x4 hired vehicle, perhaps not the best vehicle for sorties into African compounds.

But how to get out of this one? There isn't any real excuse other than: we don't want to go, or we don't feel safe going there. But then a wee small voice whispers tantalisingly, 'Come on, Moira, call yourself a writer? How many writers get the opportunity to enter an African compound? After all, it's not on the average tourist itinerary.' And the wee small voice wins.

Tresford on the other hand is delighted to be riding high in the 'mzungus' hired vehicle. He climbs in front in order to guide Bob to Kalingalinga compound. I sit behind reflecting, there has to be a first for everything . . . kissing an African, sleeping under the same roof as one and now heading out to a compound. Twenty-four hours into a trip intended merely as a trip down memory lane, I'd not expected to head into the unknown hazards of an African compound. The expression 'baptism by fire' springs unbidden to mind.

Leaving the area around the Cathedral where Ali's office is located, we immediately enter another world. Suddenly everyone's livelihood depends upon the side of the road where a veritable hive of activity is underway, everything from making and selling doors and beds and tables to complete suites of furniture in lurid shades of green, purple and tan. Women are busy chipping rocks into gravel by hand, while piles of chipped stones, sand and gravel stand ready for would-be builders to buy. Dotted here and there amongst the carpentry and building materials, children sometimes as young as six or seven or women with babies tied on their backs, sell piles of over-ripened fruit and vegetables crawling with flies. The whole scenario is bizarrely punctuated with signs advertising coffins for sale. Literally: Get your coffin here! Best price in town! Not to be beaten!

Driving though these unfamiliar scenes, Tresford enlightens us as to what it means to be HIV+, the reality of living with Aids and of the effect it has had upon his family. It is difficult to imagine the same conversation back in the UK where Aids still remains a taboo subject.

Not so with Tresford, he seems bent on proving that people can and do live with this terrible virus. He shares the most intimate details of his illness as if he was relating the tale of a bad bout of flu.

"In fact myself, I am also a counsellor for people living with Aids," he announces proudly.

"So what does that involve?"

"Where there is a person who is thinking of testing, but is not sure whether that is the right thing for them to do, then I will tell them to go ahead and that it is possible to live with the disease."

"How is that possible?" Tresford is amongst the lucky few whose treatment is being funded privately. Government supplies are currently erratic, so that even if a person knows their status, there is no guarantee that they will receive the treatment they need from a government clinic.

"Firstly it is important to have a good and balanced diet," Tresford explains, "and not just 'nshima' all the time. They must eat plenty of fresh fruit and vegetables and some little protein. Then they must take some small exercise like walking or playing a little football. Me, I also am playing football. Which team do you support?" he shoots at us suddenly.

We demur, not being great fans of football.

"Ah, David Beckham," raves Tresford oblivious to any lack of enthusiasm on our part, "one day maybe I get to see the great David Beckham play football in the UK."

"Maybe . . ."

"Then it is important for a person with the illness to think positively. Indeed, that is our message, think positive! A positive state of mind will keep a sufferer in good health for longer."

As opposed to thinking negatively? This is all so unreal. I've never met, shaken hands with, let alone sat in a vehicle holding a conversation with a person with Aids before, nor discussed their needs and agreed to meet their family. Where is all this leading? Is this really careful, cautious Moira who never takes a single risk with her health?

We turn off the main tarmac and plough into the uncharted depths of Kalingalinga. Immediately the vehicle becomes the subject of great interest. Round eyed and barefoot children race after it on skinny legs. Women stare in blatant curiosity, while men in apologies for clothes weigh up the odds. I don't suppose they see many 'mzungus' in 4x4s down their street. Hardly surprising given the potholes and trenches and running open sewers the hired Toyota Hi-Lux contends with as it heaves and lurches its way to our destination. Jeremy Clarkson rated this vehicle indestructible. Maybe he didn't test it over the potholed roads of an African compound!

The Toyota grinds to a halt outside Tresford's family home. No imaginatively named 'Dunromin' or 'Four Oaks' here, but merely house number B4/82/24 in a road of houses all drearily and depressingly the same. On the other hand, neither is it a shack and it's certainly not as bad as we might have feared. But then, we have yet to go inside.

Grace, Tresford's mother, is waiting on the concrete doorstep to greet us. She is clad in a red skirt and yellow blouse with a blue headscarf tied around her tight black springy curls. "Welcome, welcome!" she exclaims though her expression says the rest for her . . . If this is the first time we have *ever* been inside an African's house, then it is also the first time Grace has entertained a 'mzungu' in hers!

Is it coincidence perhaps that her name is Grace? There but for the grace of God . . . Could her name possibly be an omen? I dismiss such fanciful thoughts. A half an hour should see us through, then back to civilisation . . .

Grace clutches my hand, at the same time drawing me inside her humble home. "God has indeed sent you to us today!" she says reassuringly.

Grace's words carry such conviction, how could we possibly doubt them? I want to say, 'Hang on a minute, God didn't send us, we came of our own accord.' Yet suddenly it's become difficult to swallow. The words simply won't emerge. Is it possible we have been sent here, indeed to Zambia, for a purpose? If so, God might have given us an inkling of the plan beforehand. And how come Grace enjoys privileged knowledge we were denied? Does she have a direct line to the Almighty?

Conversation is stilted. Grace doesn't have much English, while Tresford's loquacity has temporarily dried up. I survey the room in which we are seated. Clearly this is their best room and a lot of time and effort, though sadly not money, have gone into its appearance. Despite the smoke-blackened walls, the uneven concrete floor and the shabby, faded upholstery, there is nevertheless an air of 'best-ness' about it. In one corner stands a glass cabinet full of prized possessions, while in another stands an electric fan. Over the doorway hangs a framed photograph of an austere looking Zambian in an ill-fitting suit. Tresford's father perhaps?

One by one silent figures slip in from the dim shadows beyond the living room to be presented to and shake hands with the 'mzungus'. No-one has suggested viewing these other rooms. Altogether sixteen people share four rooms. Apart from the parents, Tresford and his brothers and sisters, there is a widowed sister and her children plus a couple of orphans they have taken in. God alone knows how they sleep, let alone survive. Tresford and his father are the only two with employment. However Tresford's is part-time, while his father's is only occasional piece work.

But then God alone seems to have the answer. The house is bursting at the seams. Its inmates have little besides poverty and the stubborn will to survive. So quite why God has dragged us into all this remains to be seen. A quick half hour and we'll be away. So the house group funds Tresford's treatment? But really, that's no big deal. Plenty of Christian groups do no more and some even less.

Half a dozen coca-colas and a packet of biscuits appear as if by magic. There is not quite enough coke to go around and younger children must do without. They eye the drinks enviously before slinking back into the shadows deprived of their treat. Yet this must be the way they decided to play it.

Nevertheless, it seems impossible to leave this situation without giving something over and above the fifty-five pounds per month already being paid for Tresford's treatment. But how much to give? I hand over a fifty thousand kwacha note. This may seem a lot to them, but is in fact barely seven pounds, the equivalent of one third of Tresford's monthly wage packet. No wonder he can't afford to pay his treatment.

The gaseous bubbles from the coke lie uneasily along with a growing suspicion that, not only do we not know why we are here today, but we really have no idea why we are back in Africa at all. Twenty-six years ago God quite firmly shut that door in our faces. Why then should he now choose to reopen it, if not for some purpose as yet not revealed?

In the dim and dingy recesses of Grace's home, for the first time I suspect there is indeed a bigger picture and that we might even be part of it. In spite of the rainy season humidity, the Spirit suddenly moves. I suppress a shiver. Tresford is one of thousands of Aids victims in Zambia. The two orphans cared for by his family are a mere drop in the ocean of Zambia's orphan crisis. Conservative estimates place the numbers of orphaned children at between 700 000 and one million. Alex is only one of hundreds of street kids. What business is all this of two past their prime 'mzungus' helpless in the face of such suffering and with barely a charitable bone between them?

The feeling of helplessness persists throughout the rest of the day, so that we retire to bed bamboozled by the whole desperate situation. Surely God in his wisdom doesn't expect *us* to tackle this mess?

Thirty years ago we used to joke, 'You can't control Africa, it controls you!' Now thirty years later Africa is at it again. Africa is controlling our footsteps, guiding our decisions before we've even had time to shake the dust of arrival from our sandals.

God alone knows where all this is leading. I only pray he has some inkling. And to think, we only agreed to come back to Zambia for a holiday!

# CHAPTER THREE: OF CHIMPANZEES AND AN INTRODUCTION TO CHEP...
## *Sunday December 15th, 2002*

Many people mistakenly believe the work of Starfish is connected to the work our daughter does in Zambia. True, God may have used our daughter as a catalyst in order to draw us back once more to the continent we left in 1976, swearing never to set foot there again.

True, the house group began paying for treatment for Tresford and continued to do so for several years. But following the initial contact with our daughter's organisation, there the association with her work ended.

So how did the real work of Starfish begin?

At the time of this first return visit to Zambia in December 2002, I was church rep for Christian Aid. Prior to the trip an intriguing letter arrived inviting Christian Aid reps to visit third world projects at their own expense. Fares were already paid to Zambia and a round robin trip visiting haunts old and new planned. Surely there was a Christian Aid project somewhere in Zambia we could simply 'drop in' on, then drive off into the sunset. I contacted Christian Aid headquarters in London.

For sure Christian Aid had partners in Zambia. They would be delighted to put me in contact with one. In fact the director of one of their Zambia projects just happened to be in London at that time.

I spoke to Alick Nyirenda, Executive Director of CHEP, the Copperbelt Health Education Project, which is based in Kitwe. Kitwe just happened to be on our itinerary, because thirty odd years ago we lived not thirty miles away from there. Moreover Kitwe possessed the only suitable hotel for us to stay in, in order to revisit the area.

For sure Alick would be pleased to welcome us to the project. We discussed dates and times and agendas. Unfortunately our only full day in Kitwe fell on a Sunday. Blink, and you miss us. If it's Sunday, it's Kitwe, Monday, we were travelling on to Kasanka Game Reserve. Alick wasn't fazed. Sunday or not, he would be pleased to welcome us in the late afternoon, after church commitments were fulfilled by those members of staff involved.

Which left one small dilemma . . . how to fill a Sunday in Kitwe when, for us, church that particular Sunday was not on the agenda?

The Rough Guide to Zambia recommended a visit to the Chimfunshi Wildlife Orphanage some 60 km west of the neighbouring town of Chingola, making a round trip of 200km. "But the road is good," we were told.

We set off later than expected. Chingola lies at the end of one of the few main roads out of Kitwe and is not that hard to find. What takes more time is finding the road out of Chingola to Solwezi. There are few if any road signs in Zambia. Either you know where you are going or it's the luck of the draw which road you take. You can of course ask somebody walking along the side of the road. However, since most people walking along the side of the road are doing so because they don't possess a car, then asking for directions is largely a waste of time, since they don't know where any other town is unless they've been there.

So we rely on the luck of the draw and end up taking a road that leads to the Democratic Republic of the Congo. Maybe not the best place for a Sunday jaunt. How do we know this? Because many years ago, when we lived in Zambia, off this road lay one of the locality's few beauty spots known as the Hippo Pool. Whether there were Hippos in it or not is debatable. There were certainly crocs in it, because the story was told of the man who threw a stick in there for his dog to retrieve. The dog never came back because a croc ate him. Maybe it should have been called the Crocodile Pool.

One quick glimpse as we flash past of a now largely overgrown Hippo Pool reveals we are on the wrong road. We backtrack to Chingola, before bandits from the DRC claim their prize. We attempt once more to locate the Solwezi road off which the trail to Chimfunshi lies. Amazingly when we find it, it is a single strip but fast and newly tarred road. We make good time to the Chimfunshi turn off which is clearly signposted and hard to miss.

However once off the tar, the road surface deteriorates. The speedometer shows barely 18kph. At this rate we'll be lucky to make it to Chimfunshi by midday. As it's taken three hours to get this far, we toss up the odds of getting back in time for a 16.00 appointment with Alick Nyirenda at Chep.

But there's always that small voice needling, 'Having gone this far, don't give up now!'

So we press valiantly on through dense bush with branches scraping the sides of the vehicle and the thought that anything could be out there. We are as deep into the Zambian bush as it's possible to be.

Just as we give up all thought of finding anything buried so far away from civilisation, a barred and fenced property indicates we're there. And if we have any last doubts, the hideous screeching and growling and banging coming from numerous caged chimpanzees all demanding their lunch, banishes these last doubts. We have arrived at lunchtime. Roast beef and Yorkshire pudding it may not be, but these guys sure want lunch.

The Chimfunshi Wildlife Orphanage was set up in 1983 by David and Sheila Siddle. It is a non-profit making refuge for sick and wounded animals. However its main residents are almost one hundred chimps rescued from poachers seeking to sell them as pets. Some were rescued from a life of misery as pets who grew too large. Others are zoo and circus rejects from around the world. The aim is to create as close an environment as possible to their native environment, with the ultimate hope of re-introducing suitable candidates to almost wild conditions. Sadly that is not the case with all of them, hence the lunchtime din from those who, for reasons of safety or insecurity, still remain in cages.

We are reminded that this refuge is not primarily a tourist attraction. Chimps and their feeding times come first. Though caged, many of the chimps remain rather too close for comfort as we pass via their cages on a narrow walkway. One irate customer, *'Hey, why leave me till last!'* lashes out with a stick as we pass by his cage. The stick catches Ali on the corner of her mouth, splitting her lip. Instantly it gushes blood.

"Are you okay?" Too late we realise what has happened.

"I think so." Blood spatters the hankie I pass her. "Maybe he mistook me for a mate," she jokes.

"Well, if that's his way of being friendly, I'd hate to encounter him when he's cross."

"*She* actually," says Sheila Siddle, the owner, coming across to see what the commotion is about. "Are you okay?"

Ali assures her she is fine and we continue the tour, this time keeping a safe distance from caged chimps and a wary eye for further advances, mating or otherwise.

Apart from the Siddle family, all the keepers are Zambian and have established an amazing bond with the chimps, fondling them and allowing themselves to be fondled even kissed. No health and safety regulations here then! The chimps are served meals of fruit and raw vegetables, followed

17

by tin mugs of milk for the younger ones who drain the cups dry then bang them on the sides of the cages begging for more of the same.

At the current time there are ninety-seven chimps at the centre. If we had more time we could visit the enclosures where conditions as close as possible to the wild have been established. Though these chimps are far removed now from their natural family groups, it is still in their nature to bond. When alternative family groups have been established, they are relocated into semi-natural conditions from which, being naturally good climbers, they could take off into the wild.

Sheila Siddle hovers by. "Are you sure you're okay?" she asks Ali once more. Perhaps even here the long arm of the compensation culture has reached and she fears we may sue her. We wouldn't, but then she doesn't know that. "Perhaps you'd like to see the photos of our early days?" she suggests.

We are making our way towards the shelter of her veranda when suddenly a commotion erupts rivalling that of an armoured tank coming through. To our shock a fully grown hippo charges onto the scene. Ali and I dive for cover behind Bob who tries valiantly to stare down the charging hippo.

"Oh no!" exclaims Sheila. "Someone's let Billy out again."

Billy is the resident hippo who thinks *she* is one of the family. She was named after one of her rescuers before her sex had been determined. Maybe her name should be spelt 'Billie'?

Billy was raised in the Siddle house along with the dogs until she became too large for the family bath and broke the settee by crashing down on it. Now she is supposed to be kept shut away when the centre is open to visitors who don't take kindly to the sudden appearance of a fully grown hippo charging in their direction.

When Billy is safely rounded up once more, we sit on the veranda of the Siddle family home enjoying a private viewing of photos of the early days, when the Siddle family first settled on the remote farmstead on the banks of the Kafue river.

Time is marching inexorably forward. It took us three hours to get here. It is now 13.30. If we are to have any hope whatsoever of keeping our appointment with Alick Nyirenda at 16.00 we must leave now. Fortunately we don't deviate via the DRC or the Hippo Pool on the way back.

Hot, sweaty, dusty and with a raging thirst we reach Kitwe's Edinburgh Hotel at five minutes to four. We race upstairs to the foyer to find Alick cool as a cucumber already waiting for us. He is still in his Sunday best, yet rather incongruously wearing trainers on his feet.

"Welcome, welcome to Zambia!" he greets us. Though he is doubtless used to dealing with 'mzungus', he must be reflecting we are amongst the most dishevelled he has ever met.

We mutter our apologies and dash up yet more stairs in order to satisfy the call of nature and gulp down some water. Shaken but not stirred, we rejoin Alick in the foyer.

"You are indeed most welcome," he starts all over again. "So, we can proceed with our programme?"

It is five minutes past four. We are mortified by our lateness. Yet if we had any inkling at that time how many hours we were destined in the future to spend waiting around in Chep's offices for things to happen, for trucks to arrive, for money to be paid out, for colleagues to appear, for interminable meetings to start, we might have felt marginally less apologetic.

But at this time we still have no idea where destiny is set to lead us. We are simply off to spend a pleasant afternoon hearing about the good works of a partner organisation of Christian Aid. Something to tell folks back home.

We troop downstairs once more and back into our car to drive two minutes away to Chep headquarters located in Diamond Drive. We pass by the African Market which, being Sunday, is virtually deserted.

"I would advise you not to go in there," warns Alick.

Not that we have any intention of so doing. Nevertheless I ask politely, "Oh, why's that?"

"Because cholera is rife in there. There is no running water and no proper sanitation for any of the sellers in there. You would be well advised to stay clear of the place."

I store up this information for future reference. But then at this stage we have no plans to return to Kitwe, nor to make forays into the market there. *If we but knew . . .*

"So, we turn left here and right here and we are there."

Alick indicates a drive leading into what was once an unprepossessing mine manager's bungalow of the colonial era, of which there are a multitude remaining, not only in Kitwe, but in the neighbouring towns of Mufulira, Chingola, Ndola, Luanshya and Kalulushi. Though it looks like somebody's dwelling, it was acquired by Chep as their headquarters.

Standing in front of the bungalow is a motley collection of Zambians. There is a hugely tall and clearly well-fed guy with wrinkly hair by the name of Isaac Mumba. Beside him stands a small lady in a long black evening skirt who is introduced as Olive Sichanga, Alick's secretary. There is an unprepossessing but well-spoken gentleman named Weston Mutale Bowa and finally a small dumpy lady with her hair scraped up on top of her head into a pineapple shaped grenade which looks set to detonate any moment. Since her grin splits her face, we hope it doesn't pull the pin. "You are most welcome," she says. "My name in Evelyn Lumba."

Secretly we are bowled over by this reception committee. It is Sunday afternoon, a time for family and friends. Yet five members of Chep staff, including the director, have turned up to welcome us. *Heavens, I hope they don't imagine we're more important than we actually are!*

They give us a guided tour of their offices. As we reach each individual office the member of staff concerned treats us to a spiel about their particular area of expertise. There is so much I shan't remember half of it, and, not having brought a notebook, nor can I write it down. I pray I will at least remember the gist when writing up my travel diary that evening. But then, given its dramatic content, how could we forget?

We are introduced to facets of life in Zambia about which we had no idea. If any lingering doubts remain since our arrival three short days ago that things have drastically changed in the country we once lived in, then these last doubts are dispelled that Sunday afternoon at Chep. Information overload? We are saturated with facts and figures to the point of drowning in a sea of misery and need . . .

- Almost one million children orphaned in Zambia as a result of the HIV Aids crisis
- Children as young as eleven and twelve heading up families where both parents have died
- Or taking to the streets of Lusaka and Kitwe because they can't live with their grief or their responsibilities
- 50% of girls in rural areas excluded from school because of caring for families or lack of funds
- Community schools in both rural and town areas which provide basic education for orphans and vulnerable children who fall outside the supposedly free state system
- One in five sexually active adults infected with the virus
- The diabolical role of traditional healers in spreading the disease by themselves impregnating supposedly infertile wives or by disgusting practices such as bloodletting
- And more . . .

"Wow, we really had no idea things were so bad," we rise to the surface and gasp for air.

"Not all is doom and gloom," points out Alick. "For example the rate of HIV transmission between adults is beginning to show signs of falling for the first time. Of course if we could really inculcate the habit here of zero grazing . . ."

"Zero grazing?" *Exactly how did we deviate to the subject of livestock?*

"Yes," continues Alick unaware of our confusion and ignorance. "Meaning a man is encouraged to have sex only with his wife or long term partner."

"Ah!"

"Then of course if he can be encouraged to fire blank bullets . . ."

But this is beyond us . . .

"Use contraception of course," Alick explains, bemused at our sheer lack of knowledge.

"And the adolescent level also is declining," adds Evelyn who is very fired up about her subject, even threatening to pop the pin of her grenade which wobbles alarmingly. Evelyn is in charge of Gender and Advocacy which department deals mainly with children, an area more interesting to us than for example that of health and safety on the mines with which Isaac Mumba deals.

"It would be so interesting to see some of your work," I murmur to Evelyn in a momentary lull. Though actually what I want is a pee and another long drink of something very cold. Any order will do.

"Ah, it is a shame that you have come on a Sunday," reveals Evelyn. "Sunday is the one day we do not go out into the field. "

*Are we back in with the cows again?* But no, 'in the field' means out amongst the nitty gritty of working with orphans and vulnerable children in community schools both in African compounds and rural areas.

"But maybe you are free to come out with us tomorrow?" she asks eagerly.

"Sadly tomorrow we leave Kitwe. We're travelling on up into the north of Zambia." *Blink and you miss us on our whistle-stop tour of haunts old and new. This is a holiday after all.*

"Maybe another time," one of us mutters politely. Ah but, who said it? Was it Bob? Or me?

"Yes next time," agrees Alick gleefully as if he has just hooked a very large fish. So he heard it also. Strange, because I don't recall saying it and Bob is looking very much as if he didn't say it either.

21

"You must inform us when next you are coming to Zambia and we will arrange a programme for you to visit our projects in community schools."

Later over mutton byriani and poppadums in the Edinburgh Hotel, we share thoughts on what a day it's been.

"Orphans all round," quips Bob, "what with chimps and child-headed families."

"There's hardly any comparison," our daughter waspishly reminds him.

"Still, it would be nice to do something to help them," I muse.

"What, the chimps or the children?" Ali is still nursing a bruised lip. Understandably she's not feeling so well disposed towards chimps right now.

"The children I guess," says Bob. "But darned if I'd know where to start."

"Uh-huh," I agree overwhelmed with tiredness and a full stomach. "At least if we ever do pay a return visit to Chep, I'll make sure next time I'm properly dressed for the occasion, not hot, sweaty and dirty after a day out in the bush. There's such a thing as keeping up appearances, isn't there?"

"Too right," agrees Bob. "Though I'd have thought making sure we're there on a weekday is pretty important too. We wouldn't want to miss going out in the field now would we?"

"And why's that then?" I ask, for the moment too tired to care.

"Well, you never know what might come of it, do you," he responds.

And, though we did not know it at that moment, never a truer word was spoken. We had no idea at all what was to come from an idle promise to come back one day and venture out into that same field.

# CHAPTER FOUR: OUT IN THE FIELD, or down into a bottomless pit! . . . *Tuesday 22nd July, 2003*

Seven months later and this our second return trip to Zambia feels like a homecoming. But can this really be so? Though we shed genuine tears on leaving Zimbabwe in 1976, neither of us shed a single tear when we quit Zambia in 1971. Yet here we are, less than a year and back again!

Zambia, home of Zamchick, Zambeef, Zamseed and Zamswipe, a crop irrigation firm, which makes irrigation sprinklers so vast they stretch from one side of an entire field to another. Now Zambia looks like becoming our second home for a few years to come.

However this is no holiday. This trip we have arrived armed with both a programme and a purpose. Copious emails between ourselves and Chep have led to us bringing 250 school bags filled with pens, pencils, rubbers, rulers, sharpeners and notebooks intended as gifts to needy children in community schools.

We have also agreed to provide desks to a community school selected by Chep. We however will select which one of six schools will receive the bags of school materials. Hence a programme grandly entitled:

## PROGRAMME FOR THE VISIT TO CHEP BY STARFISH PROJECT REPRESENTATIVES

**MONDAY:**
AM - TRAVEL LUSAKA TO KITWE
PM - ARRIVAL & CHECK IN AT EDINBURGH HOTEL (A Stranger only once!)

**TUESDAY:**
AM - MEETING WITH CHEP MANAGEMENT/VISIT TO CHEP UNITS/VISIT TO TYFOTAP CENTRE RE MAKING OF DESKS

PM - VISIT TO MUSONDA COMMUNITY SCHOOL

**WEDNESDAY:**
AM – VISIT TO MCHINKA COMMUNITY SCHOOL/ DISTRICT OFFICES
PM – VISIT TO KAPUTULA COMMUNITY SCHOOL

**THURSDAY:**
AM – VISIT TO IPUSUKILO COMMUNITY SCHOOL/ VISIT TO COMMUNITY SCHOOL FOR CHILDREN OF PARENTS WITH MENTAL ILLNESS
PM – VISIT TO KAMAKONDE COMMUNITY SCHOOL

**FRIDAY:**
AM – DEBRIEFING AT CHEP
PM – RETURN TO LUSAKA

Goodness, this all makes Starfish sound very official!

Since our visit last Christmas, along with the Wednesday House Group, Starfish has raised enough money to buy the bags of school materials plus funding for the desks. There is currently £600 in the Starfish Bank account in the UK. Yet one thing niggles . . . does Chep, which boasts as its overseas partners such 'biggies' on the charity playing field as Christian Aid, Norad and Unicef, perhaps mistakenly believe Starfish is in the same league?

On Tuesday morning bright and early we present ourselves at Chep. This time we are not only punctual, but also presentably dressed. We are also equipped with notepads and biros in order to write everything down. In other words we look the part, even if we don't entirely feel the part.

The morning begins with endless visits to the same departments and offices we toured last Christmas. Eventually we wonder if we will *ever* get out into what Evelyn so tantalisingly called 'the field.'

The tour ends in the Accounts Department where we sign over a fistful of travellers' cheques brought to finance the making of the school desks. Hands are shaken, photos taken, making it all very official. Why then do I experience a momentary stab of unease . . . *Heavens, this is other people's hard earned money we are parting company with. Do we really know what we are doing?* Then I smile as the camera clicks, the deed is done and the moment is recorded for posterity.

"Of course we have facilities here at Chep for receiving money any time you should wish to send it for programmes, yes please," enthuses Evelyn.

"Is that so . . ." I respond cagily.

"For example, should you wish to set up child sponsorship programmes, you can send the money directly from the UK into the Chep bank account."

"I don't think as yet we really have any intention of going down . . ."

"For which we would provide regular half yearly or quarterly updates. Even myself I would see to it."

*Whoa, hang on a minute! Evelyn is racing ahead faster than a racehorse on a winning streak while we're still under starter's orders . . .*

"Plus we can send photos of what Starfish money is spent on via email."

"Is that so?" Evelyn's exuberance makes Starfish sound a lot more official than is the case. And what about us, two very green charity workers who walked into these offices at 9am this morning? Can Chep really have no inkling that we have never done anything like this before? Apart that is from shoving envelopes through people's doors for Christian Aid Week!

"But for now we must go to where they are making the school desks for you." Evelyn carries on regardless of our faithless thoughts.

So this is it, finally out into the field. Shivers of excitement course down the length of my spine. The desks are being made at a centre called TYFOTAP, a community based programme located in one of Kitwe's many African compounds. Tyfotap provides literacy and training skills for women and youths. Its motto is: THINK, ACT, REFLECT, REFORM. Any profit from the construction of desks and other items is ploughed back into the project.

The carpentry workshop is run by Mr Justice Katungulu who is so proud of the skills he is imparting there, that he feels impelled to tell us all about his project, show us not only what is being made, but also photos of everything which has been made there probably since its inception.

Time is ticking by with no sign of any let up in Mr Katungulu's spiel. Worse, any time he does pause for breath and before I have time to butt in with, *'I really think we should . . .'* Bob asks *yet* another question which causes Mr Katungulu, grateful for such an avid audience, to launch forth *yet* again.

Eventually we corner him at the spot where Starfish desks are under construction. The desks are assembled as an all in one construction incorporating seat and desk. Each desk will seat up to three children during the morning session and a further three for the afternoon session. Thus they are well worth the investment of sixteen pounds per desk.

"As you can see, ten desks will be ready for tomorrow," explains Mr Katungulu.

We run a hand along the as yet unvarnished and uncompleted desks assessing the workmanship. There still seems to be a way to go even before these first ones are completed. "And the others?" I ask tentatively.

"Ah, for sure they will be ready by Friday."

"Which is good!" exclaims Evelyn delightedly. "That means you will be able to hand them over at Musonda on Friday." Musonda is the community school selected by Chep to receive the desks, though we have as yet to visit it for the first time this afternoon. Hence an almost indecent haste to get out of here and away ever deeper into the field!

"But will there be time on Friday?" Our packed programme states there is to be a debriefing at Chep before the 250 mile drive back down to Lusaka. And we certainly don't want to be travelling that road in darkness.

"For sure there will be time," says Evelyn encouragingly. We are quickly learning one fact . . . Evelyn makes time for *everything*.

Back at Chep we have barely ten minutes in which to wolf down disgusting 'vegetable' sandwiches specially made for us by the chef at the Edinburgh Hotel. Maybe it is the fact that he has made them literally with cold cooked vegetables from last night's dinner and not with lettuce, tomato and cucumber as requested. Could this represent a serious communication problem between ourselves and the hotel catering staff? Let's hope Mr Katungulu has understood somewhat better our insistence that the desks are ready by Friday.

The vegetable sandwiches are lying heavily as we finally head for Musonda Community School in Musonda compound. The approach to the compound lies along tree-lined streets of neat bungalows behind high fencing and security gates. However we are soon off the beaten track and bumping along a narrow dirt road leading into the compound. Small houses stand cramped one against another between which narrow tracks thread their way in an endless maze. Children race ragged and barefoot out of houses and yards, then stand and stare at the novelty of a vehicle scattering chickens and dogs alike in its passing. Dust and dirt and litter and filth abound, creating an overwhelming air of dejection and extreme poverty. It's very different from the hive of activity in Kalingalinga compound where Tresford and his family live.

The school is located in a converted beer hall, which still has all the appearance of a beer hall. As if the transition to community school proved one step too far and it prefers to wear its former identity like a favourite overcoat. Though doubtless a lack of funding has far more to do with the appalling state of disrepair into which it has fallen.

We enter through a narrow doorway, along a dark and dingy corridor before squeezing into a poky room no larger than a small bathroom. The head teacher, Mr Banda, wears an air of sleepy indifference. He has no proper desk. Paint peels from the walls and the floor is bare and uneven concrete. In the corner stands a second hand photocopier, which seems encouraging till we learn the school has no electricity, along with no running water and no sanitation.

Yet there are more than 700 children on roll here. Of these 568 are orphans and of these 212 are double orphans, that is children with both parents dead. A total of 248 are classed as vulnerable because of poverty, disease or abuse . . . and sometimes incredibly because of all three.

To cope with this nightmare scenario, the school runs a two shift day from 07.30 until 17.00. Half of the pupils attend in the morning and half in the afternoon. There are only six teachers, some of whom work both shifts, while some only work afternoons. Not one of them, including Mr Banda himself, is qualified. They do not receive any salary from the government. However Chep pays them a monthly incentive of about eight pounds.

"But it is not enough!" Mr Banda shakes his head sorrowfully, then eyes us expectantly. "In fact I am behind with my rent and the landlord says he will evict me, for sure, at the end of the month if I do not pay."

However we do not let ourselves become sidetracked by this issue, and instead ask him what the immediate needs of the school might be?

"Textbooks," he exclaims immediately. "We have only one textbook for Maths, one for English and one for Science for the entire school. Always the teachers are complaining because they have to share this one book."

"Do none of the children have textbooks?" I ask naively.

Mr Banda looks at me as if I have taken leave of my senses. "Then there are exercise books," he says. "The children don't have exercise books."

"Also we need pegboards and desks, at least 60 to 70 desks," adds one of the teachers who have joined us inside the cramped head's room where we are sitting knees touching. It's all too close for comfort and certainly too close to the very real problems here at Musonda School.

"Maybe you saw our staff-room as you came in?" asks another laughing.

Indeed we did. The staff-room was in fact the narrow unlit passageway overshadowed by the monstrosity of a rusty and long since defunct water tank which we were forced to squeeze past in order to reach the head's room.

27

We remind them that the first desks will be arriving on Friday, while mentally we resolve to try to do something to solve the chronic shortage of exercise books. A source of textbooks can perhaps also be investigated.

"And a room divider would be good," reveals Mr Banda hopefully.

We are bemused as to the need for a room divider and so he invites us to visit what passes for classrooms. Totally unprepared, we follow him into the first room. In all our years of teaching, neither of us has ever seen anything like it. There are three rooms devoted to teaching. Mr Banda proposes to divide one of them into two with the room divider. Not one of the rooms has seen a lick of paint for years. Not one of the classrooms contains any proper desks, tables or chairs. Instead they are furnished with cracked and chipped oddments clearly salvaged from the local dump. Some of the children have nowhere to write, so they either write on their laps or leaning against a wall or an adjacent concrete pillar. One child is even writing on the pages of a *used* receipt book. Their pencils are mere stubs.

Yet some of the classes contain more than sixty children. The pupils eye us warily. It is impossible to assess how old they are since most are undersized because of illness and malnutrition. There is no doubt they rarely see any 'mzungus' here. And if we had any doubts before, this confirms our resolve to satisfy more of this school's desperate needs than simply with the gift of a few desks.

"About the room divider, what exactly did you have in mind?" we ask Mr Banda, imagining he may want something rescued from a scrap merchant.

But no, he describes a simple construction of bamboo canes and reed mats. It will be used to divide the classroom currently containing the youngest and largest group of children into two groups and will cost about four pounds.

"But what will you do for a teacher when you have an extra class?"

He shrugs in resignation. "Maybe someone can do an extra shift. Even myself I can teach them."

The visit to Musonda draws to a close. This has been the first of the six school visits programmed for this week. Yet already emotion overload is threatening to overwhelm us. And then I spy a child's drawing pinned up on the wall. In a childish hand the lettering underneath the picture proclaims, 'Jesus loves you!' This almost finishes me off, but then I wonder if perhaps these words are an indication as to why we are here? That Jesus does indeed love these children? And that he is asking us also to hold them close to our hearts?

"So, what are your first impressions?" asks Evelyn when we are once more closeted inside the vehicle and bouncing our way back to sanity.

"It's hard to put them into words," I say.

"I think we can honestly say . . . we've never seen anything like it," manages Bob, which is an understatement if ever there was one.

"Ah but you will see worse tomorrow," Evelyn promises blithely as if revealing an even greater treat to come from this toystore of hardship.

"There is worse?" I am incredulous at the prospect.

"For sure," she responds brightly. "Even tomorrow you will see children who don't have anywhere to sit at all."

But will we be able to take any more? After only one day we are already overwhelmed by a situation that beggars belief. I don't know about 'out in the field', because today has seemed more like a descent into a bottomless pit!

Yet tomorrow is always another day, and at least we have the promise of getting out of Kitwe for the day. Tomorrow we are heading for the rural district of Lufwanyama, and, if we but knew it, where God is surely leading us.


## NOTE:

*Visits to Mchinka and Kaputula Community Schools are already described in chapter one of 'Bwanakula Thandi . . . the story of the building of Kaputula School', and therefore not included again here. Suffice it to say, we did see worse. We still had a mere £600 in the bank. Yet somehow by the end of Wednesday, we'd agreed to build a school at Kaputula in the heart of the Zambian bush.*

# CHAPTER FIVE: LEAVING STARFISH STRANDED ON THE BEACH . . . *Thursday 24th July and Friday 25th July, 2003*

Our week visiting community schools in Kitwe is flying by. Following yesterday spent travelling the roads of Lufwanyama, and the momentous decision to build a school at Kaputula, the night was spent tossing and turning . . .

"Did we *really* agree to build a school for the Kaputula Community?"

"Yes, I rather think we did!"

So, we face Thursday's programme with some trepidation, not in any way eased by the trials of breakfast at the Edinburgh Hotel. Fed up with mince on toast, I ask, "Is there any bacon?"

"No madam, there is no bacon," comes the response.

I settle for a boiled egg with a scone while Bob orders two poached eggs. Aeons later, when the boiled egg and scone have long since disappeared, and while Bob is *still* waiting for his poached eggs, two plates of bacon arrive.

"Sorry for the delay, we had to defrost the bacon."

"And the poached eggs?" But the waiter denies all knowledge of these.

Bob demolishes his bacon while I stuff mine inside today's unappetising sandwiches . . . sliced tomato and toast already deteriorating into a soggy pap. At which point, two totally unwanted poached eggs appear. Sod's law, it would appear. But since 80% of Zambians won't have eaten anything this morning, there is an obligation to eat the darned things.

All of which makes us late arriving at Chep for Thursday morning's visits. With us this morning are Chris from Chep and a huge pastor from Evelyn's Bread of Life Church named Pastor Bwalia.

Both schools scheduled for this morning lie deep in Kitwe's compounds. The route leading there meanders through a bewildering maze of unsurfaced tracks, barely wide enough for the vehicle. Just as well we don't have to locate these places on our own, we'd never find them.

Eventually, after much deviating because of unmanageable and impassable roads and negotiating a densely packed market place with stalls and chickens and produce spilling onto the road, we reach the first of today's schools. Though from the din blaring from a loudspeaker system across the way, how any lessons take place is questionable.

Ipusukilo Community School is the largest school visited this week. It has 1068 children on roll, of which a staggering 336 are orphans, while many of the others are classed as vulnerable. There are only seven teachers running a three shift day, from 07.30 until 12.00, from 12.10 until 14.00 for beginners only, and then from 14.30 until 17.00. Yet amazingly it boasts a 90% pass rate for the grade seven entry exam into secondary education.

We crowd into the cramped office of the head teacher. If this is the largest school visited, then Mr Joffrey is the youngest head so far. Apparently he was appointed head because he's the only qualified member of staff. He is very keen to tell us of the school's needs . . .

"Materials and desks, yes please, and some chalk."

Still jittery from yesterday's spur of the moment agreement to build a school at Kaputula, we are reluctant to commit.

"And we are also needing a new building," Mr Joffrey informs us.

"Is that so?" Since we don't as yet have the money to build one school, it would be foolishness in the extreme to show more than polite interest in the construction of a second one.

Mr Joffrey offers to show us round. Outside his office the noise is deafening. It is change over time for lessons. Children swarm everywhere. Teachers are shouting, ringing bells and trying to round up several hundred children. Over and above it all music is still blaring outside the school gate.

"The problem is the lunchtime shift is already arriving," shouts Mr Joffrey above the racket, "even before the morning one has finished."

We squeeze past serried ranks of children into the first classroom housing a grade three class. Children are squeezed five and six to a desk. In a second equally crowded class the only natural light comes from one small window high up in the blackened wall. It is almost impossible to see.

"Is there any electricity on site?" I guess the answer will be no. Best then not to ask what 1068 children plus seven teachers do for toilet facilities.

It is the same story in the other classrooms, dark, crowded, roofs leaking in the rainy season. Thoroughly dispirited we follow Mr Joffrey back to his cramped office. "As you see, we have many needs."

Nevertheless, there is a need to ascertain the facts. "Do you receive any support at all?"

Surprisingly the school has received assistance from the British Council and has a twinning arrangement with a school in the UK. Mr Joffrey, young as he is, clearly knows some of the rules on the charity playing field.

Yet in having sufficient nous to obtain some help for the school, he has, by the same token, sealed its fate. Things here may be far from ideal, yet the school is better off than either Musonda School visited on Monday, or Kaputula School visited yesterday.

We leave knowing that Starfish money and energies will be directed elsewhere. Sadly this early into the charity game, we are already learning that not every starfish will end up back in the water.

From Ipusukilo we travel on to Twatasha School. The Pastor has said little while at Ipusukilo. Yet it is soon apparent he and his church have an interest in Twatasha. It was described as a centre for children of mentally handicapped parents. *Not my choice of words!* However, though, it turns out to be a pre-school for beginners and reception class children, a staggering 30% of the parents suffer from mental health problems.

"Stop the car one moment!" exclaims Pastor Bwalia suddenly, though we are currently on a dusty track with not much in sight. "Only here we have acquired a plot of land for the building of the new school."

We clamber out and politely express interest. The same thought is running through both our minds . . . *Even if we had the money, which we don't, because there is still only £600 in the Starfish kitty, then this is the third request to build a school in two days!*

Pastor Bwalia extracts some papers from his shabby briefcase. "These are the facts and figures. I have ascertained ready made bricks can be purchased at a cost of K300 per brick. We shall need 10 000 bricks in order to construct the school, making a cost of K3 million."

"Surely you need more than bricks to build a school?"

"In fact yes," he concedes, "we also need cement and roofing materials."

We don't ask how much these cost. We may still be very green about building community schools in Zambia, but we do know he will need a lot more than bricks. And that it will cost a great deal of money.

"Sorry, but we're not in a position to commit to anything," I tell him.

"In fact only yesterday we agreed to build a school at Kaputula," adds Bob.

Pastor Bwalia's face clouds with disappointment. Too late by a day to grab the prize! "Ah well, then let us proceed to Twatasha."

We park outside the school and walk across a rickety platform over a storm drain. The school is in a rented house containing four rooms. It currently has sixty children in pre-school, nursery and reception. Some come from normal homes. However many are from homes of parents suffering from mental illness, or who have been raped or abused. Admirably the Pastor's church raises a levy on its congregation in order to send children on to basic school.

If we expected any resemblance to pre-schools in the UK, then our illusions are soon shattered. The school possesses one blackboard between four classes. There are no desks or tables, no reading books, visual aids or other stimulating materials. Yet bizarrely each child is seated on a brightly coloured plastic chair. We admire the chairs, which represent the one bright spot in an otherwise bleak environment.

"But you will see what happens," says Pastor Bwalia enigmatically though declining to elaborate.

And we do see. After the children have sung and recited nursery rhymes and poetry, it is time for them to go home. They stand as one, each placing a chair on his or her head, before filing out.

We are bemused. "What is going on?"

"There are no doors inside the building nor indeed any locks so we cannot keep the chairs here overnight. Thus each child must take their chair home overnight."

"Won't the landlord do something?"

"Nothing, because if he were to rent this building as a house, he would get more rent than he is getting from us."

The mind boggles how anyone might live in this building. The floors are uneven and broken up. There is no paint on the walls and no doors or windows, let alone electricity or sanitation. A cold wintry wind penetrates through unglazed windows passing clean through the building.

"Which is precisely why we are needing a new school."

Questions need asking. "Do you receive any assistance at all?"

"As I have already said, people in my church donate K1000 per person per month. Also we receive an allowance from the Mental Health Patients' Association."

"And there are how many people in your church?"

"There are one thousand people."

So, it is a big church, possibly one of the Pentecostals originating in Nigeria and now sweeping across the continent of Africa. Maths is not my strong point, yet one thousand multiplied by itself does make one million, does it not? Which question I put to Bob over lunch and he confirms as correct.

"So, the pastor has one million kwachas coming in every month? Which in three months makes enough to raise K3 million for his school."

"Supposing that his sums are correct, which we have no means of verifying, unless we take matters further."

We are both confused "The whole business is a minefield," I say.

"Which unwittingly we've stepped into," Bob responds.

"Better not tread on any mines then," I say gloomily.

Lost in thought, we sit outside Chep munching soggy cold toast, tomato and bacon sandwiches. "One more school to go this afternoon," I remind Bob. "But can we take much more?"

"As long as we're not asked to *build* any more schools," he quips.

We travel with Evelyn Lumba to Kamakonde School located in a township across the rail tracks and outside Kitwe. Our sixth school visit, yet again we are caught by surprise. Some of the children are dressed in such tattered rags they barely cover their decency.

"Have they nothing else to wear?" I ask.

Evelyn regards me blankly. "For many of these children what you are seeing will be the only clothes they have. In fact, on the day when their clothes are washed, they will absent themselves from school because there is nothing else for them to wear. Is that not so Gibson?"

Head teacher Gibson confirms that is indeed so, thus ranking these children the poorest seen so far, even in comparison with those in Kitwe's most densely packed compounds.

Yet Gibson stands out in a class of his own. One of only two trained teachers on the staff, he is keen his voluntary teachers benefit from Chep's programme to train a couple of them each year before returning them to the community school they came from.

Gibson also has a chicken rearing programme planned to generate income for children who pass the grade seven exam to continue on with their education in government schools. His plans reach further, to setting up an orphans' centre so that orphans with no other relative to look after them can be cared for yet still remain part of the community.

We sense ourselves getting caught up by Gibson's enthusiasm. If we're not careful . . . But there is unfortunately still only £600 in the Starfish kitty, not enough to build Kaputula School let alone an orphans' centre as well.

And so we say, "Sorry, we would very much like to be part of your plans but . . ."

That night I pray, *Lord, why are so many starfish left stranded on the beach? Because what this week is teaching us, is that we can NEVER hope to rescue them all.*

Friday is our last day. There is not only melon for breakfast, but also toast made with brown bread. Though since brown bread in Zambia is only white bread dyed brown, that rather takes the edge off its attraction.

We check out of the hotel and reach Chep by 9am along with one thousand exercise books and six hundred sweets, only to find . . . "In fact the desks they promised are not yet ready." Evelyn's expression is as sorrowful as the magician who fails to pull the rabbit out of the hat.

Not only that but the rabbit may also have died. "Even the ones which were ready, have not yet left Tyfotap for Musonda School."

With a handover ceremony plus a 250 mile journey to Lusaka, today was destined to be tight. But a handover ceremony minus desks for handing over just will not do. Time to head for Tyfotap.

On spying our vehicle, Mr Katungulu visibly cringes. He skitters about more nervously than a horse under starter's orders, waving his hands in the air and making rash promises he has no hope whatsoever of fulfilling.

"Look Mr Katungulu," I tell him, "what we would prefer is that the job is done properly."

"Really?" His expression reveals that he can't believe what he is hearing. Could this be the way 'mzungus' handle failure to deliver the goods?

"It is far better to take your time rather than rush the desks and spoil them," explains Bob. "We want them finished properly."

"Oh well, if that is the case." The sun emerges once more on Mr Katungulu's features.

"So where are the nine completed desks?" we ask.

"Oh, they have gone already to Musonda School," he replies, which means someone got their wires crossed earlier.

We arrive at Musonda School to find Mr Banda frying out in the hot sun and standing guard over nine newly varnished desks. Each one is capable of seating three children in the morning session and a further three in the afternoon. Mr Banda wipes the sweat from his brow. The geese that lay the golden eggs have arrived. Already in our short acquaintance he has made it plain that is how he views us.

What he does not yet know, is that we have also brought one thousand exercise books with us today.

"Aieeh, they are for us?" he beams in delight when he sees them. Then he proceeds to count them lest even golden geese get diddled in the shops in town. Worse, attempt to diddle him!

The time comes officially to hand over the desks. Evelyn insists I tell the Starfish story. Most of the assembled crowd of orphans and vulnerable children have never ventured outside the compound or out of Kitwe, let alone as far as the big wide sea. Teachers eye us suspiciously. Even Mr Banda appears uncertain what might come next. Golden fish perhaps?

Fortunately one person present, apart from us, has seen the sea. Evelyn has been to the UK. As I tell the Starfish story for the first time to a Zambian audience, she translates it into Bemba with much embellishment in order to put the message across.

"Ah, that is very good," says Mr Banda.

We follow Mr Banda around the back of the school to the room to be divided. The poles, which will support the structure, are already in place. "And the mats?" we ask.

Mr Banda wrings his hands forlornly. "Unfortunately the mats are not yet purchased. For that they are asking a further K63 000. The original quote was for poles only. The cost of the mats was not included."

Do we smell a rat? Surely Mr Banda would not risk trying any tricks with his precious golden geese? There is however no time for debate. The cost is a mere £9, so we hand over a further K63 000, on the agreement that Evelyn will provide a receipt from Chep and will further check the mats are purchased. She will also check the remaining desks arrive, that exercise books are distributed one to each child and that the afternoon children also get sweets.

As we climb into the vehicle ready to depart, Mr Banda gazes rapturously at us as if he can hardly believe the events of today. "How can we ever thank you?" he says. Could that be a tear in his eye, or merely a glitter of comprehension that he and his school are amongst the lucky starfish rescued and thrown back into the water.

As for us, our week 'in the field' is now over. Our emotions have ridden the highs and lows of a roller coaster, while our hearts and minds have been opened to the sheer scale of need amongst Zambia's poorest children.

Yet sadly also, the week has created the realisation that we are leaving starfish stranded on the beach. Worse, we will *never, ever* pick up every last one.

# CHAPTER SIX: EVERYTHING HAS ITS PRICE . . .
## *Monday July 19th, 2004*

By 2004, visits to Zambia begin adopting a regular pattern. Gifts of furniture and school materials are made to Musonda, Twatasha and Kaputula Community Schools. Building work commences at Kaputula and, as news of Starfish and its work spreads, requests for assistance inevitably start coming in from other Copperbelt based projects.

As building work at Kaputula progresses, one person becomes key to its success. However, as well as project managing the Kaputula building project, Mr Mbai also manages the Salem Centre for Street Kids, located on the outskirts of Kitwe. Before long he invites us to visit his project. How can we refuse? In two short years he has become the linchpin for the work of Starfish.

In July 2004 travelling in a hired single cab pickup, it is somewhat squashed in the front with the gear stick protruding between my legs. Thank God for wearing trousers today! Every time Bob coaxes the car into second gear, I have to prop one leg up on the dashboard.

Today is our first visit to Salem. Also on today's agenda is a need to verify the price of bags of cement to ensure Starfish is not ripped off on the Kaputula building project. But first it's off to Salem.

We leave Kitwe on the main Chingola road, though soon abandon the tarred surface for the corrugated and broken road leading through Mindolo North compound.

"Your centre is some way out of Kitwe then?" My voice judders in tune with the vehicle heaving its way over rock strewn hillocks in the road surface.

"That is for a reason," explains Mr Mbai. "Children who stay at the Salem centre are picked up from the streets of Kitwe where they are begging or even stealing. If we were not so far out of town then, given a chance, these kids would head straight back for the streets."

We first came face to face with the reality of street kids on meeting Alex on our first day back in Zambia. Yet we still struggle with the enormity of the problem. They swarm around the vehicle at traffic lights or pester for money to guard the car outside shops in Kitwe. They sleep rough in shop doorways or under an overpass in Lusaka where they can be seen smoking illegal substances. In the wrong part of either town there is an ever-present risk of mugging.

Yet the phenomenon of street kids in Zambia is relatively new. Thirty years ago there was no such problem. If a child lost its parents, then it was given a home by other family members. In Zambia every sister of the mother is also a child's mother, and every brother of the father is also a child's father. Thus the extended family has since time immemorial reigned supreme.

However, with the advent of Aids, compounded by ever-present poverty, the extended family system is crumbling under pressure. Conservative estimates place the number of orphaned children in Zambia as between 700 000 and one million. That is a lot of children being cared for by aunts, uncles and ailing grandparents.

"How do these people cope?" we ask Mr Mbai.

"The problem is they don't," he responds. "Frequently the grandparents become sick. Then the position is reversed as the child ends up caring for them."

"Some of these families must be stretched to the limits?"

"Indeed. Sometimes the aunts and uncles have already taken in other orphaned children and can take no more, or else they treat the orphans less well than their own children."

"Is this why these children take to the streets?" I recall Alex whose story is sounding less like a fairy story by the minute.

"That is so, but also sometimes when there is no adult family member to look after them, children as young as ten, eleven and twelve find themselves as head of the family."

"It's hard to believe what you are saying."

"Yet increasing numbers of these children can no longer bear their way of life and so run away from home and take to the streets of the capital Lusaka or else the larger towns of the Copperbelt."

"Do the kids you pick up come voluntarily to Salem?" Bob asks.

Mr Mbai chuckles. "Hardly, because even when they are brought here, they are wanting to return to their lives on the street. Either they are picked up from the streets by our own outreach workers or else the police round them up and dump them on the centre often in the early hours of the morning."

"But why should they want to return to living on the streets?" I say.

"Many are addicted to illegal substances. On the streets they beg for or steal money to pay for them. However at Salem we don't allow these substances. They have to go, how do you say . . .?"

"Cold turkey?"

"Exactly, cold turkey, which is hard for them because all the time their bodies are craving the substances they are addicted to."

"Such as?"

"Lighter fuel, kerosene, whatever they can lay their hands on or steal."

"How many children do you have at Salem?" we ask.

"We have some four hundred children at the school," says Mr Mbai.

"All of them street kids?"

"At any one time we have between thirty-five and forty-seven boys sleeping at the centre. Then there are also twelve to fifteen girls in a separate house as well as up to four hundred local children attending the school."

"So Salem is also a school? We hadn't realised this before."

"Indeed, it is a community school for children from the neighbouring compound. We have over four hundred orphans and vulnerable children who attend the school, as well as the boys living on site and the girls living nearby."

"Are there many girls living on the streets?"

"Indeed yes. Many young girls take to the streets because of rape or abuse, even within their family. Some of them, in common with the boys, are HIV+. Even we have had the first case of a baby born HIV+ on the streets."

Which knowledge stuns us into silence until we reach the gates of Salem. The centre lies on the outer edge of Mindolo North compound and thus also the outer edge of Kitwe. It is housed within a former sports ground surrounded by eight feet high walls and entered by solid double iron gates. Inside is an oasis of calm. A vast sports field sprinkled with scant grass cover fills the centre of the plot. Around the edge stand various outbuildings and temporary structures. Yet the first impression remains that of an oasis of calm in the midst of a troubled and uncertain world.

One large blue and white building dominates the others. On the wall is painted in large red letters: GOSPEL MISSION SPORTS OUTREACH.

"The name is that of the organisation set up to run Salem," explains Mr Mbai. "Our centre was originally founded by Pastor Joseph Mwewa, a former professional footballer turned pastor. He believed the way to reach disadvantaged children was by means of sport, hence the title."

Pastor Mwewa emerges from the main office building to greet us. He is a small softly spoken Zambian, yet he possesses considerable presence. With him is the social worker, a young man who is HIV+. We sit together under an open shelter while they fill in more details. Apart from being HIV+ many of the children also have TB or sexually transmitted diseases. Stories of abuse, defilement, poverty and sickness rightly fill us with horror.

We are now into our third year re-visiting Zambia. If we'd expected by now to become inured to such suffering, then this morning's visit demonstrates how far removed we still are from that point. It would be all too easy to become demoralised faced with such suffering. Yet should we give into pity, we would become useless at what we are attempting to do.

Nevertheless, I can't help tossing up the prayer . . . *'God, where are you in all this? What exactly do you want us to do?'*

Yesterday was Sunday. For the first time we stayed over the weekend in Kitwe instead of travelling down to Lusaka. We tried to discover God in several Kitwe churches, ranging from neat white stuccoed buildings to red brick monstrosities, from Anglican to Baptist. Yet we failed dismally.

*'Now today, Lord, what are you about?'* I pray silently, *'Are you leading us into yet another overwhelming situation and expecting a response?'*

Already in the short life of Starfish, we are committed to building a seven classroom school at Kaputula with not a clue where the funding will come from. Now, confronted with this, we feel powerless. Does God seriously intend Salem to become another project, when we still don't know where the means to complete the first is coming from? Or do we turn our backs and leave yet another Starfish stranded on the beach?

Spirits already low, the guided tour of Salem commences. However our spirits only plummet ever lower as the tour progresses. Next to the main office block stands the boys' dormitory. Row after row of wooden bunk beds stacked so close the boys can reach across and touch each other's hands. They resemble bunks at Auschwich-Birkenau. Each bunk is covered with one tatty blanket while a meagre bag of belongings hangs on a hook on the wall. Worse, some of the smaller boys sleep two and three to a bunk. There is an overpowering stench of urine, sweat and filth, which sends us out gagging for fresh air.

"They wet the beds I presume?" I can't help asking.

"Indeed, because for some it is the first time they have slept in a bed or

40

used a toilet." Mr Mbai doesn't offer to show us the toilets. He doesn't need to. Their location is obvious from the stench emerging from them.

"If you like, maybe one night you could accompany our outreach workers?" suggests Mr Mbai.

Before we left home, someone blithely quipped, "Have a good holiday!" *Holiday?* Perhaps reading this dispels any last illusion that we go to Zambia on holiday. This is no holiday, but emotional meltdown. Yet we must remain strong if we are to achieve anything.

The guided tour continues into the dining hall, temporarily converted into a sewing room. Here vulnerable women from the neighbouring compound learn to use sewing machines. Items they make can be sold to earn a living. This empowers women who have been abused or raped, who are widowed or HIV+ to earn a living. *This tour simply gets better by the minute!*

In the open kitchen area food for forty boys is being prepared, 'nshima with beans or kapenta and little else. There is a carpentry shed where older boys acquire skills, again to help them earn a living. Along one wall of the plot is a garden where they attempt to grow enough vegetables for food, but with an inadequate water supply the results are not encouraging. There is one completed and operational chicken shed. The other partially completed shed lacks roofing and plastering.

"This also would be income-generating," explains Mr Mbai. "Sadly however, we ran out of funding."

Along one wall of the plot stand four immaculate and almost brand new classrooms, gift of the Beit Trust. However, next to these still stand four ramshackle huts open at the sides and with ragged black polythene sheeting fluttering like widows' weeds from the thatched roofs. Amazingly classes are still taking place in three of these.

We are puzzled. "Why are you still using these shacks when you have bright new classrooms?"

"Because so many children in the compound now want to come to this school, as fast as we pulled down the first classrooms thinking we would not need them any more, these became filled with pupils again," explains Mr Mbai.

Children sit clustered on makeshift benches twenty, thirty and forty to a hut. Except for one class which is having its lessons outside.

"There is an infestation of insects inside the hut," explains the teacher, "so today the children must learn outside."

It is evident the school urgently needs another four classrooms to replace the remaining thatched structures which leak like a sieve in the rainy

41

season. It also needs roofing and plastering for the poultry shed to enable the school to generate much needed income. And that's not to mention: clothing, medicines, blackboards, blankets, books . . . and a cooker for the girls' accommodation.

*But how to achieve this?* We pray silently for a solution to this dilemma.

However Mr Mbai has yet another trick or two up his sleeve, should we still not be convinced that, even with insufficient money in the bank to meet Starfish's current commitments, we *cannot* turn aside from the desperate needs here.

"The children would like to perform for you," he announces. "But first let us go and see where the girls live."

To do this we leave the security of eight feet high walls and walk a short distance into the neighbouring compound. Mrs Mkuba, who is in charge of girls' welfare, accompanies us.

"You don't keep the girls on the same site then?" we ask.

"Ah no, it is better to keep them at some distance away and where they are all girls together," Mrs Mkuba informs us. We can only imagine why this is.

The girls' house is a small unpretentious building a short distance from the school. It is sparsely furnished with bare essentials, chairs, table, iron bedsteads or wooden bunk beds and an ancient electric cooker. From the kitchen emerges the overpowering odour of dried kapenta, a small fish similar to whitebait fished in vast quantities in Lake Kariba then dried and sold. It is the cheapest form of protein available in Zambia. Its stomach-churning stench makes me glad we're not invited for lunch. The meagreness of their existence is overwhelming. *But this is better than life on the streets, isn't it?*

We return to the main school site. By now the whole school has filed out from classrooms both old and new. The pupils take their places on concrete seating which was once spectators' seating, when the centre was a sports ground. We are given a place of honour in the midst of four hundred black faces eager with expectation of a performance.

*Or does the prospect of a miracle the 'mzungus' might perform also have something to do with it?*

The show begins. There is music, drama, dancing, mime, poetry, speeches, a wide variety of entertainment from children of all ages. Yet it bears one common and tragic theme . . . the devastation on people's lives caused by HIV Aids.

At times the mime and dance become so sexually explicit as to be embarrassing. Yet who are we to turn aside preferring not to watch? These children face this threat every day of their lives. If they need to act it out in mime and dance and drama, then who are we to turn aside?

And so we watch a performance which beggars belief, during which children as young as five and six laugh because they understand what the sexual connotation is all about. The performance at times surpasses our limited comprehension.

Will we help them? By the end of this harrowing performance we know we will. *Yet how?* A lot depends on how much of Starfish funds Kaputula swallows up. Which reminds us that later today, we still have to check up on the price of cement, which task seems mundane after what we've just seen.

We drop Mr Mbai at Chep headquarters and head for Shoprite, Kitwe's one supermarket. With wallets and purses bulging with kwachas, we buy what we want and retire to the flat where we are staying this trip. The veranda, where we sit to eat lunch, overlooks the swimming pool. No need to worry where our next meal is coming from, it's waiting in the fridge. Unlike the children we met this morning for whom, until Salem took them under its wing, the struggle to find their next meal had become a daily battle for survival.

We once commented, perhaps unwisely, to the PCC at our former local church, that as a community we should consider ourselves lucky.

"And why is that?" a leading PCC member was quick to demand. His puzzled expression clearly demonstrated an utter lack of comprehension as to why this should be so.

We were so taken aback that, for a few precious moments lost for words, we sought round for how best to respond: water, sanitation, food in our bellies and fridges, money in the bank, electricity on supply, a roof over our heads . . . The list is endless of things which people in developed countries take for granted. Yet people who have never struggled for these necessities of life, have no concept of what it is like to be deprived of them.

Tonight we don't feel so lucky. Rather we feel amongst the unluckiest people in the world, given that God seems to expect us to share the responsibility for dealing with this mess.

"Why us?" We gaze bleakly at each other.

"Search me," is Bob's uninspired response.

"It's not as if we have the heart for the task. We have no experience of problems as immense as these . . ."

"Or that we're particularly charitable people."

43

"The sort who take up other people's causes."

"Definitely not us! Besides, we've enough on our plates already with the Kaputula project . . ."

"Then there's paying for Tresford's treatment . . ."

"How much time and energy are we supposed to devote to all this?"

"Not to mention our finances. We can't keep running backwards and forwards to Zambia trying to set the world to rights, now can we?"

Stunned into silence by the enormity of it all, I begin writing up today's diary entry. In a flash of inspiration. I entitle it . . . 'Everything has its price!' Today was also supposed to be about verifying the price of cement so that Starfish does not get ripped off on the Kaputula building project. By accident or design we never got around to pricing cement today.

However since our visit to Salem, we do know how much it costs in Zambia to have sex with an underage girl. About K2000, the equivalent of 25p! And girls as young as nine and ten sell themselves for so little because money in their pockets means food in their bellies.

For dinner tonight we have two large frozen Kariba bream. Unfortunately after defrosting and opening the packet, one gives off a rank and foul smelling odour. Despite copious washing and trimming of dubious looking bits, the fish still stinks. There is nothing for it but to bin all 80p worth and share the one remaining fish between us.

The broccoli has frozen to the bottom of the fridge, which inversely freezes at the bottom and merely chills in the ice compartment. The carrots have a hard green core. However with a gigantic pink grapefruit and a crumble made in a cake tin bought yesterday and which leaks all over the electric oven, we eat more than most people in Zambia will do tonight.

The choice of TV channels is limited in Zambia. One which invariably works well, is TBN or the God channel. Tonight a firebrand preacher holds forth on the merits of giving as opposed to receiving and of the just rewards awaiting the generous giver in their heavenly home. All the while he is speaking a message is relayed across the foot of the screen informing those watching of an address in Lumumba Road Kitwe where pledges for the work of the church may be made. The suggested amount is K200 000, about £25.00. That is one hundred times the amount a girl of ten might earn tonight in exchange for selling her body to an adult male.

"I wonder how much of the money raised ever finds it way to Salem or other such organisations?" I muse.

"Everything has its price," responds Bob.

"Even charity?" I can't help adding.

The final insult comes as I flush the toilet and turn the taps on to run a bath. The water emerges brown and stinking. "Oh no!" I groan.

"What's up?" calls Bob.

"The water is running dark brown!" I nearly say nigger brown, but that's not at all PC, even to think let alone voice it.

"You're not complaining, are you," Bob chides. "I mean . . . at least we have water!" Which sobering thought is the final straw in a day where everything has indeed proved to have a price.

# CHAPTER SEVEN: WILL YOU BE MY MOTHER?
## *Tuesday August 3rd, 2004*

'Things can only get better." So run the words of a well-known song. Oh that those lyrics applied to Zambia! Just at the point we decide we simply CANNOT take on another project, or cannot POSSIBLY see anything worse than we've seen already, along comes yet another wake-up call.

Since we have just enjoyed four days break from the rigours of charity work along with a birthday celebration, you would imagine we'd be raring to pick up the reins once more. In fact the opposite has occurred. We have reached poverty saturation point.

"I'm dreading today," I groan on waking. "The last thing we need, is yet another needy community with yet another catalogue of desperate needs."

"Agreed! We've enough on our plates already, what with starting the building work at Kaputula, trying to fulfil Musonda and Twatasha's many needs, not to mention Salem . . ."

"It's all very well, the Starfish ideal of picking up one stranded starfish and tossing it back into the ocean, but where does it end? How many will we actually succeed in tossing back into the ocean?"

"And what about all the ones left behind, what difference are we making to them?"

We stare gloomily at each other across the breakfast table. Poverty saturation point well and truly reached.

"Well, however desperate the needs we encounter today, I shall inure myself to them, vaccinate myself against them. I simply shall not be moved, not one little bit," I announce with conviction.

*If only, in Zambia, things were so simple!*

We have arranged to meet Mr Quistin Chalwe of Chilumba Orphans' Centre at 09.30 at Chep. In common with several other people, Mr Chalwe has heard what Starfish is up to in and around Kitwe. On several occasions he has waited for several hours at Chep trying to make contact with us. Yet unlike many of the others, Mr Chalwe did not give up. Nor was he put off by such comments as . . .

"Starfish is really only a very small organisation."

"And we're already fully committed for some time ahead . . ."

"We cannot possibly take on another project at the present time . . ."

"Maybe we should just call and cancel," suggests Bob.

"Maybe we shouldn't have agreed to visit his project in the first place," I add gloomily. "Or agreed to travel in his vehicle. That puts the ball rather too squarely in his court."

"So shall we cancel?"

"It's too late for that. Maybe things won't turn out as bad as we expect. Surely it won't be worse than what we've seen already?"

In this none too cheerful frame of mind we head for Chep to meet Mr Chalwe. Perhaps the fact he is there on time is too good to be true . . .

"I just need to drop something off at a friend of mine before we travel," Mr Chalwe informs us, before driving to the opposite side of town. He parks outside his friend's house leaving us outside in the car to wait.

Twenty minutes later Mr Chalwe emerges. "Sorry to keep you waiting," he says. "Now we make our way to Chilumba."

Seated silently in the back we reflect on the error of not travelling in our own vehicle. Perhaps it's because the car does not belong to him, or because he's not a very experienced driver, but Mr Chalwe drives slower than a snail on vacation.

We reach Kalulushi and its treacherous speed bumps. These he negotiates at the daring speed of 5mph. On the broken tarred stretch out of town he manoeuvres each individual pothole at 10mph. At the police post marking the junction with the Kaputula road, he turns left onto a red dirt road and accelerates to 20mph. Red dust flies up on either side of the car obscuring the view. Hence even more caution is required. At this rate it will be time to make the return journey before we even arrive.

Eventually Mr Chalwe pulls off the dirt road and parks in front of a small red brick building. It has all the appearance of a tavern or bar, and indeed it once was. Now its two tiny rooms house Chilumba Orphans' Centre. One filthy blackened room is designated as the classroom, while the smaller room serves as sleeping accommodation for up to twelve orphans.

"Do the children who sleep here come from far away then?" I ask naively.

"In fact, no," responds Mr Chalwe enigmatically.

"So why are they sleeping here?" I persist.

"For some children, there is no-one left to look after them," he reveals.

"Either both parents are dead, or else no other living relative can be found, or is willing or able to take them in."

"And so they sleep here?"

"That is so. In fact there is also a grandmother in a hut nearby who has some eight or nine children staying with her. We try to home as many of the orphans as possible in a family unit, but there are so many orphans around here." Mr Chalwe waves his hands vaguely at the surrounding bush. "Some are still living with one parent, some living with another member of their family." Clearly the orphan crisis here is so vast that Mr Chalwe has no idea of the exact numbers involved. At Chilumba they are wallowing in orphans.

On the outskirts of Lusaka stands a large and fairly new SOS Children's Village. It has brick built classrooms, dormitories, offices, the whole complex surrounded by security fencing and gates. But this is Chilumba, not an SOS Children's Village. Chilumba is the sharp end of Zambia's orphan crisis where the stark reality is worse than anything we had anticipated or seen to date.

Worst of all is the exceedingly high rate of double orphans in this community. Double orphans are children who have lost both parents. Deaths from HIV Aids and associated illnesses have decimated the adult community. Education, prevention and treatment of the disease, in this area, are almost non-existent. The children staying at this school are truly at the bottom of the pile, the dregs of the dregs, whom no-one wants.

"Shall we go inside then?" Mr Chalwe gestures towards the one classroom.

Totally unprepared for what lies ahead, we enter the classroom. The first thing that hits us is the overwhelming stench of poverty combined with sickness, disease and hunger, the stench of people who no longer have any control over their own fate.

And then what strikes me is the blank expression on every single child's face. Not a glimmer of curiosity as to why we might be there, not a flicker of the novelty at seeing 'mzungus' so far off the beaten track. Even in the poorest of communities such as Kamakonde, there was always a glimmer of hope or of curiosity, the joy of touching or shaking the 'mzungus' hands, as if we were a talisman, destined to change their luck.

Yet here at Chilumba there is nothing. Not even hope.

Correction, they do have some things: TB, malaria, sexually transmitted diseases, coughs, colds, open and weeping sores on their legs. Yet few if any can afford treatment for their ailments. If they develop full-blown Aids, they quite simply die.

Yet the room we have entered is full to bursting point with children of all ages from tiny tots to older teens. Without exception they are dressed in rags and without shoes on their feet. Many appear severely malnourished. Several have swollen infected eyes round which flies swarm, yet the kids don't appear even to have the energy to brush them away.

The speeches begin, welcoming us there today and expressing a hope as to what we might do for them. As the village elder's voice drones on, translated at length for our benefit, a small child in the front row keels over face forwards. An adult steps forward and hastily removes the child from the meeting. Then another tiny tot whimpers, searching the room for a comforting face and a pair of arms to pick him up. He crawls across outstretched knees to reach the lap of his older brother.

"In fact for that one, the brother is his one remaining relative," Mr Chalwe informs us in a stage whisper.

It is horrific. I can't take any more. Tears well, choking back down and blocking my throat. My breath comes in gasps. Yet there is no way out. We sit there, two white stooges drowning in an untold ocean of human suffering. And most incredible of all, according to the man speaking, *God has sent us here to them!*

*'Well okay, God,'* I scream silently, *'if you really want us to do something about this, how about giving us the wherewithal with which to achieve it? Because right now, we're committed to building at Kaputula, trying to fulfil some of Twatasha and Musonda's needs and struggling to find some means of helping Salem. How then do we cope with this? Now you've landed us with yet another situation we cannot walk away from!'*

"Did you say something?" Bob's voice is also choked.

"Not me, not a word!"

A second village elder takes the floor to inform us the community would like a school, a clinic and a borehole. He doesn't specify the order, but maybe that's just a technicality for the requirements placed before us today.

"Perhaps you would like to say a few words?" suggests Mr Chalwe. "It would make them very happy for you to address them."

*Like what? Does anybody here realise how much all that would cost? That we come from a small group in a small church in a small village?*

I rise shakily, ungluing my trousers from where they've long since stuck uncomfortably between my legs, but whether from the stifling atmosphere in the cramped, airless and overcrowded classroom or from the length of time we've been sitting there or nervousness, or all three, I couldn't say.

"I would like to tell you a story," I hesitate uncertainly. This is the least likely audience yet for the starfish story, but here goes . . .

*'There was once an old man who lived beside the sea. Every morning he would take a walk along the beach before settling down to his work.*

*One morning as he was walking along the beach, he saw a strange sight ahead of him. A strange figure was leaping and dancing and picking things up and tossing them back into the sea. Intrigued, the old man hurried to catch up and see what was happening.*

*To his surprise, the strange figure turned out to be that of a young man who was bending and stooping and picking up starfish, which had been stranded by the tide, and tossing them back into the ocean.*

*"What do you think you are doing?" exclaimed the old man. "Don't you know there are miles and miles of beach and thousands upon thousands of stranded starfish? What difference can you possibly make?"*

*In answer the young man bent down and picked up one lone starfish and tossed it back into the water. "Well for that one it sure made a difference!" he exclaimed.'*

I gaze around at a sea of unreadable black faces. Impossible to tell how well received this story was. Not one person present can ever have seen the ocean, let alone the starfish which swim in it.

Yet something clearly strikes a chord. Over in the far corner an old wrinkly grandmother chuckles and wipes a tear from her eye with the corner of her 'chitenge'. Then realising she has grasped the significance of the story's message, she lets out a whoop of joy, ululating and prancing round the room.

"Mr Cooke, would you also like to say something?" asks Mr Chalwe above the din.

I know what Bob's going to say even before he opens his mouth. Yet it has to be said. "We are only a very small fund," he begins. "Moreover we are already committed to a building project at Kaputula. Therefore I am afraid at this present time . . ." He warms to his theme. "In fact it's not even my wife and myself who make the decisions as to what projects Starfish undertakes, but the committee back in the UK." All of which is the long way round of telling this desperate community, sorry, no can do.

I recall my words of earlier this morning . . . WE SHALL NOT BE MOVED! Well, strictly speaking, that's not true. We *have* been moved, more probably than either of us can put into words, but without funding . . . WHAT CAN WE DO?

It makes not one jot of difference. As far as the community is concerned, we are their saviours, sent by God.

"The problem is," Mr Chalwe's voice cleaves into our thoughts, "so many people come here, then they go away and we never see them again. But we know that with you and Mr Cooke and the Starfish, it will be different. Ah, that story! Because of it, I know, you are indeed our saviours!"

It is time for the giving of presents. Mr Chalwe has brought gifts for the children, cheap plastic toys purchased from a market stall. One orphan wanders off clutching a packet of marbles. Another tries on an outsize pair of orange plastic sunglasses, while a third sports a purple bead necklace.

*For heaven's sake,* I want to scream, *they can't eat marbles or sunglasses or purple bead necklaces!*

We also have gifts. Concerned that we were arriving empty handed, on the way here we flagged down a bread delivery van and purchased one hundred bread rolls from the bemused driver. Now these also are distributed to the children. They stand around clutching bread rolls like manna from heaven. Yet they don't immediately tear into the bread, as starving children might do. Rather they stare as if they can't believe what has happened.

"Go on, you may eat," encourages Mr Chalwe. Only then do a few allow themselves a tentative nibble. The majority still stand around gazing at their prize uncertainly.

Outside in the hot noonday sun, children mill around aimlessly, still clutching their bizarre collection of trophies. Eventually one child, a girl of seven or eight with a mop of frizzy hair, sidles up to me. Very unsure of herself, she nevertheless plucks up enough courage to hold out one hand in order to shake mine. She is the one and only child to connect positively with our presence here today. She asks something in Bemba, the local language.

"What did she say?" I turn to Mr Chalwe.

Mr Chalwe looks embarrassed. "I don't think it is so important," he waffles.

"I want to know what the child said," I insist. "She may be begging for money or sweeties, but nevertheless, I want to know what she said."

"The child has no mother. She asked, 'Will you be my mother?' "

I gasp, turning aside, completely overcome. *God in heaven, where are you in all this? That a child as young as this approaches a total stranger, a 'mzungu' at that, and asks, will I be her mother!*

"Tell her I'm old enough to be her grandmother," I quip, then instantly regret this crass response. Fortunately Mr Chalwe declines to translate and instead shoos the child away to join the other children.

"We would like to show you our orchard," he proposes in a masterly change of direction.

We allow ourselves to be steered around to the rear of the school building and away from the mêlée of orphans. I suspect, lest one of them is tempted to ask for something even more outrageous than a substitute mother.

To the rear of the school lies a partially cultivated plot, which Mr Chalwe refers to grandly as the orchard. Sometime past an Australian charity visited the site and provided them with fruit trees. The fruit trees were intended to provide supplementary food for the orphans. Then the Australians went away and were never seen again, an all too familiar story in Africa.

We stumble about over hillocks of half tilled soil trying to establish which are orange and which are lemon trees, and summoning up enthusiasm for apologies of paw-paw and mango trees as well as sickly banana plants. Only one variety of tree is thriving which we establish is a macademia nut tree.

"The problem is the village goats," explains Mr Chalwe. "They keep entering the site and eating the leaves from the young trees before they can grow enough to bear any fruit."

"Is there nothing can be done to stop them?" I ask.

"We can ask the chief to tell the people to stop letting their goats come into this place. But I don't know if that can work."

"For heaven's sake!" Bob explodes. "Why not build a ruddy fence around the orchard? That will stop the goats from getting in. There's ample wood around here." He waves his hand at the encroaching bush, which surrounds the orchard on three sides.

"Even just a small picket fence around the base of each tree," I suggest since Mr Chalwe is looking extremely daunted by the prospect of constructing a fence around a one and half acre plot.

"Mmmm, yes," Mr Chalwe concedes. "Maybe that would be a good idea . . . but there is also the problem of the water supply."

We shake our heads in disbelief. This is African fatalism at its worst, where communities are unwilling or unable to perform even the most elementary tasks to help themselves.

*And they want us to build a school for them?*

Time is ticking rapidly away and along with it all thoughts of being back in Kitwe in time for lunch. Mr Chalwe is now deep in conversation with a community elder whom he introduces as both the Pastor of the local Baptist Church and also his father.

It appears Mr Chalwe grew up in this community, not as an orphan but within a slightly better off family, where both parents have survived into old age. He was educated at the local government school and later went on to secondary school. Mr Chalwe was able to better himself. Now he wants to do something for the less fortunate members of the community where he grew up. His intentions are admirable but . . . *how about an orchard fence for starters, Mr Chalwe?*

As we wend our way back to Kitwe, Mr Chalwe entertains us with stories of his youth while we share out biscuits amongst the three of us. Eating anything at Chilumba was out of the question. Most of the children and adults there enjoy one meal a day, and sometimes not even that.

Back at the flat that evening I cook lamb chops with gem squash and pears with chocolate sauce, except the chocolate burns in the microwave leaving a bitter aftertaste in the mouth. Or is it the bitterness of futility that however hard we try, we will never ever meet the needs of this country?

Over supper we return to this morning's harrowing visit.

"Somehow it no longer seems enough to save lone starfish. What on earth do we do about the thousands left stranded on the beach?" I ask gloomily.

"You mean Chilumba and the like, which we'd like to help, but simply haven't got the resources to do so?"

"The trouble is, we slung out a hook, expecting to land a little minnow, and instead we hauled in a ruddy great whale which threatens to turn us and the boat over. What are we supposed to do, throw it back in the pond?"

"Sea," says Bob matter of factly. "Whales live in the sea. And in any case we were rescuing starfish, not minnows."

"Minnows, starfish, whales, what does it matter? Do we say, sorry, we never meant to land so many or such big ones?"

"Not exactly . . ."

"So we leave yet another messy load of blubber stranded on the shore waiting for somebody else to do something about it?"

But there is no easy answer and so we leave the whale washed up on the shore along with all those stranded starfish and retire to bed . . .

03.45 is a lonely hour of the morning at the best of times. At the worst, it's hell. But God is speaking, time to listen. I think at first it's all the cheese and chocolate I ate yesterday causing a spell of wakefulness. Thoughts race through my mind faster than a dervish with a spinning top. If I go back to sleep and wake feeling okay, then I'll know it was God putting the thoughts there. If I don't and feel lousy all day, then I'll know it was the cheese.

But I wake up with a head as clear as a bell and an even clearer idea as to what needs to be done. Now to put these thoughts into words . . .

"We mustn't let ourselves become discouraged by conditions here. Instead we must make a plan . . ."

"Or two." Ha! Has Bob experienced the same divine conversation in the night?

"You're talking about Chilumba, I presume?"

"And Salem and Twatasha and Musonda."

"Taking on Zambia on a much larger scale than we have up to now?"

"Or maybe let's start with Chilumba," suggests Bob. "At least then we'll feel something positive came from yesterday. Even providing some orchard fencing might restore their faith that people will do something to help them."

"In fact I was just going to suggest the same thing myself."

Which proves God *is* on the case after all. Though hopefully he has some clearer idea than we do where all the money might come from to pay for it. Because right now, we haven't got the vaguest idea!

# CHAPTER EIGHT: OF THE BIG PLAN and juggling too many balls. . . *August 4th -> 13th, 2004*

And so the 'big plan', consisting of three parts, is hatched. Maybe it should be called the 'grand' plan, because it is infinitely grander than anything we have tackled to date.

Firstly there is a proposed programme to enable Musonda Community School teachers to obtain the necessary qualifications for entry into teacher training. Our first visit there revealed that, not only was there not one qualified member of staff, but also that several of the teachers didn't even possess the necessary qualifications for entry into teacher training.

Secondly, we are proposing interim measures for both Salem Centre for Street Kids and Chilumba Orphans' Centre. Hopefully these small measures will help them realise that Starfish has taken their desperate needs on board and may even undertake something bigger at a later date.

However, the third part of the plan grows infinitely grander and involves what to date we have not dared to do, that is look to the future. At present Starfish is heavily committed with the Kaputula Building Project. Money is currently in hand to cover stage two building work. However, disputes and delays have meant the community is not likely to reach stage two this year. Might the UK committee approve commencing a second building project in the meantime?

"That's a daunting prospect," says Bob guardedly. "Especially if we end up with a community as difficult as Kaputula! Or one that causes even more problems!" Is that possible? Silently we mull over the disturbing prospect of a community even more difficult than Kaputula.

"Besides, where will the money come from?" asks Bob finally. "Since any money currently on hold is destined for Kaputula."

"We started Kaputula with barely £600 in the bank," I remind him, "So, step out in faith once more and the money should keep on coming."

And so today, there are people to talk to and to bring on board, if we are to have any hope of getting this grand plan off the ground.

But first we must pass by the accounts office at Chep, there to pay in money for nursery tables and chairs, which Starfish has already agreed this trip to provide for the nursery unit at Twatasha. However Pastor Bwalia seems confused about the carpenter's payment, even thinking he may have been paid twice. I inform Mrs Musangaila head of Chep accounts.

"Then he is mistaken!" Mrs Musungaila retorts frostily. "Myself, I have no recollection of this. Even I think there may be a shortfall."

This is not good news. Just as we are all fired up to commence the 'big plan', Twatasha clearly requires another visit. However, as we leave Mrs Musungaila's office, we bump into Evelyn Lumba, with whom we are anxious to share our big plan.

As Evelyn listens to the proposed plans for the Musonda teachers, her cheek-splitting grin causes her pineapple headpiece to wobble excitedly. "This is excellent, especially since two of those unqualified are also WOMEN!" She claps her hands in delight. "What better way of empowering women than by education!"

"And not forgetting head teacher Mr Banda also," we remind her. "But how do you suggest we go about it?"

"In fact it is quite simple. Those teachers will require coaching from a local secondary school which offers grades nine to twelve."

"But won't going back to school prove difficult for them?"

"Not so difficult, because lessons will take place from 17.00 until 19.00 hours, after their teaching day is over, maybe three times a week. When each teacher reaches grade twelve standard, they will sit for the exam in the normal way and obtain the necessary qualification for entry into teacher training."

Evelyn makes it all sounds very simple, though perhaps also expensive. We put the cost factor to her.

"Chep will pay the examination fees along with teacher training. If Starfish comes up with the tuition fees and maybe a learning incentive to encourage these persons to stick with it, then it will work. So what we must do now, is head out to Musonda to break this good news."

It is a tight squeeze in the single cab pickup hired this trip. Had we anticipated transporting such 'traditional' Zambian ladies as Mrs Musungaila and Evelyn, we may have considered a larger vehicle. With every bump and grind of the vehicle, the soft folds of Evelyn's ample flesh threaten to engulf me.

To our surprise Musonda School is deserted. However Mr Banda soon shuffles along the dusty path leading to the school. Did he perhaps get wind of our coming by bush telegraph? We follow Mr Banda into the cramped and dingy confines of his office, there to outline the plan for his betterment.

His slow smile broadens into a wide grin. "Me, I am delighted!" He rubs his hands together in glee, but whether at the prospect of bettering himself, or at the prospect of a small incentive allowance each month, is not clear.

"When you are fully qualified, you will be earning K600 000 (about £75) a month," I inform him.

"Then I will be a rich man for sure!" he exclaims.

Richer certainly than he is right now! However frequently months pass by when government teachers, like the police, receive no pay at all. But instead of reminding him of this, we spell out the need for thorough preparation to reach grade twelve standard. But Mr Banda has no qualms and promises to enquire at a local secondary school with regard to himself and the two ladies starting lessons there.

"Indeed, I will do so this very afternoon," he assures us, "and myself report back to you later at Chep."

Back at Chep there is just time to set a second ball rolling. We catch Isaac Mumba, who not only has dealings with Chilumba Orphans' Centre, but also knows where it is. Mr Mumba is extremely large, perhaps indicating he enjoys a lifestyle unknown to impoverished Zambians in rural locations such as Chilumba.

"Yes, I have visited that place for the purpose of giving advice regarding matters of health." Since Mr Mumba's voice is as ponderous as his gait, this conversation could take all day.

"They have an orchard there in which the young trees are currently being eaten by village goats," we inform him.

"That is most unfortunate!" He shakes his immense head.

"So we propose assisting the Chilumba community with the construction of a fence around the orchard to protect the trees."

"Then I suggest we obtain wood off-cuts for free from the local Forestry Commission Depot. In fact the director of the Kitwe forestry office is a friend of mine. I will undertake to contact him on your behalf. Leave it with me. I will get a letter off straight away today and report back to you tomorrow."

Dare we hope the provision of an orchard fence is that simple? Even better, that the two additional balls now spinning in the air along with the

Twatasha and Kaputula balls, will stay there? We watch Isaac Mumba's vast bulk as he shambles off. Chilumba's fate now lies in his immense hands. We can but hope and pray.

Yet the following day brings disappointment. There is no Isaac Mumba.

"Mr Mumba has gone to Chililabombwe," we are told in Chep. Chililabombwe, apart from being unpronounceable, is miles away from Kitwe on the border with the Democratic Republic of the Congo and nowhere near either the Chilumba project, or the Forestry Commission Offices from where the wood for orchard fencing is to come.

However Pastor Bwalia is at Chep waiting for us, agitatedly waving the Twatasha accounts book our way. "I am insisting you must see this."

Despite Mrs Musungaila's assurances to the contrary, there definitely is a discrepancy! But then, balancing the Kaputula books caused Mrs Musungaila many a headache, so why should the Twatasha account prove any different? We write everything out in full for Pastor Bwalia, including $97 paid into Chep yesterday, which quite definitely puts the Twatasha account into credit and not shortfall.

Is this a genuine mistake? Either way, we definitely need to visit Twatasha again next week, even though we already have enough on our hands juggling all the balls in the air and trying not to let any of them drop.

The rest of that day is spent ferrying river sand for the Kaputula project. It is past closing time when we return to Chep to find both Isaac Mumba and Mr Chalwe waiting. Goodness knows how long they have been there.

"I am pleased to inform you we have obtained the fence posts for free from the Forestry Commission," announces Isaac Mumba ponderously.

"There is only one problem," interjects Mr Chalwe. "We are wondering if you can assist in the matter of transport?"

We are both filthy dirty and only want a shower and a long cool drink, not to become enmeshed in Mr Chalwe's convoluted web of problems. I groan inwardly. Yet another hired truck to pay for! The current cost of truck hire to ferry materials out to Kaputula would almost buy us a truck of our own! We suggest our hired vehicle will be perfectly adequate for the job.

Then there is the question of which day. Tomorrow we are scooting down to Lusaka lest our family forgets we are still in Zambia. On Monday we travel back, hopefully laden with books for Copperbelt community schools, of which more later. Tuesday is set aside to get things underway at Salem, while Wednesday has been allocated for setting up the Musonda teachers' programme. Thursday is yet again a Kaputula day. Life has suddenly become hectic and time all too scarce.

"Sorry, we can't do anything before Friday next week," we tell them.

Mr Chalwe and Isaac Mumba look glum. Clearly they were geared up for a trip to Chilumba tomorrow. Maybe we're trying to do too much at once? However I keep these thoughts to myself. I know deep down Bob shares the same sense of achievement at what we've accomplished this week. And hopefully still more to be achieved next week . . .

Unfortunately over the weekend I develop flu. By Tuesday morning I don't feel well enough to stand around builders' yards haggling over the price of roofing sheets and nails. These we have promised Mr Mbai as part of the grand plan, and as an interim measure to roof the chicken shed at Salem.

There is only one small problem . . . as yet neither this, nor the orchard fence at Chilumba, nor the Musonda Teachers' Programme have been approved by the UK house group. We pray that, when we do tell them, they will support this sideways channelling of funds to set yet more balls rolling.

"So, can you handle the purchase of the Salem materials alone?" I put to Bob over breakfast, knowing that in Zambia, two heads are always better than one.

He surveys my flu-ravaged features. "I'll give it a go, but what will you do?"

The living room of the flat is currently filled to overflowing with over six thousand life skills books, which need counting and allocating. "I think I've enough here to keep me occupied," I say.

No sooner has he gone, than he is back again with a sheepishly humble Mr Mbai in tow. "Apparently they need not just roofing sheets and nails, but also plaster sand and cement to complete the external and internal walls of the chicken shed," Bob explains. "And . . . it's going to cost about £250 all together."

"Which we haven't exactly got," I hiss at Bob, all the while smiling sweetly at Mr Mbai. "So what are you going to do, disappoint him?"

"I was going to take the surplus out on my credit card," says Bob. "Except ATMs here don't seem to like Mastercard so . . ."

"You want to use my Visa card?" *Got it in one!*

He departs along with my Visa card and Mr Mbai, while I reapply my splitting head to the task of counting books which, by now, are swimming before my eyes.

By lunchtime roofing sheets, nails, twenty pockets of cement as well as river sand are on their way to Salem Centre. Finally the 'Big Plan' is well and truly underway. Except that . . .

"Have you ever considered just how much Starfish needs to raise for this 'grand' scale plan?" Over dinner Bob puts the question we've both been avoiding.

"You mean to complete Kaputula, not to mention giving further help to Musonda and Twatasha, then to build at Salem and possibly even Chilumba? Maybe around £50 000 pounds?" Airily I toss off a figure, though frankly I haven't a clue.

"More like £150 000," he says gloomily. "And goodness knows where that sort of money will come from."

Such thoughts do not bode well for a good night's sleep. Figures swirl around our heads all night. Have we bitten off more than we can chew? Have we finally overreached for the impossible? Worse, dropped all the balls before we've even started?

Coughing and protesting loudly, I surface to face another long day. Not helped when we reach Chep to find Evelyn looks positively grey under her black skin. "I hope you haven't caught what I've got?" I sympathise.

"In fact no, since I have been unwell since the middle of last week." Which means I probably caught it from her before heading down to Lusaka.

At least she assures us Mr Banda has obtained the information about evening tuition. Inside Evelyn's office we pour over the information recorded in Mr Banda's spidery scrawl.

"Perhaps they will also teach him handwriting when he goes back to school!" I joke.

According to Mr Banda's records, three of his staff possess grade twelve and would qualify for teacher training, though not all at once. Mr Banda and two ladies however need to attend classes. Now we need to confirm with the school where these classes are on offer.

Squeezed once more into the single cab pickup, and trying not to share any more bugs than we have already, we head for Mitanto Secondary School. Then on to Musonda to confirm arrangements with Mr Banda, still grinning from ear to ear and anxious to assure us that his life is set to change.

"Dare we congratulate ourselves?" I ask Bob cautiously later.

"Not yet," says Bob guardedly. "They've yet to attend the classes *and* pass an exam!"

"Plenty of time later to pop the corks if this and all the other projects work out."

*Not to mention, not dropping any balls in the process!*

For the moment we're off to sort out Twatasha this afternoon. Since all I can do is cough, cough, cough, I don't at all feel like tackling dusty and bumpy compound roads, which in places are not even recognisable as roads at all. But hang on . . .

"Shouldn't we be going *that* way?" I point beyond Pastor Bwalia's immense bulk.

"Indeed yes," he responds. "But today maybe we should take this route."

*The scenic route perhaps?* One compound road may look much the same as another, nevertheless we complete a full circle before approaching Twatasha along a different route. At least this allows opportunity to agree the 'discrepancy' is now sorted to everyone's satisfaction and the record set straight. Though it is still taking a long time to get there . . .

After we have verified that the school has received one hundred nursery chairs and money has been handed over for twelve tables, even leaving enough for a blackboard, I check, "Do we take the same route back?"

"I think perhaps there is no need," says the Pastor.

"So, was there an obstruction, which has now cleared?" If you don't ask questions, and this of the man who requested a school when he already had sufficient money coming in from his church, you don't get answers.

"It was because of the carpenter," says Pastor Bwalia enigmatically.

"The one who made the chairs?"

"Not the one who made the chairs, but the one who was going to make the chairs."

This is developing into a Zambian conundrum. "So if the one who was going make the chairs, did not in fact make the chairs, who did make them?"

"A second carpenter made the chairs."

"But why, since the first carpenter lives just down the road?" Indeed, we went to his house to arrange it, only he wasn't there. However his obliging wife assured us he would be happy to make the chairs. She even let Bob take a photograph of her husband's workshop, another snap for the album.

"It is because of the photograph," reveals Pastor Bwalia. "It was taken in the absence of the carpenter."

"But his wife said . . ."

"It is no matter what the wife said. The carpenter feels that you have stolen his heart with your camera. Since that time he has been sick and unable to work. Even he has been saying he will stone any vehicle which comes this way."

I cast an anxious glance around, checking for lurking carpenters and flying stones. "Do you think perhaps we ought to get out of here?" I squeak.

"I think so," agrees Pastor Bwalia.

"And the tables?" I ask as Bob revs the engine, skidding the wheels and creating a veil of dust under which we make good our escape.

"The second carpenter will also make those. There will be no problem."

*No problem? Only the threat of being stoned, if we set foot or wheel near Twatasha again! Whoops, have we just dropped one ball?*

Which still leaves the orchard fencing for Chilumba, to stop goats from feasting on their fruit trees. And this, on Friday the thirteenth! *But then, we're not superstitious . . . are we?*

However, we are spending the day with Mr Chalwe. Past experience has shown days with Mr Chalwe have a habit of disappearing down a black hole. The plan is to ferry wood off-cuts from the Forestry Commission depot at Kafubu back to Chilumba Orphans' Centre. However to date, Isaac Mumba, who was supposed to set all this up, has failed to confirm the arrangements.

We arrive at Chep at 9am to find Mr Chondoka and Mr Mbai busy loading a lorry with building materials for Kaputula. Seizing the chance, we draw Mr Mbai to one side in order to share with him an even grander idea . . . that we will do all we can to get agreement from the UK committee to build a further two classrooms at Salem.

"Ah Mr and Mrs Cooke!" Mr Mbai is so overwhelmed at this news, he all but falls to his knees in gratitude. He wrings both our hands at once. "How will we ever thank you!"

By this time Mr Chalwe has appeared. "You have permission to collect the wood off-cuts?" It's always wise to check such things before we depart.

"Indeed, we can proceed straight to the sawmills on the Ndola road," he answers.

"But surely we're going to the sawmills at Kafubu? They're almost on our way."

"In fact that is not the case." To which there is no answer.

Ten miles out on the wrong side of Kitwe, we reach the sawmills on the Ndola road. "It will be better if I deal with this by myself," announces Mr Chalwe. Since prices may rise dramatically if our white faces become evident, we readily agree.

Mr Chalwe is gone for ages. Suddenly he reappears on the far side of the sawmill only to disappear again leaving us sweltering and fuming in the car still on the wrong side of town.

"I'm going in after him!" Bob leaps out and sets off in hot pursuit. He returns thunder-faced and alone. "So much for Isaac Mumba fixing it all up. There is *no* letter, *no* agreement and as yet, *no* wood."

While Bob was gone, I watched Zambians materialise from nowhere, help themselves to copious bundles of wood off-cuts and equally mysteriously vanish with their bundles, all with no sign of any money exchanging hands. "Why don't we just help ourselves, load up the pickup and go?" I propose.

"Because Chalwe still reckons all is in order and we are having 'special' wood," says Bob. "Though goodness knows what special wood is!"

Eventually Mr Chalwe waves us around to the far side of the sawmill, where an argy-bargy erupts between him and the man dealing with it who has suddenly decided we are no longer entitled to 'special' wood. *Or would he prefer 'mzungus' cough up for special wood?*

By the time the pickup is loaded with wood, it is 10.30. There is no longer time to transport three loads of wood that side today, three loads being the amount estimated to fence around the orchard.

"It would have been possible from Kafubu sawmills," we remind a crestfallen Mr Chalwe, "but certainly not from the Ndola road sawmills."

"In fact you are also an illegal load," the guy from the sawmills adds unhelpfully. "You require a red flag on the rear of the vehicle."

We end up with a bright yellow and red Shoprite bag dangling from our rear end as we crawl ten miles back into Kitwe. There we take the ring road, praying a policeman doesn't spot our illegal load, before crawling all the way to Chilumba and trying not to leave a trail of wood off-cuts sufficient to provide firewood for every villager along the way. *Oh joy!*

We reach Chilumba Orphans' Centre after midday. All of the children have gone. Nothing stirs, except . . . *what is that smoke over there?* A chill of fear clutches my heart arousing a distinct sense of déjà-vu. Haven't we been here before? Didn't a convenient fire demolish the temporary school at Kaputula just at the point we pulled the plug on the funding? Is the Chilumba community up to similar tricks here, burning down an orchard they can see no use for, when what they really want is . . .

We follow the trail of smoke over to the orchard where a fire smoulders under some logs, right in the middle of the windbreak, which is supposed to protect the trees from fire. We smell more than drifting wood-smoke. Mostly the trees are unscathed though some have suffered fire damage.

"Maybe you can communicate your thoughts to the community," suggests Mr Chalwe since both children and adults have begun gathering back at the school.

We sit in front of a silent and sullen community. All of them are eyeing us suspiciously. But then we also eye them suspiciously. Neither of us feels particularly communicative. We have no idea what we are dealing with here. Is the construction of an orchard fence beyond them?

Mr Chalwe, who is seldom lost for words, starts up. On and on, chilapa-lapa, chilapa-lapa. Suddenly I quite clearly detect the words 'kitchen', 'blackboard' and lapa-lapa 'log delivery tomorrow.'

"Hang on a minute!" I interrupt hotly. "Those off-cuts aren't intended for firewood!"

"Nor for building a kitchen!" exclaims Bob who has quite clearly heard the same. Has a kitchen hut just now been added to the lengthy list of requests made on our first visit here? Does the community consider the use of wood off-cuts for orchard fencing as a waste of resources? Once our backs are turned, do they intend using them for something else? *Firewood perhaps?*

"Besides, tomorrow is Saturday," we remind Mr Chalwe. "We cannot deliver tomorrow." *Logs, firewood, wood off-cuts or special delivery kitchens!*

The journey back to Kitwe is a silent one. As we stop to buy 5kg of nails, we wonder again whether this wood will ever end up as fencing, or simply the equivalent of Möben kitchen hut in rural Zambia. We part on cool terms.

"We would hope to see the orchard fence in place next time we come," Bob reminds Mr Chalwe.

"Unless it is, sadly Starfish couldn't consider any further funding to Chilumba," I add, thus hammering home a few of the 5kg of nails and in the process dropping the Chilumba ball.

A borehole, a clinic and a school they asked for on our first visit here. Now a kitchen, a blackboard and transport were added today. Which begs the question as to who is right and who is wrong. Is the community right for presuming what they are given can be used for whatever purpose they want it for? Or are we wrong for not asking in the first place before handing over what we thought they should have? Maybe there is a lesson to be learnt here! *And we thought we had a heart for this work?*

But for now, we must leave Chilumba and its hypothetical orchard fencing, Mr Banda dreaming of his proposed betterment, as well as Salem and its chicken shed along with the prospect or not of greater things to come. Not forgetting the carpenter at Twatasha, who has threatened to stone us, should we ever set foot there again.

*Who said this was going to be easy?* So many balls to keep juggling at one and the same time! Though hopefully God's capable hands are also in on the juggling act.

So much for the 'big plan! The big question is, will any, or all of it, succeed? And what if anything will happen in our absence? Time alone will provide the answers, and hopefully keep you reading on!

## CHAPTER NINE: A GHOST TOWN FULL OF MEMORIES . . . *Monday August 16th, 2004*

Visits to community schools reveal schools with no desks, tables or chairs, schools with no textbooks, exercise books, pens or pencils, schools with no water, electricity or sanitation and schools with no qualified teacher on site. Yet every school visited is packed to capacity with orphans and vulnerable children who fall outside the state system of education.

It would be hard to categorise these schools' greatest area of need. They need so much. Following the commencement of the 'big plan', Starfish began redressing these shortfalls with gifts of desks, tables, chairs and exercise books to Musonda Community School, nursery tables and chairs to Twatasha Nursery School and bags filled with school materials to Kaputula Community School. We investigated the possibility of orchard fencing at Chilumba and funded roofing and plastering a chicken shed at Salem Centre for Street kids.

Yet one need Starfish has found particularly difficult to satisfy is the desperate need for textbooks. In some schools the entire supply of textbooks would fill one small suitcase. This meagre supply is often shared between six or more teachers forced to teach by rote or blackboard, always supposing they have a blackboard. As for one textbook per child, forget it! In Zambia, it's a dream that doesn't exist.

Imagine then our surprise, when visiting the Zambia Organisation for Community Schools (ZOCS) in Lusaka, and upon raising the issue of the chronic lack of textbooks in community schools on the Copperbelt, we are told . . . "Ah, but they have hundreds of books at the Zambia Community Schools Secretariat (ZCCS). Even thousands! I'm telling you they have a storeroom with books stacked from floor to ceiling."

At ZCCS we are directed to the office of a Mrs C whose glare is so threatening, she possibly suspects we're after the family silver. We explain who we are and why we want books.

"We have books," she concedes guardedly, "But you cannot have any."

*Could that be because we are not there officially, but as rather better off beggars?*

"How can I give you any books without first receiving a letter of introduction telling me that you are bona fide in your request, huh?"

In Zambia nobody gets anything unless their request is copied out in triplicate, and duly signed and stamped to authenticate it.

"You know these people in community schools," expands Mrs C, "most of the time, they don't know what they are doing."

We resist the temptation to tell her in most of the schools we have visited, not only do they know what they are doing, but they are also doing a fine job, albeit under difficult circumstances.

"Always they are saying, 'Give us more textbooks' when in fact, because these teachers are not qualified, they are not knowing how to get children to share books one between two," complains Mrs C.

Unable to remain silent I say, "If a class teacher has only one book per class, how can they possibly get children to share textbooks?"

"Ah me!" Suddenly Mrs C buries her head in her hands before taking off on a different tack. "If it is not that my poor mother died in June and still my head is not straight from my loss! Then my father also is having a stroke."

"We are sorry for your loss," we tell her. "Nevertheless . . ."

"You are wanting books," she sighs. "Maybe you can ring me in two weeks. If you bring a letter, I will see what I can do."

Which is small progress. However it means another trip up to the Copperbelt in order to obtain a letter from the acting ED of Chep . . .

"First *you* must write *me* a letter," she announces, "requesting *me* please to give *you* a letter of permission for the secretariat."

We shake our heads in disbelief. Nevertheless we write the ED a *letter* requesting a *letter* to which she duly responds with a *letter* sanctioning our request. All this must then await our next trip down to Lusaka where we present Mrs C at ZCCS with our letter duly signed, dated and stamped. After surveying our letter critically, she finally shows signs of softening, so we ask, "How many books can you give us?"

"That I don't know." Mrs C is obviously not going to part with books that easily. She is guarding them more cagily than drug addicts their precious stash. "Maybe you must give me time to sort it out."

"Will an hour be enough? Only we are off to the Copperbelt today and it really would make a lot of people happy if we took them some textbooks."

Miraculously we return to find two immense piles of books. True, they're not Maths, Science or English textbooks, but books on Life Skills such as the importance of good hygiene, and nutrition, Aids Awareness and other skills for survival. In a country where the average life span is a mere thirty-seven years, these are important skills. We guess there are a thousand or more books. Certainly they fill the back of the hired pickup. The difficulty will be deciding which schools in Kitwe receive the books.

Since this makes us late leaving Lusaka, Bob puts his foot down and is speeding along nicely when suddenly out steps a policeman hand raised bringing us to an ignominious halt.

"Oh no!" groans Bob. "Aren't we in the 100kmh zone yet?"

Our daughter is of the opinion that politeness towards the Zambian police lets you get away with murder, if not speeding infringements. To date this strategy has failed dismally for us. This is not the first time we've been caught. Nor is it destined to be the last. Bob winds down his window, preparing to argue the point.

However politeness is not on this particular policeman's mind. Maybe, as so often happens, he didn't get paid at the end of the month. "You have exceeded the speed limit for this stretch of the road."

"I have?"

"The speed limit here is 80 kph and in fact you were doing 85 kph."

"This is a hire car. There must be something wrong with the speedometer." Bob attempts to bluff his way out of the charge.

"I can assure you sir, you were doing 85 kph."

"Perhaps there's a fault with your speed camera?" Perhaps not the wisest remark to make to a Zambian policeman currently in control of Zambia's one speed camera.

"If you would step out the vehicle, then the officer there will write out your charge."

But Bob is having none of it. "You can't charge us, we're charity workers. We don't get paid for our work, how can you fine us?"

"Then you can discuss your case with the senior officer over there."

The senior officer is installed behind a table and chair away from the dust and dirt of the highway. He glances our way, perhaps wondering why this particular 'mzungu' hasn't paid up and shut up. After all, a fair cop is a fair cop. Or is it? Fines are supposed to be fixed amounts. However at 'unofficial' roadblocks cash often changes hands and nothing further is said. Unfortunately, offer twenty pin to the wrong policeman and we're done for.

I sit sweltering in the car while a little charade is played out at the roadside table. Will Bob get away with it? Is the fact that he's returning to the vehicle alone a good sign or not? "Well?"

"I gave him all the excuses. We're charity workers, carrying books for orphans and vulnerable children. He said 'such things should not be used as a scapegoat' . . . then he let me off saying it is *not* to happen again."

All this makes us late arriving at Kitwe. Darkness is falling as the gardener and the maid at Rosewood Flats unload our baggage, piling the books high along one wall of the living room in the flat.

"That's a lot of books, certainly more than we'd expected!"

"How many do you think there are?" I ask.

"A couple of thousand or so, perhaps we ought to count them?"

So, tired as we are, we count the Life Skills books. . .

"What on earth do we do with *six thousand* books? There's enough and more for Kaputula, Musonda and Twatasha. Even some for schools we haven't been able to help so far like Ipusukilo, Kamakonde and Mchinka . . ."

"Then there's Salem and Chilumba."

"Even so there'll *still* be some over. Just like it, now we're wallowing in books!"

The following morning I set about counting out books while Bob deals with building business. For each school I count out fifty books each for grades one, two, three and four plus three teacher manuals for each.

Over the next few days we touch base with Kaputula, Musonda, Twatasha, Salem and Chilumba, variously handing over an allocation of books. Without exception they are delighted. Without exception, it is the most books any of them have seen to date. Unfortunately this first distribution makes little impression on the book mountain. We still have almost five thousand books left!

Then Chileshe of Gender and Advocacy at Chep comes up trumps. "Maybe some schools in Mufulira or elsewhere would be glad of some books."

"So what is it like now in Mufulira?" we ask cautiously yet intrigued.

Mufulira is the Zambian town we lived in over thirty years ago. Our son was born there. However, on our whistle-stop tour of old haunts in December 2002, we found Mufulira had become a ghost town. Gone was the thriving town of neat avenues lined with jacarandas, flamboyant and flame trees. When the bottom fell out of the copper market in the 1970s, Mufulira mine was hard hit. Now mine workers' and teachers' houses have become homes for squatters living in them like slums. Whether any 'mzungus' still live there is doubtful. Hardly a shop remains in the once bustling main street. Yet now another trip looms large.

"It is okay," responds Chileshe cautiously, indicating more might be said, but she prefers to keep it to herself. "But there are other places where also you can donate books. I will make a list."

It is Friday and Kaputula day before Chileshe produces her list. Since one of her *other* schools lies out Kaputula way, Chileshe is only too happy to have a day 'out in the field.' The problem is finding Mpandala Community School.

"It lies that way," announces Mr Chipotyo climbing uninvited into the back of our pickup as we prepare to leave Kaputula. "In fact, since I am coming with you to Kalulushi, I will myself show you where it is."

By now the Kaputula community views us not only as benefactors, but also as providing a free shuttle service to Kafubu Depot, Kalulushi or Kitwe. Generally without asking, workers or their wives climb up into the back of the pickup with anything from babies to bicycles to sacks of mealies. Mr Chipotyo in particular always seems to have business somewhere en route.

"You do know where Mpandala School is?" I ask. Beyond Kaputula lie vast, impenetrable forests of pine and eucalyptus. Roads into the forests are mere dust tracks. Get lost in there and we could be gone forever.

"For sure!" Squinting through over-sized glasses, Mr Chipotyo's pained expression suggests: *how could I even ask!*

"Mr Chondoka mentioned a shortcut," I hazard.

"I know of no shortcut." Which lack of knowledge is discouraging, since we are barely four kilometres distant from Kaputula.

We drive back up to the main road, then plunge off onto a forest track. Eucalyptus trees tower high above us covering the forest with eerie shadows. Gradually the track becomes narrower and sandier. "You're sure this is the way?" I ask Mr Chipotyo.

"I think so," he says, "but in fact, Bwanakula Thandi, I am not sure."

On and on we plough through ever thickening forest. "You have been to this school before?" I check with Chileshe.

"In fact yes, but from the other side where the road is better."

*Now she tells us!*

Just as we think the road will peter out completely, we emerge into a forest clearing containing nothing but a cluster of primitive mud huts. Can this be a school? Yes, on the other side of the clearing is a larger mud hut bearing a sign proclaiming: MPANDALA MIDDLE BASIC SCHOOL.

"You are most welcome!" A little wizened old man rushes out to greet us. His effusive greeting suggests this head teacher hardly sees anyone.

Since it is past midday, there are no children on site, but still he must show us his school. It is the most delightfully simplistic school we have seen. When we hand over two hundred life skills books, the old man is overcome. "What a difference your gift will make! How can we ever thank you!" he says.

*Actually by telling us there is a loo here!*

There are two spanking clean pit toilets round the back of the school with an open view of the vlei to die for. However closer inspection reveals a perilous balancing act is required in order to stay poised over the pit. All that separates the user from a fate worse than death, is one precariously balanced log over a hole dropping away into infinity. But relief is more important than irrational fears, and the view to die for is worth the fate worse than death, though I wish I'd worn a skirt, not bush trousers.

Back on track, lunch is in danger of becoming a distant memory. Since neither Chileshe nor Mr Chipotyo has any food with them, it's a case of share what we have. We park up in the midst of the forest and open up the dusty rear guard of the pickup. Using it as an impromptu table I lay out bread and butter, crisp-breads, two hard-boiled eggs, two juice drinks, two small bottles of water and four pieces of pineapple which might decimate our rations, yet provides a veritable feast for two people who have not eaten all day.

Around us there is not a sound of civilisation, just the rustle and settling of uninhabited bush, the soughing of tall trees. Memorable moments like this in the middle of the bush and away from the bustle of Kitwe will stay with us forever and make it all worthwhile.

It is Monday before we pick up the book distribution programme again. At least the pile is diminishing and Chileshe is dangling the Mufulira carrot once more. "I have eight more centres to which we can deliver books. However there is one problem . . . they lie in two different directions out of Kitwe. It will take time and effort to achieve what we set out to do. Oh and the school holidays have begun and I have been unable to contact any of them."

*Right then, that shouldn't be too difficult!*

Our first drop, Fisenge Community School, lies on the Luanshya road, which is virgin territory. We arrive to a deserted and locked building, though very soon the first ragged orphan appears. He assures us he knows where one teacher lives and races off on bare feet to fetch him. In no time a straggle of curious onlookers arrives, bemused by two 'mzungus' and a posh pickup. Could a spaceship landing in their compound appear more alien?

When the teacher turns up, we hand over the books and take a picture to make the donation official. The children also want their picture taken, then peer excitedly at themselves on the small screen at the back of the camera. Already we are running over time and still seven schools to go.

The next two should be easy. Chep has a branch office in Luanshya where Chileshe has arranged to drop off a box to be shared between two schools. But is anything *ever* easy in Zambia?

Chep's branch office is located in a tiny house far away from the centre of what used to be a busy mining town. Luanshya like Mufulira has seen its heyday come and go. In charge of the office is a young man called Payne whose welcome is so overstated, his opportunities for social interaction must be severely limited. "But you must stay for a cup of tea, I insist."

It is a tempting offer. "I'd like a tea with no milk," I say without thinking.

Payne summons Chileshe's assistance in making the tea. But have I created a dilemma? "What if they don't have any milk?" I mutter to Bob. "How can they offer tea with or without milk if they don't have any?"

"I don't mind mine without," he says.

"But they don't know that. Now they probably feel they have to give you that option, regardless of whether they have any milk or not." Does he get the point? "Just *don't* ask for milk, wait and see what comes."

The tea takes a long time. Have they sent out to buy milk? In comes another member of staff to entertain us. We comment on the visible changes since the 1970s in towns like Mufulira and Luanshya.

"That is the fault of privatisation on the part of the government . . ." He launches into a lengthy diatribe concerning the ills of Zambia in general and the evils of privatisation in particular.

*And we thought Zambia's ills were due to poverty, disease, corruption, HIV Aids, malnutrition . . .*

"Ah, the tea!" In come Payne and Chileshe bearing a kettle, three mugs, a choice of teabags, instant coffee and CREMA instant milk powder.

We sit sipping tea and discussing Zambia's many problems, though somewhat guardedly. The different political agenda here is maybe something to do with depressed towns where there is no longer any employment.

Time is advancing rapidly. Since we are half way to Ndola, it seems sensible to continue along this road to the roundabout on the outskirts of town, then branch off onto the Mufulira road which runs along the Congo border.

"Aaaghh, but we cannot go that way!" shrieks Chileshe.

"Why ever not? We travelled along that road two years ago on our first trip back to Zambia. There wasn't a problem, though it was a bit quiet."

"*Quiet!*" screeches Chileshe. "Aieeh, you are not knowing people have been attacked on that road? Even a minibus was stopped by bandits, who stripped all the passengers of their clothes and their valuables, then stole the minibus leaving the people stranded by the side of the road."

Stunned into silence, we reflect on our narrow escape. "And we thought the road was quiet because of the mine closure."

"No, it was quiet because it is dangerous! Today we have no choice but to go via Kitwe onto the Chingola road, then turn off to Mufulira."

"But is that road any more safe?"

"Safer than the road which you and Mr Cooke travelled before when you were not knowing," chides Chileshe.

The long drive back allows time to reflect that we really should have thought twice about using that road two years ago, or at least tried to confirm whether it was safe.

Over the past couple of years we have come to realise how different Zambia today is from Zambia thirty years. During school holidays we used to travel long journeys down to Rhodesia and even Mozambique. Because of the distances involved, we often set off in the middle of the night attempting to reach the Rhodesian border before dark the same day.

On one trip our small son was asleep in his carrycot in the back of the car as we travelled that same road from Mufulira to Ndola in pitch darkness, not a vehicle nor a light in sight. Suddenly on the road ahead appeared two Africans swathed in greatcoats and mufflers. One held a huge bazooka type gun and the other a sturdy stick like a knobkerrie. They indicated the vehicle should stop. Police officers or villains, how were we to know?

As Bob slowed, I squealed, "Don't stop! Put your foot down and drive on!" My thoughts were for the safety of our son sleeping in the back of the car.

"Don't be so stupid!" Bob retorted. "They're police officers. If I don't stop they'll shoot at the vehicle."

"Police officers, on the Ndola road at four o'clock in the morning? Now who's being stupid?"

"I'm not taking any chances." And he brought the vehicle to a standstill.

One of the two men indicated he should wind down the window. "We are police officers," he said. "We need to see what is in your vehicle. You must get outside the vehicle."

It is hard to argue with a bazooka at 4am. Nevertheless, for our own sake and that of our son, I had to try. "But officer, our baby is asleep in the back of the car. If we get out, we will wake him."

A crack appeared in the hollow of the African's face. Was it a grin? He stuck his head up close to the open window, assailing us with his foul smelling breath. I tried not to cringe. "Ah, yes, indeed you have a baby in the back. In which case you may drive on."

Bob wound the window up and eased the car back into gear. We drove off trembling. "They were no police officers. They were after the car and money and all our stuff."

"So what do you think saved us, Andrew asleep in the back?"

"I guess so, after all . . . Zambians love babies."

"They weren't Zambians! They were Congolese car thieves or I'll eat my hat! And I guess that puts paid to us travelling this road at 4am again."

Which it did, though that same recollection didn't stop us two years ago from using the very same road without checking its safety. Hence the need for a detour today and taking the long way round to Mufulira via Kitwe.

Since we're already going back via Kitwe, it makes sense to complete the Kitwe drop-offs, then tackle Mufulira in the afternoon. It is almost noon and very hot. Two more drop-offs remain before lunchtime, fortunately located near to each other. The Kwacha II Centre is for young children only so we just leave books for grades one and two. The second is a familiar name . . .

"We have been to Ipusukilo School before," we tell Chileshe.

"Then you will also know it is tricky to reach." Which is an understatement. Either the vehicle is bigger or else the roads are narrower or there are more stalls littering the sides of the road and spilling over into the road. The same music is blaring at deafening pitch outside the school, though since it is the holidays there are no kids on site.

Mr Gibson the head teacher looks as young as ever. But hang on a minute, *isn't that a familiar face?* "Mr Banda, we didn't expect to see you here?"

"I am visiting my good friend Mr Gibson," Mr Banda head teacher of Musonda Community School informs us. "He has been good enough to assist me with my education."

Does Mr Banda mean Gibson is teaching him? But there is no time to pursue this now. We have already mooted the possibility of Mr Banda and other teachers at Musonda pursuing studies for grade twelve. Maybe Mr Banda has already started by helping himself.

Finally after lunch we are en route to Mufulira where we need to find two schools. The first, Kawama, lies in a vast compound or rather shanty town which certainly wasn't on the outskirts of Mufulira thirty years ago. As soon as we enter the compound bad vibes emanate from all sides. People stare with suspicious eyes. Groups of youths hanging around on corners weigh up the car. Unfortunately our hired car lacks the protection of UN or UNICEF or WORLD VISION emblazoned on the side to protect us from attack. Unfortunately also the school is well and truly shut. What to do now?

"I'm not really sure we should be here in an unmarked car," I murmur.

"Maybe we locate the head teacher's house and leave the books there," suggests Bob.

"It is important to leave the books with someone we can trust," insists Chileshe. "In fact a Catholic sister co-ordinates this place. Maybe she is the best person with whom to leave the books."

Bob is turning the car around when I observe a man wearing an ugly expression heading our way down a narrow track between the rows of houses. He starts shouting and gesticulating, then bends down and picks up a large rock.

"We must get out of here . . . FAST!" screeches Chileshe.

Bob also catches sight of the man as a stone whizzes our way. As he bends to pick up second one, Bob's foot hits the accelerator and we zoom off leaving a cloud of dust. I glance into the wing mirror to see the man standing in the centre of the road shaking his fist at the receding vehicle.

"Yes, well they can be a bit hot-headed here in Mufulira," squeaks Chileshe.

The convent is mercifully in a quieter part of town away from the compounds. The Sister there promises that the children will have the new books at the start of the new term.

"So you used to live In Mufulira?" asks Chileshe.

"Our son was born here, thirty-four years ago."

"Maybe we should find the place where you used to live."

"Is that wise when someone's just tried to stone the vehicle?"

"I think it is okay in the centre of town."

However 56A Lumumba Avenue proves a little difficult to reach, since most avenues off the centre of town are blocked off with concrete blocks. But whether to keep cars in or keep thieves out, who can say? Once beautiful tree lined avenues are now pock-marked with potholes. The whole area resembles a Nazi concentration camp, not the pleasant town we once lived in.

We fill up the car with petrol. Few people are around in the centre of town and not a white face to be seen. Thirty years ago Mufulira contained one of the largest expatriate communities on the Copperbelt. There was a library, theatre, swimming pool, cinema, even a restaurant. All have vanished. It has indeed become a ghost town.

"What will happen to these places?" we ask Chileshe.

"Maybe that young man at Luanshya with all his politics has the answers," she says sadly. "Me, I don't think things can improve unless they produce copper once more. And for the moment that does not seem likely."

Driving out of town, we accept this will be our last visit here. The main road is no longer safe; even the town itself is not safe. Yet we are leaving part of ourselves behind in this ghost town.

"But we still have one more place to go to," says Chileshe brightly, perhaps sensing our feeling of loss. "According to Mrs Lumba it is half way along the road between Mufulira and the Kitwe turn-off." Which is of no help since Mrs Lumba is not in the car with us. "I think maybe we can ask these roadside sellers," proposes Chileshe.

We pull up beside colourfully clad women in 'chitenges' selling cabbages, rape, spinach and tomatoes. Immediately we are besieged with arms thrusting cabbages and other vegetables in through the open car window. "Here!" "Me, me, me!" "Buy this one!"

"Sorry, we don't want vegetables. We're looking for a school called Mwambashi."

There is much muttering between the women, maybe because we don't buy their vegetables, maybe because they have an inkling where the school is. A hasty conversation ensues between Chileshe and the women.

"Mrs Lumba was clearly wrong in her directions," announces Chileshe. Just how wrong becomes apparent, as we drive another ten kilometres onto another road entirely before turning off into an unrecognisable world of affluence and comfort, of large houses, verdant lawns, swimming pools and even horse riding and tarred roads. Beautiful homes, for beautiful people.

"This is Garneton," says Chileshe, "where people from Kitwe who have a lot of money live."

Even the school is easy to find. "But why a community school here, in this affluent environment?" We are puzzled.

"Even these people have their needs," Chileshe tells us. "It is a school for the hearing impaired."

And so our task is done. We have distributed almost four thousand books. The remainder will be left with Chep for distributing to other needy schools in the area. In all some nineteen schools have benefited from receiving the books.

What's more, Copperbelt teachers are now aware that there are books aplenty and for free in Lusaka. All that is needed is a couple of stubborn 'mzungus', a pickup, someone with a sense of direction to ferret out the schools, plus an endless supply of petrol, time and energy.

Not much really, but all that goes a long way to explaining why schools in Lusaka lack for nothing, while schools in Kitwe lack everything. The reason being that nobody bothers sufficiently to shift much needed materials from Lusaka up to the Copperbelt. No wonder teachers on the Copperbelt feel hard done by!

# CHAPTER TEN: OF FISHPONDS AND FAITH and a pair of misplaced cuckoos . . . *May 3rd, 11th and 13th, 2005*

By spring 2005 the 'big plan' is well underway. And if at times we feel like circus performers spinning plates and trying not to let any fall, well . . . who said retirement would be a doddle anyways!

In late April we return to Zambia, exchanging the burgeoning UK spring for the tail end of the Zambian rainy season. Winter may well be on its way, but for the moment the skies are clearing and it's pleasantly warm if not downright hot.

Unfortunately we return to find not only Kaputula project at a standstill, but both the teacher training and the pupil sponsorship programmes at Musonda have gone pear-shaped. Worse, no-one seems willing or able to give satisfactory answers and Chilumba STILL has not constructed the fence around the orchard.

There is however one bright star in the firmament. Salem has done all and more of what was expected. Because their organisation possesses a properly functioning bank account and accounts department, Starfish has transferred money out to them so work could start on the construction of two classrooms there.

So, even if lack of progress on our other projects makes us feel like getting on the next plane back to the UK, the prospect of a visit to Salem on Tuesday forestalls any thoughts of premature flight.

As usual we meet Mr Mbai at Chep though, since he slips the noose several times, it is 10am before we have him the vehicle. Even then someone else has clambered into the back with him.

"So Mr Mbai, how goes it at Salem?" I ask.

"Very well, Mrs Cooke. We so appreciate you and Mr Cooke and the Starfish for what you are doing," Mr Mbai responds

"And you are already in the final stages with the two classrooms?"

"Indeed, we are just now starting glazing and painting."

"That is incredible!"

Just how incredible is almost beyond belief! Because of the need to get approval from the UK committee, then to transfer funds out to them, the Salem project started a full five months after Kaputula. Yet it is already in the finishing stages, and all without going over budget.

"It is truly amazing!" We stand on the far side of the sports field which constitutes the greater part of the land area at Salem and gaze across at the newly constructed two classroom block which has replaced the tattered shacks which formerly served as classrooms there.

"How come you have succeeded where Kaputula failed? Is there is a magic formula we could transfer to Kaputula?"

Mr Mbai may be modest, nevertheless he knows the answers. "Here *everyone* chipped in to get the work done, acquiring new skills in the process. Even the older boys who stay on site have been learning brick-making and bricklaying in the process."

"That's amazing!" The more we hear, the better it gets.

"Also we kept employment of outside people to a minimum, using those same skilled workers to train others . . ."

"Tactics which might well have been employed at Kaputula?"

"Indeed, but then Kaputula is a very different and difficult community." Which rather sums them up . . . a very difficult community.

Mr Mbai leads us with pride across the sports field to visit the new building. It consists of two immense classrooms and an office. Even the workmen have smiling faces.

"The good news is the government has agreed that if we can turn part of the office into a secure storage area, we may be entitled to register as an examination centre," Mr Mbai informs us. "Then the school will no longer have the expense and trouble of sending children to government schools in order to sit the grade seven exam."

"That is good news."

"And, once registered, we can charge other schools to take the exam here, thus generating much needed income."

Ah the Holy Grail of income generation, one sure way out of the twin traps of poverty and dependency. Mr Mbai has certainly got his head screwed on.

"But now we must visit the chicken shed which also is completed and fully operational."

This tour gets better by the minute. We follow Mr Mbai's slight figure across to the chicken sheds. No mistaking the smell hitting us from several yards away. But yes, there are now two operational chicken sheds. We squeeze inside each shed in turn. Inside they are well maintained, though the smell of ammonia combined with chicken poo is overpowering. One shed contains birds ready for selling while the other contains birds a few weeks old.

We are thankful to escape, gagging for fresh air. "So now, when you sell off the larger birds and empty out one shed, you have a second lot coming on in the second shed?"

"Indeed that is so."

"So how much do you sell a bird for?" I ask.

"They are K20 000 cash and K22 000 on credit."

"You give credit?"

"Indeed, Mrs Cooke. That way we make even more money for the school."

I take my hat off to this man.

"But now Mr and Mrs Cooke, the children have something to perform for you," he tells us.

We return to a classroom to find four chairs placed throne-like at the front of the room. "They are so pleased with their new classrooms, that the kids wanted to prepare an entertainment for you," confides Mr Mbai.

Oh dear, I pray it won't be as 'heavy' as the previous performance which put across the dangers of HIV Aids to children as young as five and six. What was truly shocking, was how perfectly at ease such young kids were with the sexual content of the performance, even the simulated act of sex.

But no, this drama is lighter in nature. The school is currently closed, so the street boys who live on site are performing. Since it is in Bemba, Mr Mbai on one side and Pastor Mwewa on the other, translate for us.

The drama tells how once there was a school, which consisted of nothing but shacks. The shacks let in rain and were infested with insects. Nobody wanted to go to this school because it had no proper classrooms. Even kids who did go there, were ridiculed by other kids who went to 'proper' schools.

One day along came a couple of 'mzungus' named 'Mr and Mrs Cuckoo' . . . yes, they really do mean us. We smile secretly at this unfortunate corruption of our name.

The street kid playing Mr 'Cuckoo' has a roll of 'chitenge' stuffed up inside his shirt to convey a large paunch, while the boy playing Mrs 'Cuckoo' adopts a simpering and distinctly feminine voice. He carries a notepad and pencil, because 'Mrs Cuckoo' writes everything down. She has however forgotten her camera so 'Mr Cuckoo' wags his finger at her and even threatens to beat her. Clearly these kids enjoy comedy and play it for all it's worth.

To everyone's great joy, the 'Cuckoos' provide nice classrooms for the struggling school. Now everyone wants to go to that school, because it is better than the other schools. Now no-one laughs at children who go there. And here is the punch-line, the 'Cuckoos' must come back because . . .

"The school is needing a library!" Mr Mbai concludes with a chuckle.

Finally all the children as well as the grownups burst into spontaneous singing and clapping and dancing. Even the 'Cuckoos' join in, swaying and wiggling and casting their innate Englishness to the winds.

Mr Mbai holds his hands up to halt the jollity. "Mr and Mrs Cooke, we are appreciating you for what you have done for us here at Salem . . . However we want you to know that we still need two further classrooms as well as a library unit."

"Er . . . maybe we will see what we can do." The 'Cuckoos' look at each other dismayed. *Did we really imagine we would get off so lightly?*

There is one further task to perform. A teenager from our local church has donated clothing for the street girls. About twelve of them stay in a 'safe' house along the road from the school, so there we must take the clothing.

"How long will these girls stay here?" We ask Mr Mbai as we go along.

"In general about three to six months," he tells us. "Sometimes longer, depending on how long it takes our counsellor to resolve the home situation and discover why the girls took to the streets in the first place."

"So you try to get them back to homes they have run away from? This seems a strange way of going about it."

"In most cases this is the best solution in order to keep them off the streets or from turning to prostitution or becoming abused."

I'm tempted to add, '*What if they were being abused within the home in the first place?*' But this is one question too far. These are Mbai's own people. It's not our place to pre-judge.

By now we have arrived at the girls' house where today the unappetising odour of Zambian beans cooking rises to greets us, marginally better than 'kapenta' and it is food.

The girls range from four years to twenty. They crowd into their one tiny living room, perhaps sensing we come bearing gifts. Many of their eyes are blanked out from the struggle to survive and what it has cost them. However when they see the clothes their eyes light up with something approaching joy. The bag contains glitzy tops and tight leggings, even a black skirt with a shocking pink zip. I fear possession of that will be hugely contested.

Finally the girls sing for us. Slow tuneful voices meld as one into a dirge-like hymn. 'Jesus has taken me and washed me and lifted me up from the problems I have.' In their case fortunately He has, since they are being given a new start in life. Oh that it was the same for hundreds of other street kids in Zambia, as well as thousands of orphans and vulnerable children wallowing in a mire of poverty from which there is no escape.

"Mrs Cooke, I am thinking you must pray for everyone," announces Mr Mbai. Somehow God provides inspiration along the lines that He indeed does hold them in his hands.

"Amen!" echoes around the room where not a single person doubts that is the case. *Oh that people in the UK had the same faith!*

Still buoyant from Tuesday's trip to Salem, we survive the rest of the week in Kitwe. And if the Kaputula account still does not balance and both of the Musonda programmes still threaten to go pear-shaped, there is the joy over the weekend of buying two sewing machines in Lusaka for handing over to vulnerable women at Bwafwano Women's Centre.

It is therefore Wednesday of the following week before we manage a trip to Chilumba to see how things are there. At first the road follows the same route as to Kaputula and Kafubu, then at the police post bears off to the left, along a red dirt road, which sees little in the way of traffic. Bob flies along, much faster than Mr Chalwe would ever take this road, scattering chickens, goats, men on bicycles, even a couple of bush pigs out for a stroll. I sense Mr Chalwe's knuckles going white with fear in the rear of the vehicle.

Since we were later leaving than intended, we meet the Chilumba children walking back from school. The school site is almost deserted. However many children recognise the vehicle and about turn to head straight back to the centre. Soon we have a veritable crowd of barefoot and ragged children around the vehicle, trailing their fingers in its dusty coating and waiting to see what will happen next.

Since last year's harrowing visit to Chilumba, we have maintained email contact with Faith Lyena, director of the centre. Also, following the harrowing request from a child there for me to be her mother, plans are afoot to set up an orphan sponsorship scheme whereby the most needy children there will be sponsored by people in the UK. There is only problem. While we are very soon awash with orphans and needy children, there is no sign of the man supposed to be drawing up the profiles.

"So where is he?" we ask Mr Chalwe.

"In fact I am not quite sure," responds Mr Chalwe. He conducts a hasty conversation in Bemba with some wrinkly and toothless grandmothers who have turned up.

Time is ticking by. We shall meet ourselves on the return journey if things don't speed up.

"They are saying everyone came yesterday because they were expecting us yesterday." Mr Chalwe appears almost as fazed as on our first visit when a young girl asked would I be her mother.

"But there was never any mention to come yesterday," I try. But there is no answer to this. The community has no phone contact, bus service, postal service or transport. Clearly someone got the wires mixed up and they weren't telephone wires. "So what is to do?"

"In fact Benny, who has the profiles for the nine orphans who are to be sponsored, lives about five or six kilometres away at Kabulangashi which is another Faith Orphanage project."

"Aaah!" A small sigh of frustration escapes. "Is it possible we might reach Benny?" Which maybe is asking the impossible.

"Only if we were to go there," replies Mr Chalwe, perhaps stating the obvious.

"But will Benny be there?"

"Ah, that I don't know." He shakes his head. "But we can try."

So we clamber back into the vehicle to continue along the red dirt road leading past Chilumba seemingly to nowhere, but in fact which leads to Kabulangashi. After a few kilometres, Mr Chalwe waves us off-road along a mere track, which plunges like a knife slicing through butter into dense bush. We hope Mr Chalwe, and also his mother who has climbed uninvited into the back of the vehicle, have got this right.

"We have gone six kilometres now," announces Bob pointedly thus revealing his mounting sense of unease. *Where are we going?*

"It is just a little further." Mr Chalwe appears oblivious to ever deepening ruts, branches and grasses whipping the sides of the vehicle and that it is rapidly approaching lunchtime.

Suddenly realisation dawns: this is developing into another 'chalwe day', what we have taken perhaps rather unkindly to calling any day when things do not exactly go according to plan. But how do we turn it around? We are currently on a track to nowhere, trying to locate someone whom we don't even know is there. We have orphans waiting back at the centre for us, which we must drive back to, and from there back to Kitwe. It is now twelve o'clock and worst of all . . . our sandwiches are in the fridge back at the flat because we thought this would be a short trip.

"We are here!" announces Mr Chalwe.

Here being a clearing in the bush in the middle of which sits a mud hut albeit of the 'posher' variety. To our immense relief a man emerges from the hut. *Bet he doesn't see many callers round here!* Could this be Benny? Cheers, it is!

"In fact yes, I have the profiles," explains Benny, "but I am not having the photos. They are still in my camera."

We tell him no matter. The profiles are what are important. We can take photos ourselves.

"Benny here is the co-ordinator of the Kabulangashi project," Mr Chalwe is keen to inform us. "Which in turn is supported by the Faith Orphanage. We are encouraging the setting up of fishponds here for the generation of income. I am wondering if you would like to see the fishponds?"

*How could we refuse!* Unfortunately reaching the fishponds involves continuing by foot along an even narrower track wending its way through tall grasses swaying way above our heads. *Oh this is fun, on foot along a pathway, along which and round any turn might lurk a gaboon viper or puff adder. Both are short, thick ugly snakes, two of Zambia's deadliest. Both strike first, then don't wait round for questions afterwards!*

The track is so narrow we are forced to walk in single file. Benny leads the way, followed by Mr Chalwe, Mr Chalwe's mother, a woman with a baby on her back who may be Benny's wife and finally ourselves. We walk and walk in the hot noonday sun till eventually we reach two fishponds.

"What sort of fish are in them?" asks Bob eagerly. Perhaps he fancies a weekend's fishing out here in this far-flung spot . . . *by himself!*

"There are no fish in them," says Mr Chalwe.

*Heck, what did we expect? This is Zambia after all! But no . . .*

"The fish, tilapia, will arrive in two weeks' time. Then one day there will be much food for the people of this area."

By now we are over three hours away from base and, by the looks of things, a further three hours away from returning there. I have one urgent and dire need. "Is there by any chance a toilet around here?"

"Ah sorry!" responds Mr Chalwe.

Which leaves two choices, one, squat somewhere round about thus risking the ire of those snakes, or two, ask to use the primitive 'facilities' back at Benny's place. I opt for the latter.

Benny's facilities consist of a pit toilet of the more dilapidated kind, a hole in the ground constructed with or without adequate supports and surrounded by a rapidly disintegrating grass palisade. It is open to the world on one side. Still, it's not my intention to linger longer than essential. I squat precariously, but as soon as my pee hits the spot, a stench of gargantuan proportions rises to reward me. Aaagh, the 'doings' of generations must be down this particular pit. I look up to see a couple of pigs and several chickens studiously regarding me. I hope the sight has made their day!

We clamber back into the vehicle now accompanied by Benny, Benny's wife and baby, two sacks of sweet potatoes, one of groundnuts and Benny's bicycle in the back. It is approaching 13.00. Lunch has become a dim and distant fantasy, not likely to be realised for two hours at least. Any water and nibbles must stay closeted in the cool-box because on this occasion there quite simply isn't enough to go around.

Back at the centre we photograph the orphans still on site. Four have wandered off presumably under the impression we are never to be seen again. At my request, Dynass, the child who asked last year if I would be her mother, is produced. She is delighted to see us and even more delighted to learn I will sponsor her. Goodness knows if she understands the concept of sponsorship, but from the look in her eyes, she clearly thinks her wish has come true . . . *she now has a mother!*

By 13.00 we are able to escape. Strategically I place Mr Chalwe in the front of the vehicle and clamber in the back where the snacks are. My blood sugar has reached an all time low. Once restored, I pass biscuits through to the other two.

"So now we must go straight back and visit Faith Lyena, the director of our organisation," Mr Chalwe announces.

"Ah no," we tell him. "First we have lunch." Though I suspect a swim is more on Bob's mind.

Back at the flat, we leap in the pool, then gobble the egg sandwiches from the fridge, at the same time reminding ourselves NEVER to get caught in the same predicament without any prospect of lunch again, before pegging it back to where we are to pick up Mr Chalwe.

The Skills Training Centre, also operated by Faith Orphanage Foundation, is located in the second class trading area of Kitwe. There Faith Lyena, founder and director of the foundation, awaits us. We are not sure what to expect. We have been told she is a former nurse, married to an anaesthetist and living in Ndola. What then is a woman of clearly better means doing based in Kitwe and running projects in such far-flung places as Chilumba, Kabulangashi, and even Solwezi?

"Ah I knew it would be you!" Faith clasps her hands gleefully. "I saw you in town the other day and I said to myself those are the people, the Cookes!"

We are bemused. "What made you so sure?"

"Because you looked like missionaries!"

Now we are puzzled. A lot of things we might be mistaken for but . . . "Missionaries? How is that?"

"Because of Mr Cooke with his hair and his backpack, then the sandals on his bare feet . . ."

I smile silently to myself, so it was *his* appearance gave us away . . .

"Then Mrs Cooke also, because of the dress you were wearing."

My spirits plummet as I resolve never to wear that particularly dreary dress ever again. I regard it as my Zambia dress. Below the knee, waisted, with small green and beige checks and clearly very drab!

"So what brings you to work in these parts?" I ask by way of diversion from a sensitive subject.

"Myself I am from those parts," Faith waves us to be seated and produces cool drinks and a packet of Eet-sum-mor biscuits. The ritual of handing these round consumes the next few minutes leaving us to contemplate how this large, well fed, well-dressed and well educated lady possibly hails from the same world as the wizened specimens of womanhood living at Chilumba. Besides, she has shoes on her feet.

"My parents were able to send me to the government school," Faith informs us. "Which was how I received my education and training as a nurse and also met my husband. Now I wish to do something in return for the people where I come from."

Which is all very commendable . . . "But what about the orchard fencing?" we ask. "It is months since we delivered the first wood off-cuts and also left behind money to transport the remaining wood."

"We are even now working on it," Faith assures us. "But the wood which you provided did not stretch the entire way around the orchard."

"So the task is not yet completed?"

"No, but we are wondering when you can start building a school for us that side?"

We defer any commitment on the grounds that maybe the community should show its commitment by completing the task in hand first. We say our farewells, noting that in the short space of time we have been there,

Faith has demolished a packet of biscuits almost entirely by herself, perhaps contributing somewhat to her well-fed appearance?

By now we are one week away from the end of another trip. And if Kaputula has as ever gone over budget and the orphan carers' support programme there seems unworkable because of all the wrangling, then not much has changed.

Not to mention the escalating cost of the Musonda teachers' programme and that the pupil sponsorship programme also appears a non-runner. Faith still hasn't produced photos for the absent orphans and Pastor Bwalia has lost track of one hundred chairs and twelve nursery tables for Twatasha. It would be tempting to do a runner, except people back in the UK may also have a few questions.

But there's still a launch ceremony at Salem to look forward to on Friday. And what if it is yet again Friday 13th, we're not superstitious, are we?

We arrive at Salem to an air of great excitement. The children are gathered on the field in front of the new classroom block. On the veranda stands a line of throne-like chairs and a table complete with white tablecloth and plastic flowers. As soon as we are seated the children erupt into joyful singing and dancing and praising the Lord for all His goodness.

"It never ceases to amaze us how people who have so little still remember to praise God," I comment to Mr Mbai.

"People in the UK don't do that?" He appears surprised.

"No, which is surprising because there they have so much."

"Here they are doing it because they are so thankful for what little they have." Which doesn't leave much more to be said.

Today I am trying out a new cine camera, so for once Bob is in front of the lens instead of behind it. We are invited to speak and to pray before keys to the new classrooms are handed over. Will the door open? It does.

The children race inside elbowing us to one side. We enter to be greeted by an explosion of sound. Drums are playing, people are singing and shouting and clapping their hands and gyrating wildly to the music. Never mind capturing it on video, we also are required to join in. Lord knows what they are singing about, but it sure sounds joyful.

In the classroom next door women from the sewing class are waiting for us. We have three new sewing machines to hand over to the fifteen women and young girls gathered. As we enter there is once more an explosion of sound this time from the women ululating and a young girl in black and white beating a drum as if trying to extract its soul. We feel so elated by this rapturous appreciation that all the dark spirits of the previous week vanish. It is pure joy to see what can be achieved by hard work.

Too soon it is time for goodbyes along with the gift of two very live chickens tied up in a polythene bag and one last song to sing. "We shall be missing you Cookes . . ." No mistaking the words to that one!

When later that same day we make yet another trip to Kaputula to find they are only just putting the roof on the two classroom block there, it is hard not to make comparisons with Salem which has done it all and more without any quarrelling or going over budget.

"Wouldn't it be simpler just to support communities like Salem?" asked one member of the house group on one occasion.

Wouldn't it just! But that's not really what it's all about, is it?

# CHAPTER ELEVEN: THE GOOSE THAT LAYS THE GOLDEN EGG, but does Mr Banda run out of second chances?
*May 5th and 17-19th, 2005 and various*
*dates -> November 2007*

Very soon it becomes apparent that some projects will prove easier to administer than others. Yet Starfish doesn't award brownie points or black marks; better by far to accept what comes. Nevertheless, dealings with Musonda Community School pretty rapidly begin leaving a bitter aftertaste.

Musonda was one of the first community schools visited. Housed in a converted tavern, there were no proper desks and very little in the way of materials. Some children were even writing in used receipt books, either resting on their knees or leaning against concrete pillars.

The school was set up and run by Mr Banda, assisted by half a dozen voluntary teachers. It received no government allowance only an initiative allowance, the equivalent of £8 per teacher per month, allocated by Chep to voluntary teachers who stayed the course. To date Starfish has provided the school with sixty-one desks, as well as providing teachers' tables and chairs including one for the head teacher.

"You look like a proper head teacher now!" we joked to Mr Banda, who merely grinned from ear to ear displaying yellowing teeth and cavernous holes guaranteed to cause any dentist nightmares.

Starfish also provided exercise books, pencils, biros and a room divider made of bamboo to divide one classroom into two. When the purchase price was double the price quoted, alarm bells should have rung, only they didn't.

Thus in May 2005 Starfish was ready to undertake two new projects at Musonda. Firstly, a teacher sponsorship programme to enable unqualified teachers to gain entry qualifications for teacher training and secondly, a pupil sponsorship programme to assist pupils through secondary education. But for now the focus centres on teaching the teachers how to teach!

Every year our partner organisation Chep sponsors certain teachers through teacher training. Candidates must possess a school certificate equivalent to grade twelve. At Musonda three teachers, including Mr Banda, did not possess this certificate and so did not qualify for teacher training. Starfish therefore agreed to fund attendance at evening classes so the three of them could study for the exam. Mr Banda was to finalise arrangements for classes, scheduled to commence in January of this year.

All should have been well. Yet earlier this week an obsequious Mr Banda presented himself at Chep and confessed that registration for evening classes was regrettably 'requested too late.' However when we expressed concern Mr Banda exclaimed excitedly, "Ah but the teachers are receiving extra classes at our own school!" Is this good news? Time for a visit to Mr Banda and friends . . .

Conditions are cramped in Mr Banda's squalid study, though he now sits proudly enthroned behind a new desk, a head teacher with qualifications equivalent to year eight in UK schools! In the corner still stands the photocopying machine, but as the school still has no electricity and still can't afford photocopying paper, its presence remains an anomaly.

Today eight of us are present: ourselves, Damson from Chep, Mr Banda, Ms Mwewa and Mrs Kasanda, the two other teachers on the programme, the deputy head teacher and a baby. Mrs Kasanda has not long given birth and is still breastfeeding even while we talk.

"So you have made an arrangement?" we ask.

Mr Banda is a man of few words when saying too much might make life difficult. "In fact four teachers from Mitanto High School are coming here to give us classes because they would not accept our registration at the school."

We are not so foolish as to presume these teachers are doing this out of the goodness of their hearts. We remind him there is only £100 available of which £75 is for tuition and the remainder for a hardship allowance while the three of them study. Mr Banda assures us this is enough. Sitting knees almost touching, we draw up a handwritten document stating what they are entitled to. With great pomp Mr Banda and the two women sign on the dotted line.

Only later do we discover I have added an extra nought in the teachers' allowance column making the three of them kwacha millionaires. Mr Banda may be walking on air tonight, but unfortunately it must be rectified, even though he also told us they have not received their incentive allowances for four months. As a result three teachers have walked out, while he has been evicted from his rented accommodation for failing to pay the rent. Great!

A few days later when we pass by Chep to pay in money for this programme, Mrs Musungaila head of accounts surprises us with, "In fact Mr Banda has already received K643 000 to pay the grade twelve examination fees at the examination centre." Bad enough news, since it amounts to more than three-quarters of the budget for the entire programme, but even worse, because Mr Banda told her Starfish had agreed to pay this.

"Sorry, Mrs Musungaila," we respond, "Starfish only agreed to pay for tuition plus a small hardship allowance. Nothing was said about examination fees." Mr Banda clearly is very plausible, even so far as convincing the indomitable Mrs Musungaila.

Later Damson, who is to monitor the programme, reveals he has not yet met the teachers who are giving the tuition, nor does he even know whether they exist, or have agreed to give extra classes for the same money as the evening classes. There is urgent need for further parley with Mr Banda.

However the next morning, before we set off for Musonda School, who should appear but a downcast Mr Banda, earnestly expressing a desire to come clean. "In fact what I told you yesterday is true. Three teachers including myself went to register for evening classes, but we were told it was too late to register. We were then sent to Kitwe Teacher Training College . . ."

"But Mr Banda, none of you has the qualifications to get into KTTC."

"No, but the people at KTTC advised us that, as we were unable to register for the classes, we should hire private teachers . . ."

Has Mr Banda any idea how much private tuition costs? Mr Banda merely shuffles his feet and stares at the ground, reflecting perhaps on a need to be economical with the truth, lest the goose that lays the golden egg should stop laying. When asked if he discussed it with anyone, he seizes this loophole like a drowning man clutching at a straw. "In fact I discussed this with Mrs Lumba who agreed the tuition should go ahead."

But did Evelyn discuss this with anyone else at Chep, because she certainly didn't discuss it with Starfish. One vital question remains . . . "Mr Banda, just how much is this going to cost?"

Mr Banda quotes a figure off the top of his head. However Maths is not his strong point and the need for transparency is wearing thin. Thus it takes the combined efforts of ourselves, Damson and Mrs Musungaila to work out that the costs amount to a staggering £555 for tuition plus a further £75 for examination fees . . . *more than six times the original budget for this project!*

This leaves two choices: either pay up and shut up, or pull the plug on the project. We must decide this without consultation with our committee, then explain our reasons later back in the UK. *Who said this was going to be easy!*

Not wanting to make too hasty a decision, we are still pondering when, early next week, three young men waylay us in Chep car park. Too smartly dressed for representatives of struggling community projects who sometimes wait for hours or days at Chep simply to beg for Starfish assistance, yet too young for senior members of Chep or other NGOs. Jehovah's Witnesses perhaps, out making house calls?

"Mr and Mrs Cooke, we are Mr Mvula, Mr Mutale and Mr Lungu."

*Should these names mean anything?*

"We are three of the four tutors hired by Mr Banda on your behalf and are here to ask when will we receive payment for the work we are doing?"

"Let's get this straight, Mr Banda told you he had authority to hire you as private tutors on our behalf?"

The three young men glance nervously one to another. Was that a plug being pulled? Personable young men, products of Kitwe's best secondary schools and with university degrees, they may be, nevertheless they clearly have a thing or two to learn.

"Gentlemen, suppose Mr Banda went into a garage and told them Starfish had agreed to purchase a brand new car for him, would you expect that garage to provide him with a car?" All three look disconcerted. "Yet on Mr Banda's word you agreed to give tuition with no guarantee whatsoever that Starfish would pay for it? I think, gentlemen, this requires further discussion."

For them also the fate of the golden egg-laying goose now hangs in the balance. Certainly it has temporarily stopped laying, though any decision must await the morrow.

But the next day brings a surprise development. During the night Mr Banda has reflected upon his wayward behaviour and written a letter of abject apology in which he confesses that he strung along those teachers by getting them to believe the money would be forthcoming, while at the same time lying to us about the registration as well as the money.

Matters are further complicated when Chep agrees to meet the cost of the examination fees, though still leaving the unresolved issue of who will pay the tuition costs when some three to four months have already taken place. On the advice of the acting director of Chep, we agree to pay the four teachers for work already done, but tell them that their request for back-pay along with continued funding must go before the UK committee. Since it will take several weeks before any decision is passed on, Mr Banda must sweat it out in fear the four young men from Mitanto might yet decide to lynch him!

It is with great surprise therefore to find Mr Banda at Chep *again* the following morning. "It is because I am wanting to say sorry myself in person." Mr Banda's head hangs so low it almost scrapes the ground.

"We appreciate that Mr Banda, yet we have letters here for yourself and the four teachers explaining the situation. Here, you can read one now."

English also is not one of his strong points. Slowly Mr Banda spells out every word until he reaches the end in triumph and with a flourish of the letter announces, "I think the committee will agree to the tuition!"

I shake my head in disbelief. "Mr Banda, what you did was very wrong. The committee may well not look upon this favourably at all."

"Ah me, I will write them such a letter they cannot but agree . . ."

The next morning, our last in Kitwe, the four secondary school teachers come to receive their share of the tuition money. If the committee agrees, the balance of their back-pay will be sent through along with permission to continue the tuition. Today they have brought the fourth teacher, a Mr Luvale. We sit in the shade of an 'nsaka' in the grounds of Chep counting out K212 500 for each of the four teachers right down to the last K500.

Mr Banda it appears is in hiding because he fears the teachers will put the police onto him, and they will lock him away for a long time. Except the young men won't, because they also have high hopes that the golden goose will once more lay golden eggs. And if it takes four or more weeks before he learns of the committee's decision, then it will do him no harm to keep looking back over his shoulder to see if indeed the police are after him . . .


The problem with the Mr Bandas of Zambia is how many chances do they deserve? Inevitably there comes a point when time and patience run out. In August 2005 we return to assess the situation. The UK committee has approved the increased cost of the programme to teach the teachers and the grade twelve teachers have received their back pay. All should be well. . .

At Musonda Mr Banda as ever is ready and waiting as we crowd into his office along with the other teachers . . . *but how goes the tuition?*

Mr Banda shakes his head disconsolately. "Myself, I am the only person able to sit for six subjects in the examination."

"And Ms Mwewa and Mrs Kasanda?"

"We are only entered for five each," one of the women declares.

"That is because when I am going with the money to register for the examination, they are telling me there is not enough money to register all of us for all of the subjects," Mr Banda hastens to explain.

"So why did you not go back to Chep for more money, then the two women would also be registered for six subjects?"

Mr Banda wrings his hands and his head droops dejectedly. "Because they were telling me, by the time I return it will be too late for registration."

*Haven't we heard this before?* "Mr Banda, you were given money for registration back in May. How come yet again you were late registering?"

Mr Banda buries his head in his hands. "Ah me, this is too much when I am not well and also the malaria is giving me headaches."

Nevertheless, we press further till he reveals that because the two women cannot sit in all the subjects, they cannot have the full certificate but must take the additional subject at a later date. Thus Mr Banda's action has ensured he is the only one with any chance of gaining a full certificate. Even that is supposing . . . "Mr Banda, are you likely to pass all six subjects?"

Mr Banda shakes his head sorrowfully. "Maybe history . . . also maths."

"And the two ladies?"

Ms Mwewa glances at Mrs Kasanda. "We have been told we can pass, but in fact we can't because we haven't got sufficient subjects." Which interpreted means they have the intelligence to pass, but Mr Banda's action, or lack of action, has effectively barred them from passing.

Yet something does not add up. Alarm bells are ringing once more. "Hang on a minute, how many subjects have you been taught in?"

"We have been taught in sixteen subjects," explains Ms Mwewa, "five for each of us and six for him."

The sums don't add up, since we have been paying for tuition in twenty-one subjects! Mr Banda looks extremely sick, but whether from malaria, or because yet another a scam is detected, who knows! Poor Mr Banda! While our hearts bleed with genuine sympathy for the underdog, common sense screams he is no such thing! Yet again it will take time and effort to sort out, and the grade twelve teachers will not be pleased at their tuition payment being reduced from twenty-one subjects to sixteen.

Later Damson agrees to deliver a stern warning to Mr Banda, but leaves us to handle the grade twelve teachers. A few days later three of them turn up at Chep, so we ask how the tuition programme is going? Their response at first is guarded. As to their three pupils succeeding in the examination . . . "Mrs Kasanda can pass, also Ms Mwewa, but Mr Banda . . . maybe two subjects, but all of them, no . . . he is not clever enough!"

Since the two ladies are not entered for all of the subjects anyways, they can't pass either, which leaves the question of how many subjects the young men have tutored in. The three men look from one to another. "Him, he has been teaching . . . while he is teaching . . . as for myself I am teaching them in . . ." Yet their combined waffle never quite reveals the total of subjects taught.

"Is it not true that you have been teaching sixteen subjects, while we have been paying you for tuition in twenty-one subjects?"

But science is treated as one subject for the exam, while it is two subjects for the purposes of teaching. Then another member of staff, Rebecca Kamboye, also joined the classes, though why should she join if she already has grade twelve? This is growing ever more complicated.

"She was joining only to revise before applying for teacher training."

Or was Miss Kamboye angling to catch the admiring eye of bigger fish? We point out what Miss Kamboye did was her choosing, but the fact remains that we have overpaid them. "Therefore payment is set to drop from now on," we announce. "Also we have here a new teaching contract." I slip across the paper outlining their new payment structure.

The three men look glum. "So we are not getting the money you promised us?" One of them extracts from his bag a copy of the original agreement signed and dated back in May. "This is a written contract which must be adhered to!" All round temperatures are rising as high as the mid afternoon sun sneaking its way beneath the umbrella shade of the 'nsaka'.

We too are angry. Not only has Mr Banda lied to us, but these personable young gentlemen may also have attempted to pull the wool over our eyes. "Perhaps you would remember that this was intended to assist disadvantaged people in your country. Is it any wonder people like ourselves pull out from such projects, if people turn out to be untrustworthy?"

"What is going on here?" Mrs Musungaila's voice, icy as the cold wastes of Antarctica, slices through the heat of the moment. The three young men wilt visibly under her frosty glare, yet don't altogether shrivel. They are after all as educated as she is. "Gentlemen, I can assure you, because I am knowing the Cookes, that you will be paid for the work you have done whether it is in your contract or not. If work is done, it is done . . . Though maybe the Cookes will agree that since two of you were teaching chemistry and physics, they are treated as two subjects, even if they are one subject

95

in the examination . . . So what is the problem?" Mrs Musungaila dares anyone to challenge such Nobel prize-worthy peace making efforts.

"In fact we have drawn up our own draft of what we are owed." Another one produces a paper out of his bag. Yet one glance reveals their total amounts to less than ours. The figures still don't add up, but is it their maths or ours? We hand over the next part of their payment, and part if not amicably, then at least less antagonistically than we might have done.

However, one of the three remains dissatisfied and waves his paper around demanding loudly, "So which contract are we on now?"

"The contract for sixteen subjects!" states Bob emphatically.

A fourth teacher still requires payment, allowing room for another surprising perspective on Mr Banda's prospects when he calls round later. "Ah how can that one pass that exam when he does not turn up for lessons?"

"What! Mr Banda doesn't turn up for lessons Starfish is paying for?"

"Always he is sick or has something else he must do. Even when he does turn up, then he fails to complete tasks set for him."

This bad news results in further audience with Damson and Mrs Lumba who declares that if Mr Banda remains in charge of Musonda, Chep cannot continue to support them. Even Damson reveals he has given him a warning to pull his socks up. "Now I shall deliver a final warning that if he does not improve, he faces demotion from his position as head teacher."

But should we continue paying for tuition when reports about him are so bad? To our surprise Evelyn says, "Having gone so far, at least let us allow him to prove himself, but he must know things cannot continue in this way."

*So what is to do?*

"I am suggesting you should write him a strongly worded letter concerning his absences from lessons which Starfish is paying for and warning him that the end of the line is in sight for him at Musonda School."

*But will that be enough?*

"I have already recommended to our ED that as long as Mr Banda remains in charge, there should be no further financial assistance for them. How can we trust a person who is positively holding back the development of the school along with the potential development of female staff in particular?"

*How indeed!* And so Mr Banda receives a strongly worded letter from Starfish and an official notification from the ED of Chep.

*But is this the end of the line for Mr Banda?*

Certainly he must watch his step. The last teacher to be paid joked that if Musonda School was upgraded to take grades eight and nine, he wouldn't mind transferring there . . . *as head teacher!* Now that would be a turn up for the books, a highly qualified and personable young man in charge of Musonda School. Young as he is, he'd do a far better job than Mr Banda!

News of the success or otherwise of the three candidates for the grade twelve exam is slow coming through. By March 2006 there is still no news. Even when we return in July 2006 we are told there is no news. Damson has left Chep and Mrs Lumba has to cope with his workload as well as her own.

Eventually in early August we learn Mr Banda has disappeared! But whether he is on the run or been arrested, nobody knows. Our programme to sponsor ex Musonda pupils through secondary education has also run into problems. With communication at an all time low, we insist on a visit to the school.

As the vehicle bumps and grinds its way yet again to Musonda School, Evelyn explains the latest developments. Chep had offered to negotiate the purchase of the adjacent plot of land for the building of a new school, which should have been good news, except that, "Mr Banda attempted to have the purchase registered in his own name and not in the name of the school, which meant effectively the land would have belonged to him and not to the school. He could have done what he liked with it, even sold it!"

And so the director of Chep was forced to follow through with his threat. Mr Banda was sacked and a new head put in place. Time to meet the new head and assess whether a new order reigns at Musonda. But the new head teacher is young as well as timid. How effective will a mouse prove here?

"So was there any success for the three teachers who sat the grade twelve exam?" Once more we are crowded into the tiny office still with the defunct photocopying machine standing forlornly in one corner, though now bereft of Mr Banda's doleful presence.

"Ms Mwewa has passed all of her five subjects," says the new head. "And Mrs Kasanda has passed in four out of the five subjects. However she can re-sit this year for the one which she failed."

"And Mr Banda?"

"Ah, nobody knows. He has disappeared. However the good news is that Ms Mwewa and Rebecca Kamboye, the one who already has her grade twelve exam, but was sitting in on the tuition classes in order to revise, they are both able to apply for teacher training next year."

So, there is some good news, but also some not so good.

There matters might well have ended, except that in Zambia nothing is ever simple. Between August 2006 and May 2007, we receive a number of disquieting emails from Ms Mwewa claiming Chep *'raided'* Musonda School and *'stole'* not only the first batch of sixty-one desks provided by Starfish, but also a later gift of twenty desks purchased second-hand from Salem Centre.

*'Raided'* and *'stole'* are strong words. A flurry of emails flies backwards and forwards across the ether, yet we cannot unearth any reason for this action, other than a promise that all will be revealed when next we come.

"Ah, that man!" Evelyn shakes her head so violently, her pineapple headpiece threatens to detonate like a hand grenade going pop. "The school was allocated money from the Global Fund for HIV education and school development. But even though he was no longer head teacher, Mr Banda remained in cahoots with some of the staff at the school."

"You mean he dared to come back on the scene?"

"He was merely hiding and when he learned money was being handed over, he returned. Even he persuaded one member of staff to present herself at Chep saying, 'I am the one to whom this money should be paid.' Then he talked his way back into the school and gained control of the money."

"But we thought he had been sacked?"

"He had, but he re-ingratiated himself with the school PTA and also with the chairman of the board of management."

"Does this explain the disappearance of the school's desks?"

"At this point Chep removed property which Starfish gave to the school in good faith, fearing that he might sell the desks and chairs, or even destroy the furniture. We also advised those teachers at the school still loyal to Chep to find another building and establish another school. Then if Starfish is willing, we will hand over the desks to that school. But as long as Mr Banda remains there . . . *nothing!*"

Later the Executive Director of Chep requests Starfish approval for Chep's action concerning the desks. What can we say but . . . . "Sadly we now accept Mr Banda for what he is, a rogue and a scoundrel. What needed to be done has been done. Indeed we hope this is the last we hear of him . . ."

But Mr Banda is a slippery customer. Even as late as November 2007 Evelyn reveals relations with Mr Banda are not yet over. "That man will end in prison! Even we thought of prosecuting him for what he did with the money from the Global Fund . . ." Evelyn stops short, unwilling to reveal more than she ought.

We scent a rat. "What can you mean? Surely that's mighty serious?"

"You were not told?" Evelyn battles with her conscience and how much to reveal to funding partners and risk finally scaring off that golden goose? "When questioned about the money taken, he assured us it would be spent on income generating for the school, and that he would prove himself and win back the approval of Chep."

"Except doubtless you're about to tell us he then bought drink?"

"His idea was to sell the alcohol for profit and the income raised would benefit the school. However, instead of buying low-priced beer, he bought large two litre bottles of expensive beer, which he could not sell for a profit. So he took the money, then bought drink for himself and became very drunk along with another person, who was perhaps the one who talked him into it."

"And this was the real reason Chep intervened?"

"Chep called the police in, thinking that finally Mr Banda should get what he deserved. However, in the end the other person was thrown into prison, while Mr Banda has never been seen since."

So is this indeed the last we shall see or hear of Mr Banda? But Evelyn cannot say, and nor can we. However if we do see or hear from him again, have no fear, you'll be the first to know about it! Though there'll be no more chances for him. Oh dear me no! For Mr Banda, the golden goose has most definitely stopped laying!

# CHAPTER TWELVE: GUESS WHO'S COMING TO DINNER?
## *Saturday August 13ᵗʰ, 2005*

Our dear friends, Mr Mbai and Mr Chama, that's who, accompanied by their wives whom we've yet to meet. Since Starfish work began, these two have become the backbone of our work in Zambia, project managing both Kaputula and Kafubu projects and escorting us on our many journeys out there. Though we're always happy to reward their hard work and loyalty with anecdotes about the royal family as well as life in the UK, the time has come to repay them in a more positive way. Hence the invitation to dinner . . .

"So what will we give them to eat?" I ask Bob for the umpteenth time since the invitation is first issued.

"Play safe with something they're familiar with," is his opinion.

"What, 'nshima' with kapenta and a bit of 'fsashi' on the side?"

'Nshima' is Zambia's staple food, made from ground mealies or sweetcorn, then cooked to a stiff glue-like porridge and served with meat or vegetable relish. 'Kapenta' are a tiny whitebait type fish, fished in vast quantities in Lake Kariba. They smell and taste revolting. 'Fsashi' is a vegetable accompaniment to 'nshima' consisting of ground fresh peanuts, onion, tomato and rape leaves. Even supposing I knew how to cook them, would I want to fill the flat with their unappetising odours, let alone eat them?

Then Bob has a brainwave, "You could try asking them what they want to eat." So I do.

"Ah Mrs Cooke, that is for you to decide," responds Mr Chama magnanimously though somewhat unhelpfully.

"We thought we ought to give you food you are familiar with," I try.

The dour expressions on both friends' faces reveal this proposal has not gone down well. But then neither might roast beef and Yorkshire pudding, nor steak and kidney pie of which Mr Cooke is inordinately fond.

"How about chicken and rice?" Which is as Zambian as you can get. Zambians who can afford such luxuries serve chicken, T-bone steak or fresh bream either grilled, roasted or fried and served with rice, chips or 'nshima', making twenty-seven variations of Zambians' favourite dishes.

"Ah no, Mrs Cooke!" protests Mr Chama, proving the more adventurous. "I think we must try some English cooking. Is that not so, Mr Mbai?"

"Exactly!" agrees Mr Mbai though not looking at all convinced.

"If we are to eat with the 'mzungus', then we must eat ''mzungu' food," announces Mr Chama grasping the bull by the horns. And so it is settled . . .

Or is it? Our rented flat in Kitwe does not come well equipped for entertaining. There is one saucepan, one frying pan and one oven dish. We have two plastic picnic boxes of our own plus one leaky cake tin, all this with which to prepare a meal for six people. *Challenging or what!*

"So, what shall we give them? Since we have next to no means of cooking roast beef and Yorkshire pudding, as for curry and rice, forget it!" But choice is eventually dictated by dishes available in which to prepare and serve, than by our guests' desire to try English food: dry roasted peanuts and barbecue flavoured crisps to nibble on, followed by beef stew, cooked long and slow since it's Zambian beef, as well as herb-crumbed chicken pieces, a variation on how Zambians prefer their chicken but erring on the side of caution, accompanied by oven-roasted potatoes, mixed vegetables and bread should our guests not like anything other than barbecue flavoured Amigo crisps which all Zambians adore, and ending with trifle and chocolate biscuit cake which will hopefully set in a leaky cake tin in the fridge.

Purchasing and preparing the ingredients swallows up Saturday morning. After breakfast I set up a trifle in a plastic picnic container, which normally serves as a lunchbox, using South African tinned fruit set in a Zambian jelly on a base of crumbled Sainsbury's shortbread biscuits. Cream? Only if we can get it from Kitwe's one supermarket, which is no place for 'mzungus' on a Saturday morning. The place is swarming with Zambians clamouring to buy a week's supply of white bread, sugar, cooking oil, meat bones and roller meal to make 'nshima'. There is no fresh cream so tinned must suffice.

Back at the flat I set the chocolate biscuit cake in the foil lined cake tin, praying it won't leak all over the fridge, then begin the mammoth task of preparing the rest of the dinner. While I dry roast the peanuts, which Zambia produces by the bucket-load, Bob prepares mixed vegetables. Mixed because there is only one saucepan in which to cook cauliflower, carrots and baby marrows, which cost a small fortune but are more English than green beans or rape, which Zambia produces more cheaply and also by the bucket load.

Preparations over, we spend the rest of the afternoon lazing by the pool. However doubts soon surface again . . . "Maybe we should have played safe with green beans? What if they don't like chicken, or beef? Or the chocolate biscuit cake is too rich? Have we too much food? Worse, not enough!"

This afternoon all is quiet at Rosewood Flats, which for Saturday afternoon is unusual. To the rear of the flats is a bar area, in theory for residents only. In practice Zambians with money stop off on their way home, flashing around their hard or not so hard earned cash. At the weekend they bring wives or girlfriends and sit around near the pool drinking coke or fanta still liberally flashing around their cash.

Today we have the pool and garden to ourselves and to the increasing worry that everything is not quite right. "Maybe I should boil some rice just to be on the safe side? . . . Are you sure I should cook the beef in beer?"

But by 6.15pm everything is ready, which is just as well because Mr Chama is already knocking on the gate while the security guard from the gate actually knocks at the flat door. "I am sorry to be bothering you." His voice emerges from within the depths of his scarf which he wears muffler style triple wrapped around his neck against the cold which makes his coal black features difficult to identify against the inky blackness of the night. "A Mr Chama is at the gate saying you are expecting him?"

We assure him that is the case and that his wife should also be with him as well as a Mr Mbai and his wife.

"Ah, there is only one Mr Chama at the gate," announces the guard.

*But where are his wife and the other two? Should they fail to appear, three of us will have to work our way through a vast amount of food.*

The security guard escorts Mr Chama to the flat door. Mr Chama is dressed in neatly pressed trousers, white shirt and tie and is indeed alone. "Ah but security here is something else!" he exclaims. "First the guard wants to know my name, then who I am here to see. And finally are you expecting me? Of course you are expecting me, didn't you invite me here to eat dinner?" Mr Chama gesticulates wildly at this blatant affront to his right of entry.

"But you are alone, Mr Chama," we say, concerned more by the non-appearance of the others than with the inconveniences of entry after dark.

"Indeed I am by myself!" Mr Chama assures us. His wife apparently is not coming. As for Mr Mbai and his wife, they are coming, but not with him.

This is a relief to hear. "I hope your wife is not unwell?" I say.

"No, she is quite well, but unfortunately I am having a big problem today, which is why I am not going home but changing my cloth-es (two syllables) in town and also why my wife is not with me."

"We're sorry to hear that."

"Yes, the problem is that myself and Mbai rescued a company which was going bust on a building project. Myself and Mbai undertook to manage the work for them and earn the money for the project." Mr Chama shakes his head gloomily signifying yet another Zambian tale of doom and gloom.

A prompt is clearly required here. "So what happened, Mr Chama?"

"Bah, that boss gets the money for the project but doesn't hand any cash over to us so there is no money for the workers' wages!" Much head shaking and tut-tutting and wringing of hands ensues. "Ah, it was so bad, I nearly had a riot on my hands when I informed the men there was even no money for wages today. Bah, they were ready to lynch me for sure!"

"This isn't good, Mr Chama."

"Which is why it *is* good that Mbai and myself have your good selves to work for!" Mr Chama's features brighten like the dazzling sun suddenly reappearing from behind an unseasonable rain cloud.

"And why is that?"

"You are not knowing?" He is incredulous. "It is because 'mzungus' can be relied upon to pay up front!" He slaps neatly creased thighs for emphasis.

At that moment there is another knock at the door. The security guard reappears to enquire whether we are expecting a Mr Mbai and wife even though we have already informed him this is the case. The good news is . . . both Mr Mbai and his wife have arrived. Only one person down is not so bad.

We have speculated a great deal as to what the wives of Messrs Mbai and Chama would be like, especially the wife of Mr Mbai, who is a teacher in a private girls' convent school. Will she be shy and reserved like himself, or a bubbling extrovert to counterbalance his self-contained personality? To our surprise Mr Mbai's wife is a stunning beauty of Amazonian proportions, at least 5ft 10ins in her bare feet. Though she is wearing very smart shoes tonight as well as an off the shoulder floor length evening gown.

While we pick our popping eyeballs up off the floor, Mr Mbai announces with great pride, "Mr and Mrs Cooke, this is my wife, Salome."

"Salome?" we repeat stupidly, recalling Salome requested the head of John the Baptist on a platter from King Herod. Let's hope this Salome never requests her husband's or indeed anyone's head on a platter!

"Bah, but the security at this place is enough to do my head in!" Mr Mbai sounds off, blissfully unaware of the dramatic effect his wife has had upon us.

"It is because of the burglary," Mr Chama drops this bombshell as if he was discussing the unseasonably cold temperatures of late.

"What burglary?" we chorus as one.

"Ah, the people here are not telling you?" Mr Chama shakes his head in surprise. "Even the guard was telling me all the flats in this block were broken into and television sets stolen from several of them, even from this very flat."

So, this explains why there was no television the first few nights here, also no replacement, why the bar area is now deserted after dark and why enhanced security measures are in evidence. A security guard is on duty both day and night. The gate is kept locked at all times, while today someone was measuring up the perimeter walls for electric fencing to sit on top of eight feet high breeze block walls with shards of broken glass and rolls of barbed wire. No wonder Messrs Mbai and Chama were challenged! Yet clearly no-one thought we also should be made aware of the need for heightened security?

A couple of years ago a burglary occurred at a guesthouse up the road. A couple of Zambians spent the day drinking in the bar getting the lie of the land. Under cover of darkness they returned armed and with reinforcements, then shot and killed the guesthouse owner. Did something similar occur here at Rosewood? At least tonight there are five of us in the flat . . .

We begin by offering drinks. Immediately this area becomes more dangerous than a minefield in Angola. We have plenty of Cokes, Fantas and Sprites, which Zambians drink by the gallon, also wine and beer, but are our guests used to such drinks, indeed have they ever consumed them?

"Ah no, not for me!" Mr Mbai and his wife shake their heads firmly. "We are members of a Pentecostal church. It is against our religion to drink.

A broad grin splits Mr Chama's face. "For me, I am a Jehovah's Witness, so no problem!" But is Mr Chama used to such drink? We'd hate to send him home the worse for wear after a night out with the 'mzungus' to a wife who missed the party because he didn't go home to change his cloth-es.

We sip our drinks in silence seeking around for conversation. For some reason it is not flowing as readily as on journeys to Kaputula, when anything comes under discussion from the royal family to the war in Iraq and why people in the UK don't go to church on Sundays. Tonight however there is the presence of the glamorous Salome whose advice must be sought on each subject as it comes up. Also there is the previously undisclosed fact that Mr Chama is a Jehovah's Witness, so by common consent religion is off tonight!

We summon our guests to the table where, in order to seat everyone, we borrowed an extra table with a wobbly leg from an adjacent flat. Suddenly confusion reigns. Salome looks questioningly at her husband who also looks perplexed. "Maybe Mrs Cooke and I will eat here?" suggests Salome clinging to the vicinity of the coffee table like a limpet to a rock at high tide.

"Ah no, we must all sit together," I reassure her, thinking perhaps she has issue with space around the table. "Though watch out for the wobbly leg!"

Salome sashays across and begins shifting cutlery and crockery until she has isolated her own place setting and mine at the bottom of the table. Too late I realise in Zambian culture women normally eat separately from men, generally after the men have finished. However, satisfied she has separated herself as far as decency allows, Salome seems willing to proceed.

We offer around chicken pieces and beef stew, along with oven-roasted potatoes, mixed vegetables and bread. Our guests tuck in with gusto. However with no forewarning they declare themselves full. We are surprised, though maybe we shouldn't be. Better off Zambians they may be, yet we have probably served them as much food as they see in a week.

Mr Mbai still has one chicken piece on his plate. "If Mrs Cooke does not mind, I will wrap up this piece of chicken for a small snack later." Mr Mbai rolls up his chicken drumstick in a paper serviette and pops it in his pocket.

"Would Mr Chama also like a little something for later?" I offer weakly.

With alacrity Mr Chama also accepts a small snack for later, rolling up two drumsticks and placing them in the pocket of his neatly pressed trousers.

"This beef stew is so delicious!" sighs a replete Salome. "But I want you please to tell me how it is made?"

I list the ingredients: beef, carrots, onions, stock, flour to thicken the gravy, though omitting to mention one vital ingredient to give the stew its true flavour . . . an entire bottle of Zambian beer! Fortunately teetotal Salome does not ask for beef stew wrapped up in a paper serviette.

As we clear the dinner plates, suddenly all three guests stand as one and leave the table. "But there is still the pudding to come," I protest feebly.

"What, still more food to come?" They seem genuinely disconcerted. "No matter, we can eat it here." And they settle once more at the coffee table.

The chocolate biscuit cake proves popular. Salome polishes off her portion in a couple of bites. Messrs Mbai and Chama declare it delicious, but themselves defeated. "Would you care to carry some with you for later?" I suggest. So chocolate biscuit cake is also wrapped up in napkins and stowed away in pockets. Perhaps like the orphans at Kaputula and Chilumba, they also want to carry away for sharing later with people back home some evidence they ate with the 'mzungus'. We say nothing and just keep wrapping up a bit here and a bit there for all tonight's unseen guests back home.

It is 9.30pm and Mr Chama has commandeered the wine bottle. Maybe he intends taking that home with him also, though his wife may not be too pleased. Our guests declare themselves ready to depart. From here they must walk to the end of an unlit and potholed road to pick up a minibus into town, then catch another minibus out to their townships. Offering them a lift home at night to an African township is too dangerous for us.

We say our goodbyes inside, because standing with the door open allows mosquitoes in and we have no wish to commit mass slaughter later. But has the evening been a success? Who can say, though their dinner at the 'mzungus' flat will doubtless give them plenty to talk about for some time.

Certainly neither of them will go hungry tonight given the amount of snacks they have gone home with wrapped up in paper serviettes and bulging from their pockets. And just how many people will finally get to nibble food from the 'mzungus' dinner party, goodness alone knows!

# CHAPTER THIRTEEN: IT'S NOT ALWAYS EASY BEING WHITE . . .

## *August -> September 2005, February & July 2006*

Starfish work is not limited to setting up sponsorship programmes, or to handling impressive building projects on the scale of Kaputula School or Kafubu Baptist Church, of which more in a later chapter. On numerous occasions Starfish has helped struggling individuals. Which principle lies at the heart of Starfish philosophy . . . picking up that one lone starfish and tossing it back into the ocean.

One hot afternoon in August 2005 finds us once more struggling to balance the Kaputula accounts. Mrs Musungaila, whose responsibility it is as head accountant at Chep ultimately to balance the books, announces there is a young man in reception whom she thinks Starfish might be able to help.

"I'm not sure we're in a position to take on anything . . ."

"Or indeed anybody more at the moment." Which unfortunately is so often our response. Zambia is full of hard luck stories. We long ago accepted Starfish sadly could not rescue every last one of them.

"But this one is different," claims Mrs Musungaila. "He is a partially sighted young albino. He would like to apply for sponsorship for the accommodation component while he pursues his studies at ZIBSIP, the business college in Kitwe."

We sigh inwardly. Is Mrs Musungaila creating a diversion away from accounts, which steadfastly refuse to balance? Nevertheless, we drop what we are doing and head outside to meet the young student. Being an albino, his skin is of course white not black. Yet its whiteness bears the unnatural pallor of crabs, which live deep in subterranean caves and never see the light of day. Worse, his skin not only lacks the pigmentation which makes it black, but which also would protect it from the hot rays of the tropical sun.

"My name is Augustine Mumba," he announces, before explaining he has passed his grade twelve exam and gained a bursary for his tuition at ZIBSIP.

"So what is the problem, Augustine?" Secretly we dread an answer destined to lead to further involvement.

Augustine wrings his pasty white palms between skinny legs clad in threadbare trousers. "The problem is this bursary is for tuition only. Myself I am an orphan being cared for by my grandmother who is also a widow. Where I am living, it is seven kilometres from the college. Because of my skin I cannot walk that distance every day in the hot sun."

"Is there not a minibus you can catch into town?" I ask naively.

"In fact neither myself nor my grandmother can afford the money for travelling every day. So I am asking if your organisation can pay for accommodation in one of the college hostels, so that I can pursue my studies?"

This is a difficult one. Starfish is by now fully committed to building and sponsorship projects. There is no spare cash. Yet there is a vulnerability combined with humility about Augustine, which speaks of a deserving case. It is difficult to imagine how hard the lot is of someone like Augustine. Most Zambians struggle hard enough. Yet being not only an orphan, but also afflicted with a painful and distressing condition which marks him out as different to everyone else, is indeed hard to imagine.

Worse, in Zambia albinos are considered bad luck. Albino babies often fail to thrive or are rejected by their family. In the hot sun their skins blister and erupt into open weeping sores. Simply to get as far as he has done, Augustine has excelled himself. Surely he deserves a chance to go further?

"Perhaps if you photocopy your college letter of acceptance and write a letter of application to the Starfish committee, then maybe someone in the UK might sponsor you. I'm afraid that's all that we can do." Which sadly is the best we can offer.

But Augustine does not give in easily, perhaps explaining an incredible ability to survive so far against the odds. Two days later he returns to plead his cause further. We agree to visit the college where he has been promised a place and check out his credentials.

To date most Starfish work has been concerned with orphans and vulnerable children in the most appalling conditions either in townships or rural areas. ZIBSIP on the other hand caters for students who have done well in the education system and who now wish to study for business or professional qualifications. It is situated just off Kitwe town centre.

Outwardly the building looks much the same as any college in the UK.

However on entering noticeable differences soon appear. Conditions are overcrowded and cramped. There is a marked lack of facilities. Rooms are filled with broken furniture, while curtains hang ragged from dirty windows and there is hardly a computer or photocopier in sight. And this is where Kitwe's more able students come to learn!

We push our way through the mêlée of students to reach the reception desk. A bimbo wearing a wig sits nonchalantly buffing her red nails, all the while studiously ignoring students clamouring for attention.

"Yes?" She spots our white faces, which for her spells a diversion.

"We have come about the registration of this student."

"He can register here," she concedes reluctantly, since her nails are evidently far more important.

"We need some information first, so that we know he is a bona fide student. Who can give this information?"

"You may go to the office of the vice-principal."

However the place is more crowded and confusing than inside a rabbit warren. We haven't a clue where it is.

"Then you may follow me," she offers with a sigh of resignation.

So, still some benefits remain to having a white face, which on this occasion is opening the door to the vice-principal's office. We follow her wiggling bottom tightly encased in stretch lycra upstairs to the first floor.

By Zambian standards the office of the vice-principal is impressive. It contains a three-piece suite, drinks fridge in the corner, hospitality tray on the side, framed qualifications hanging on the wall and a gown hanging behind the door. That the curtains hang in shreds at the windows and the walls have not seen paint since colonial days seems not to matter.

The vice–principal shakes hands and waves us towards the faded velveteen sofa. He is fat and healthy, a sure indication he is also wealthy. "How can we help you?"

We note his use of the royal 'we'.

"We have come about this young man. We understand he cannot take up his bursary because he cannot afford to pay either accommodation fees or to travel in daily by minibus."

The vice-principal peers knowingly at Augustine. "I already know this fellow. I have seen him around. So you are wishing to register him, also to pay his accommodation fees?"

"I . . . er . . . we . . ." An amazing turnabout has just occurred. Initially we intended merely verifying Augustine's credentials. Now it seems we are here to register him as a student. Where will the money come from?

God alone knows! But since God found the money for our other projects, we reckon He might also provide money for Augustine's accommodation.

"Starfish would like to pay his accommodation so that he may take up his place at college." There, we've said it. Another lone starfish rescued from the beach and tossed back into the ocean.

The vice-principal instantly becomes most co-operative. He writes out a letter for his secretary to type stating Augustine is a bona fide student. Then he photocopies Augustine's documents. Now all that is left is to pay the money for his accommodation into accounts.

We squeeze our way back down the crowded staircase and through the press of Zambian students crowding the corridors of ZIBSIP to reach the accounts office situated at the end of a dark pokey corridor. Inside are two dodgy characters, more like characters from a gangster movie than accountants to whom we are about to entrust Starfish money, when we don't even have committee approval to do so. They delve deep into their filing cabinets to unearth Augustine's records.

"In fact this guy's bursary is only for tuition," announces one of them with a knowing grin.

"We are already aware of that," we respond. "We simply wish to pay his accommodation fees."

"There is also his registration fee, library fee, student union fee, medical fee . . . and examination fees."

We glance nervously from one to another, the same thought crossing both our minds as to whether this request for more is bona fide or an attempt on their part to feather their own nest. "We know nothing about these other fees, which incidentally amount to how much?"

Much calculating takes place on the other side of the counter. They tap figures into calculators and check lists and information stored on an ancient computer so large it almost fills the entire desk. "That will come to K2.3 million," announces one.

"Though in fact because of his bursary, the government will give an allowance each year for part of his exam fees," adds the other. "But not for the whole amount."

"So, how much then?"

Another lengthy calculation converts what is due into an extra £300.

"I'm sorry, we don't have the authority to agree to that."

Nor to any of it, if the truth were known. As with so much in Zambia, putting Augustine through college will cost a lot more than we were led to believe.

"Sorry, Augustine," we're forced to say, "but we need a rethink. Maybe Chep can help . . ." This is a long shot, but at least it gets us out of ZIBSIP, with Starfish money intact and not squandered unwittingly.

Thoroughly disheartened, we return to Chep, there to broach Mrs Musungaila. She may not yet have balanced the books, but she nevertheless frequently provides the right answers.

"Mrs Musungaila, do you think Chep might assist with Augustine's examination fees?" we ask.

By now Augustine must feel he is riding on a roller coaster. One minute his future looks rosy and the next storm clouds gather once more. Yet stoically he clings on, riding life's hills and hollows.

Mrs Musungaila ponders before conceding albeit guardedly, "I think that will be possible. If Starfish will cover the accommodation fees as well as other small fees, then Chep will agree to pay the balance of the examination fees."

Up soars Augustine once more into seventh heaven, riding on the crest of the big dipper . . .

"Only what about your books?" demands Mrs Musungaila looking pointedly at Augustine. "Do you have any books?"

I groan inwardly. What books are these? Huge great tomes and textbooks or something more modest? And where will *this* money come from? Mercifully Mrs Musungaila is only referring to exercise books and writing paper. "In fact we have a stock here at Chep. Myself, I will see he gets all the exercise books and paper he needs."

*Ah, behind that navy blue serge bosom beats a heart of liquid gold.*

I could hug her! Instead I stand aside while she frogmarches Augustine off to supply him with paper and books. When he returns, arms laden with reams of paper, he looks like a proper student.

We head back to ZIBSIP, only to find accounts has closed. However someone claiming to be the bursar offers to complete the necessary paperwork. We hand over the money and demand evidence that we have paid for Augustine's accommodation. This must be photocopied so that Augustine also has the evidence, otherwise they may not let him into the hostel.

Finally he is given a timetable. "Congratulations, Augustine!" we say, "You are now registered as a full time student of ZIBSIP."

Augustine grins from ear to ear. He thanks and blesses us at one and the same time, so that we wonder how we will ever escape such gratitude.

"I just pray we've done the right thing," I say to Bob when we are alone.

"Time will tell," he responds. "Though if the committee won't agree to what we've done, then we'll just have to bear the cost ourselves. However there is one further problem . . ."

"Which is?"

"We've paid Augustine's first semester which takes him up until December. But his next semester will be due for payment in January . . ."

"But we don't come to Zambia in December . . . "

"Or January. So what do we do?"

"Sweet-talk Mrs Musungaila to see if we can send the money through to Chep wrapped up in one of our other payments, then they pay the college on our behalf." Since Mrs Musungaila has a soft spot for Augustine and is determined to see him through his course, she readily agrees.

However fate sometimes deals a hand. Circumstances later dictate that we are back in Zambia in early February 2006, and still in time to pay fees for Augustine's second semester ourselves.

Firstly we need an update on Augustine's progress from Mr Reuben Phiri, head of Business Studies at ZIBSIP. But Mr Phiri is an elusive customer and not easy to catch either in his office or lecturing or indeed anywhere until finally . . . we run him to ground in the college car park.

"Ah, I am delighted to see you again!" We only met Mr Phiri once before, yet he greets us like old friends. He is a small, round man with a small, round shiny face who beams continually with a grin spreading from ear to ear. Zambia's many problems clearly do not weigh too heavily on the broad shoulders of Mr Reuben Phiri.

"We just wanted to know how Augustine is getting along?"

"Fine, fine, I am delighted with his progress." Mr Phiri radiates gladness.

"And how are his grades?"

"Fine, as I say I am delighted with him." He spreads his hands wide.

"So can you tell us what his grades are?"

"Myself I don't have them." Mr Phiri's grin shrivels. "But we are delighted here that you are paying this guy's tuition . . ." Beams once more.

"Accommodation," I correct him.

Mr Phiri looks puzzled.

"We are paying Augustine's accommodation fees. He has a bursary for tuition," we remind him.

"Ah yes, that is so. But there is just one, no, maybe two matters which the college wishes to raise with you. Firstly the college minibus."

*Oh, oh, here we go! Doesn't everyone have a request in Zambia, even government funded colleges?*

"I'm afraid our charity doesn't supply college minibuses. Our work is concerned mainly with orphans and vulnerable children who have nothing."

"No, no, you misunderstand me. What I am saying is that the college has placed a levy on every single student in order to raise the money to purchase a minibus. What we are asking is if you will pay Augustine's contribution for him."

"How much will that be?"

"Fifty thousand kwacha."

This converts to about six pounds, which we agree to pay.

"Then this guy also needs a pair of glasses."

"Glasses?"

"In fact yes, because he can neither see at the front of the room, nor at the back of the room. As with many albinos the eyesight deteriorates rapidly as they get older. Without glasses Augustine cannot pursue his studies."

"But how has he coped so far?"

"At the moment he listens to the lectures, then in the evening he borrows notes from his fellow students and copies them up at the hostel."

"Yet in spite of this handicap, he still achieved good grades?"

"That is so."

"So how might we obtain a pair of glasses for Augustine?"

But Mr Phiri is no help with such practicalities. Once more it's back to drink from Mrs Musungaila's boundless fount of knowledge.

"That cannot be a problem." *But then, is anything ever a problem for Mrs Musungaila, except maybe balancing Starfish books?* "He can go to the eye clinic for an eye test. Maybe they will give him the lenses for free, then he can pick up a pair of frames for next to nothing in the African market."

That sounds simple enough. Yet in Zambia, nothing is ever simple. Augustine has his free eye test, but does the Eye Clinic perhaps sniff 'mzungu' money behind his request for glasses? They tell him, "Sorry, no free lenses. Your glasses will cost K265 000."

That is almost fifty pounds, to which, towards the end of this trip, the Starfish budget will not extend. Augustine must continue to copy up notes in the evening. At least until we next come . . .

When we return in July 2006, fees for Augustine's third semester are due. This week is not only registration time for Augustine, but for every single student on the ZIBSIP campus. The queue at accounts snakes down the pokey corridor, all along the main corridor and out the main door of the college.

"What do we do?" I say to Bob.

A student standing nearby overhears and says. "Myself, I had to get someone to keep my place overnight. Already today I am here for five hours."

He *should* be joking . . . only he's not! The college in its wisdom refuses to open the accounts office before the term starts, yet it won't allow students onto their courses until their fees have been paid. Thus chaos reigns for days.

There is nothing for it; we pull rank and head for Mr Phiri's office. Unfortunately Mr Phiri is not there. "Wait here," says his obliging secretary. "I will see what I can do."

Five, ten, fifteen, twenty minutes tick by. There is no sign of her return. Every few minutes someone knocks at the door so we call out from inside, "There's nobody here!" Nobody seems to find it strange that if there is nobody there, how come a disembodied voice informs them that is so from inside the room.

Eventually Mr Phiri's secretary returns to say, "If you come with me, I can do something." This being to push us to the front of the queue, where the guy who has already waited five hours is still there. We are treated to dirty looks, even mutterings as the only white people there pushing their way to the front.

Mr Phiri's secretary is not in the slightest fazed. "You should not be saying these things," she berates the assembled crowd. "These people are like your parents. You would not expect your parents to wait in this queue."

"Even grandparents, " I mutter under my breath hoping this might rouse more sympathy.

Of Augustine there is no sign. In this crowd it would be like trying to spot a needle in a haystack except, being an albino, makes Augustine easier to spot than most Zambians! We leave a message to say we have the money for his glasses and will catch up with him next week.

It is nearly three weeks before Augustine catches up with us, but at least he knows where to go for the glasses. He directs us to an optician's in the centre of Kitwe. The place looks a little pretentious. "Possibly not the place to purchase a pair of glasses for fifty pounds," we tell Augustine.

"He has told me he will do them for that price," Augustine assures us.

*Maybe . . . until the optician also sees 'mzungus' paying!*

The optician is Asian. He stretches forth his hand in greeting, at the same time eyeing up my glasses. "Very nice glasses," he says, "varifocals. How much you pay?"

I quote an exorbitant price by UK standards, never mind by Zambian.

"Next time I make you a pair exactly the same for a fraction of the price."

I remind him we are here to sort out Augustine's needs, not mine.

"Ah yes, this one!" He tosses Augustine a withering glance. "He has already been here many times."

I fear Augustine has been pestering him, yet the optician seems to have the measure of him. There ensues a long conflab about Augustine's glasses. Being an albino, Augustine's eyes can only get worse. The optician wants to give him a pair of moderate strength glasses, which will suffice both for reading and distance work. Augustine however has his own ideas. He wants his glasses as strong as possible and for reading purposes only.

"What about your distance work seeing the blackboard?" the optician asks him.

"I can manage," claims Augustine stoutly.

"But Mr Phiri says you are copying work up in the evenings because you cannot see the board," I remind him.

"That I can do!" insists Augustine.

"Look Augustine, this man really does know what he's talking about."

Augustine peers myopically at the man who knows better than he and concedes grudgingly that he will have the mid-strength glasses given that they are costing even more than the fifty pounds budgeted for them.

"And you will wear them for both reading and distance?" I ask him.

"I will wear them," he mumbles.

"Even outside when you are walking along the road?" asks the optician.

Augustine does not respond. Maybe wearing glasses outside remains one stage too far.

"Here is your receipt," says the optician. "The glasses will be ready next week."

"You must take care of the receipt," I say. "You will need to produce it to claim your glasses or in case you need a repair or . . ." I hesitate to say in case they don't suit you. Given half a chance I fear Augustine will swap the glasses for extra strong ones.

"I think you must take charge of the receipt," says the optician maybe reading my thoughts.

"Aieeeh, then how will I get my glasses?" wails Augustine.

"Look man," the optician finally loses patience and snaps, "I know you. I will recognise you when you come for the glasses, okay?"

Somehow I suspect he recognises Augustine not just because of the colour of his skin, but more because of this young man's determination to get what he wants. And if he did come back to change the glasses for stronger ones, then neither we nor the optician would be all that surprised!

# CHAPTER FOURTEEN: YOU SHOULD BE SO LUCKY!
## *February 23rd & 24th 2006*

"Myself, I am very lucky."

*Did we hear correctly?*

True Brenda Naomi Kabwe is softly spoken. Only lately has she gained enough confidence to look us in the eye when speaking and gained sufficient command of English to hold a conversation with us. When we first met her, she would not look us in the eye and only gave monosyllabic answers to questions. Now there is no stopping her . . .

"I am very lucky," Brenda continues, "because I have a place in school and every day in the morning I am going to school."

"What time do you get up to go to school?" I ask her.

"I rise at 5am every morning," answers Brenda.

"Do you walk to school?"

"Yes, I walk." Her tone suggests 'what else?' "I walk for one hour and twenty minutes in order to reach school."

"What time does school begin?"

"My lessons begin at 07.30 and last until 13.00."

"And then?"

She gives the same bemused look once more. "I walk home again."

"For one hour and twenty minutes?"

"For one hour and twenty minutes."

"There's no bus?"

"There is a minibus, but I don't have money."

"Do you carry your lunch with you?"

"I have no lunch. Sometimes I might have K500 (about 4p) to spend on frozen sugared water which street sellers sell outside the school. They sell other things as well, but I don't have money for other things."

"So what do you do for food?"

"When I reach my home in the afternoon, my mother will have prepared our daily 'nshima' which we eat with some vegetables."

"Do you have meat?"

Brenda solemnly scrutinises my face, assessing whether I am serious. Probably she concludes I am not. "Sometimes there is meat, but mostly there is no meat."

Presumably she means there is meat at Christmas time. I don't press further, but ask instead, "Do you get your homework done okay? You must get a lot of homework now from this school."

"There is much homework," she says. "Mostly I am okay. I work after dark by the light of a candle . . ."

"You can't do your homework in the afternoons?"

"Sometimes I can, but sometimes I must sell vegetables at the market or look after my younger brother or sister. Then I cannot do my homework until after darkness falls."

Like many people who live in the densely populated African compounds surrounding Kitwe, Brenda lives in a house with no electricity and doubtless with no running water or sanitation either. Or else her family cannot afford to pay the bills to connect them.

"And you consider yourself lucky?" I repeat this question, in order to be absolutely sure. For sure not many people reading this would consider Brenda lucky!

"Oh, I am so lucky!" Brenda's eyes shine with the wonder of it, even as she says it.

Brenda Naomi Kabwe is one of a group of pupils formerly from Musonda Community School in Kitwe. These pupils are being given a real chance in life. Where once she and the other girls on the programme had little hope other than an early marriage or turning to prostitution, now she realistically dreams of becoming a nurse or a teacher. The boys, who may have turned to the streets or to a life of crime, now talk of becoming policemen or doctors.

But how did this miracle come about? For a miracle it surely is.

If the construction of Kaputula Community School proved our most difficult project to manage, then the rehabilitation of Musonda Community School always came a close second. Not forgetting that head teacher, Mr Banda, already encountered in earlier chapters, also qualifies as our trickiest customer to date . . .

In truth not all was ever doom and gloom at Musonda. Following the supply of their first ever desks, tables and chairs as well as school materials from Starfish, pupils subsequently obtained their first passes ever in the grade seven exam, which qualifies pupils for entry into secondary education. Community schools such as Musonda provide free education, generally in appalling conditions, for orphans and vulnerable children. These children cannot afford the shoes, uniforms, fees and books necessary to attend government schools, which fall within the state system.

However community schools only cater for children up to grade seven, when pupils must sit the grade seven exam. Passing this exam entitles pupils to enter Basic School and continue through grades eight and nine, eventually entering High School for grades ten, eleven and twelve. In practice very few orphans and vulnerable children achieve this, because of the insurmountable issue of paying for shoes, uniform, fees and books.

Back in December 2005 twenty-two pupils from Musonda Community School passed their grade seven exam. Damson from Chep, acting as school liaison officer, reported that eleven of these pupils were unable to take up the offer of a place at Basic School. A further four had paid for places, but were unable to pay for uniforms. The government schools were threatening to boot them out. Since the school year had already started, time was against us when early in 2006 we visited the school to try and remedy the situation . . .

We reach Musonda Community School at 09.30 on a cloudy February morning. Cloudy, because this is the height of the rainy season, and perhaps not an ideal time of year for a trip to Zambia.

This morning we need a plentiful supply of both time and patience. Mr Banda has already proved himself a tricky customer over the teachers' tuition programme. There is no reason to suppose he will prove any easier over the matter of school places for needy ex-pupils.

We head straight for his den of an office to the rear of the school. At least now Mr Banda sits at a proper table and chair enabling him to look like a proper head teacher, even though he may still not yet be qualified as one, nor indeed entirely behave like one. Though we already know the facts, it is important to hear them from Mr Banda. He may be a rogue, but he is also at this stage, and in spite of the threat of demotion, still the head teacher.

"So Mr Banda, the pupils have done well in their grade seven exam?"

Mr Banda grins cheesily. "Indeed yes, thanks to the Starfish injection of desks and school materials, twenty-two pupils passed their exam."

"But they haven't gone on to Basic School?"

Mr Banda shakes his head sorrowfully. He is a master of the art of bathos. "Alas no, only eleven have gone on."

"And the others?"

He wrings his hands for good measure. "Ah, they are not able to go to school. In fact they are even now waiting outside with their parents and guardians to see what the Starfish might do."

*So, another tricky situation for Starfish to resolve!*

Together with Mr Banda and Damson we head back outside. A line of chairs has been placed in the dust and dirt, backs to the school and facing a motley collection of ex-pupils along with their parents and guardians. Some are with mothers or grandmothers, some with uncles or fathers. The adults eye us suspiciously, while the pupils studiously avoid meeting our gaze. Most have little if any experience of dealing with 'mzungus'. Who's to say a white face guarantees us as trustworthy?

Damson introduces us, saying what we might do. Bob then explains our willingness to help, while I outline what we hope to offer them. Since most of those present have a poor command of English, everything is translated into Bemba so that they understand our offer.

"Our aim is specifically to help the eleven children excluded from school."

To our surprise this produces much muttering amongst the audience. "What is the problem?" we ask Damson.

"They are saying some of the other children also need your help."

"But we understood the other eleven were in school?"

"In fact four have since been excluded because they have no uniform."

"But their fees have been paid?"

"That is so."

"So if they had a uniform, they could continue with their place?"

"Indeed."

We confer with each other. Phone a friend or ask the audience? Not a hope, we're on our own. Will it be so hard to find money for four extra school uniforms? Probably, given the tightness as ever of the Starfish budget. Yet how can we pay for eleven pupils, only to leave a further four excluded? Four starfish left stranded on the beach. We agree to purchase uniforms for the four pupils excluded.

This produces smiles and claps. So, a success . . . er, not quite!

A large woman wearing a colourful 'chitenge' tied around her waist and with a baby tied on her back rises to her feet. She exclaims loudly in

120

Bemba, at the same time pointing at us and at some of the other children and their guardians.

"What is the problem now?" we ask.

Damson struggles for words. "I think she is saying she would like to transfer her child from the school where he is, to either Ipusukilo or Lulamba School, because these two schools are where the children being supported by Starfish will attend."

"Whatever for? Her child is already in school. She's paid his fees and he has a uniform, doesn't he?"

Damson grins sheepishly. "Indeed yes! However she feels that if her son transferred to one of these schools, then he also would have his fees paid as well as receive the other benefits."

We shake our heads in disbelief. The expression 'give an inch and they take a mile' springs to mind. Not that such thoughts help. The woman simply cannot understand why, what has been offered to some, is not on offer to all. We ask Damson to explain that Starfish is not at present able retrospectively to help those who have already paid fees.

This does not go down well. More people join the woman on her feet shouting and gesticulating. The gist being that they have scrimped and saved to pay fees and buy uniforms, so why are they being penalised?

Why indeed! Life is never fair in Africa where the slice of the pie is never big enough to go round. Both Damson and Mr Banda rise to their feet attempting to quell a burgeoning riot.

"The most we can promise is that since these people have already paid for this year, next year we will review the situation equally for all twenty-two pupils," I shout above the fracas.

Will this do the trick? Fearing we may get lynched if we remain on site any longer, we decide to beat a retreat in the hope that things will calm down.

Getting away however is not easy. Musonda School lies down a beaten earth track on the edge of one of Kitwe's African compounds. Heavy rains over the past few days have ensured that roads leading into it are awash. Our vehicle is parked facing a deeply dark and stagnant pool of rainwater. There is no way through it or round it. The only option is to reverse down the track by which we came until we find a turning place. But first we must reverse over a ridged bank in front of the school. However the car will have none of it. It stubbornly refuses to manoeuvre both front and back wheels over the ridge and ends up straddled across it, as helpless as a beached whale.

"That's done it," I say. "Now we really will get lynched."

We get out the vehicle to inspect the damage. The middle section of the vehicle is buried in the ridge, while the front wheels have sunk into mud and water. The rear wheels hang suspended in the air. "Could somebody give us a push?" we try.

Fortunately Zambians like nothing better than getting their hands on 'mzungu' vehicles, especially to push them out of tricky situations. Parents, guardians, orphans, teachers, all lend a willing hand. All, except the woman making all the noise at the meeting. She now stands to one side, hands on hips. A gloating smile flickers across her face as if to say, 'Now look at you!'

In the great push to get us going one of the parents, who clearly went to a lot of trouble to dress for the occasion when the 'mzungus' came to his son's school, ends up with his best suit spattered in mud as our vehicle struggles to release itself.

But we are free and off to our next port of call, a visit to the Basic Schools which have indicated their willingness to accept children from community schools. Surprisingly not all government schools will do so. These children have poor health and attendance records, as well as frequently dropping by the wayside before reaching their goal.

First on the list is Ipusukilo Basic School, not to be confused with *Ipusikilo Community School*, one of Kitwe's largest community schools, taking one thousand or more pupils in three daily shifts in classes of up to seventy children. They are crammed into a dilapidated building with no light, water or sanitation. Teachers are voluntary and the head is barely out of his twenties.

On the other hand, Ipusukilo Basic School is a white-washed government school with neatly cut lawns and flowerbeds. Classes boast fully qualified teachers, even if they are under-staffed by UK standards.

"It's like entering another world," I comment as we enter the building.

"Or stepping back in time," Bob responds. "Back to the days when there was no need for community schools, since every child had the right to free education. How did it all go so wrong?"

How indeed! A polite and well-spoken lady greets us and invites us into the staff-room. It is comfortable by Zambian standards and a world away from the stark reality of Musonda. She is painfully thin, but then teachers in all Zambian schools are still dying of Aids faster than funds and training of new teachers can replace them.

"In fact we have already spoken." Damson reminds her of his previous visit to prepare the ground.

She nods assent.

"So we are now asking if you will offer places to seven of the eleven children which I spoke to you about?" Niceties must be observed and nothing taken for granted. "These children will be sponsored by the Starfish Fund which will pay their fees and provide their uniforms and books."

She agrees to accept them and provides us with a list of requirements and fees charged by the school. In theory education in Zambia is free, though in practice it is not. The PTA and governing body of each government school determine nominal charges for entry to their school. Though charges are modest, around £45 per annum, they debar most OVCs from entry. Nevertheless the visit has gone well. Seven children are promised places.

We travel down the road to Lulamba Basic School. The close proximity of the two schools will make monitoring easier for Damson. In our absence he will visit at least once a term to monitor the pupils' needs and progress.

Our first impression of Lulamba School is that it is not quite as far up in the school hierarchy as Ipusukilo. But then nor is it as far down the scale as Musonda. Again the deputy head greets us. He has his own office, where first he must switch off the radio to which he was listening. Only then can he hear our request that three Musonda pupils are granted a place here. He readily agrees, provides us with information identical to that from the first school, then doubtless switches his radio straight back on again once we have left.

But seven plus three makes ten, not eleven. One pupil, Bathsheba Sibanyati, has passed for Mitanto High School. Mitanto is one of Kitwe's most prestigious schools and caters for children up to grade twelve. Bathsheba scored 721 in her grade seven exam, an exceptionally high score by any standards and possibly a first for a pupil from a community school.

Though still in a compound, Mitanto really is another world. Set behind double iron gates and approached by a drive that sweeps up to a car park, the classrooms on two floors are set around a quadrangle filled with luscious tropical plants and flowers. Set upon a plinth at the entrance to the school, are twin statues of a boy and girl in the distinctive apple and bottle green uniform of Mitanto.

*Oh Bathsheba, that you should be so fortunate to have gained entry into these hallowed halls of learning!*

Again the deputy head teacher welcomes us, so that we wonder . . . *do any of the heads actually do a day's work?* He is well spoken and clearly a well educated Zambian. We are struck by the immensity of the gap between here and Musonda, between pupils who qualify for entry and those who don't. For a mere £50 a year Bathsheba has gained entry into this other world. How will she cope? We cannot begin to guess.

Bathsheba is a softly spoken and self-contained girl. She looks about ten or eleven, but is actually thirteen going on fourteen. In common with most OVCs she is under-nourished and thus under-sized. Children should enter school at six in Zambia, but effectively they enter school when their parents or guardians can afford to send them. Their class placement depends on their number of years in school rather than on chronological age or attainment. It is not uncommon to find pupils aged twenty or more in grade twelve.

There are smiles and handshakes all round as we say goodbye in the car park. Suddenly, who should appear on the scene but three of the grade twelve teachers, hired (sic!) to provide tuition for Mr Banda and Co at Musonda. They are all dressed as ever in well pressed dark trousers, spanking white shirts and ties befitting the privileged world they work in.

"Mr and Mrs Cooke, fancy seeing you here!" they greet us jovially.

"And Mr Banda, he is with you?"

"Ah that man, what a merry dance he led us all!"

The deputy head teacher looks bemused, until we fill him in on our prior association with these presentable young men, Zambia's educated elite.

"So you have been in Zambia already?" asks the deputy head.

"Many times," we assure him.

"Then you know our ways?" he asks.

"For sure this couple knows us and our ways!" laugh the three young men. "Especially the ways of the Mr Bandas of Zambia!"

We say goodbye, leaving the deputy head in no doubt that we are not simply green do-gooders on their first trip to Zambia. Rather we have by now become somewhat experienced in the ways of Zambia and of its Mr Bandas.

All that remains is to pay the money for the pupils' sponsorship programme into Chep accounts. Damson will then withdraw a chitty for the correct amount to pay school fees for each of the eleven pupils plus their uniforms, plus uniforms for the additional four. Each pupil will also need a pair of shoes, A4 exercise books and hard-backed report books. School bags, maths sets, pens and pencils are to be provided by the parents. As these can be obtained cheaply from the local market, the cost should not weigh too heavily upon them. Since we are travelling the next day to Lusaka, wrapping it all up is left in the capable hands of Damson.

"So we've finally got the eleven pupils into school," I say to Bob later that evening as we weigh up the successes or otherwise of yet another trip.

"And now it's up to them," he responds. "How will they cope? What if they're like fish out of water? Or the other kids ostracise them because they're from poor homes?" He is voicing doubts we're both experiencing.

"And will this programme run any more successfully than the Musonda teachers' programme?" Which maybe is our biggest worry but, as ever, these are questions to which we don't know the answer.

"Well, we've given them a chance," says Bob, " and it's chance they never had before. Certainly, if they make the most of it, then they'll succeed in educating not only themselves, but possibly in enabling their entire family to escape forever from the poverty trap."

But will these kids indeed succeed? Time alone will reveal that answer.

# CHAPTER FIFTEEN: A 'CHALWE DAY', or the day everything goes pear-shaped . . . *Thursday March 2nd, 2006*

Today we are once more visiting Chilumba Orphans' project with Mr. Quistin Chalwe. Unfortunately days spent in Mr Chalwe's company have developed a habit of disappearing unerringly down a black hole. We have taken, perhaps rather unkindly, to calling any day when things go awry, a 'chalwe day'.

So far this particular trip things have gone rather too well. Could a day spent with Mr Chalwe perhaps redress the balance?

Travelling with Mr Chalwe and Faith Lyena, director of the Faith Orphanage Trust, the plan is to assess the viability of a building project at Chilumba. However, since they have *still* not completed fencing their orchard, any decision to build still hangs very much in the balance.

Chilumba Orphans' Centre is located some fifty kilometres from Kitwe along an atrocious road. Once out of Kitwe the tarred surface quickly becomes pockmarked with potholes. Over the final twenty kilometres it degenerates into an unsurfaced road, which alternates between loose gravel and rock-hard ridges destined to jar the teeth and rattle the bones. Then there are vast swathes of sand over which it is difficult for any vehicle to maintain purpose or direction. Adding to the problems of today's journey is the fact that it is still the height of the rainy season. This regularly renders this particular road impassable to all but the hardiest 4x4s.

Mr Mbai, project manager of our Kaputula and Kafubu projects, is also accompanying us and will add his expert opinion as to the viability of a future Chilumba building project.

Not only that, but we are attempting the impossible. From Chilumba we plan to travel on to Kafubu Baptist Church to show the community there plans for their proposed new church which Mr Mbai has been up until 4am completing. From there it's on to Kaputula to show Faith and Mr Chalwe what has been achieved there. We also plan to hand over fifteen pairs of orphans' shoes and to collect a sign-writer whom, you may remember in **'Bwanakula Thandi'**, was left at Kaputula overnight along with his mosquito net and the *absolute* assurance we would return today to collect him. So, a tightly packed schedule which needs everything in our favour in order for it to succeed.

The first part of the road to Chilumba follows the same road as to Kaputula and Kafubu.

"The road has deteriorated steadily every day this week," we point out to Mr Chalwe. Not wishing to put a damper on things, nevertheless we feel it necessary to ask, "Do you think it wise to attempt Chilumba today?"

"In fact there is no problem," Mr Chalwe assures us. "I went there myself only last week."

*But that was last week Mr Chalwe. A week is a long time in the Zambian rainy season . . .*

However, despite ridges, potholes and bumps guaranteed to wreck lesser vehicles, we make good progress over the first stretch. Even when the road becomes red gravel, we still travel well. Suddenly we reach a sheer expanse of water glistening in the morning sun. It stretches across the whole width of the road.

Bob brings the vehicle to a halt and surveys the water critically. "Maybe it's time to turn back?"

"No, no, it's quite okay," insists Mr Chalwe. "If you just drive straight through, you can follow the tracks out the other side."

True, there are tracks emerging on the far side of the water. But whose tracks are they? How big was the vehicle that made them? We are travelling in the 'heffalump', the same ill-advised and fated vehicle which last year suffered a close brush with its maker on the road from Chipata to Lusaka.

"I'm not at all happy about it," persists Bob.

"You will be okay. Just maintain your speed as you go through," advises Mr Chalwe. Rich indeed, since he himself rarely exceeds twenty miles per hour even on the best road surfaces.

The 'heffalump' dips its front wheels gingerly in the pond. Immediately water sprays up on either side mounting higher than the wheel arches. Bob inches forward while I hold my breath, praying faith with a small 'f' will see us through.

It does. The 'heffalump' emerges unscathed on the other side. Yet any relief is short-lived for immediately the road surface deteriorates even further. Deeply rutted ridges of red squishy mud wedge the wheels in a vice-like grip making escape impossible and forcing the 'heffalump' to slide and slither along a pathway to destruction with us inside helpless to desist.

Suddenly there is a hideous clanking noise, undeniably terminal. *Haven't we been here before?* The vehicle lurches to a shuddering halt skewed diagonally across the road and effectively blocking the road to all other traffic of which so far this morning there hasn't been any.

"That's done it!" explodes Bob.

A Zambian on a bicycle races up from behind waving his arms and shouting, "Crankshaft gone, crankshaft gone!"

"Hardly surprising!" Bob glares at Mr Chalwe daring him to challenge this undeniable fact.

The five of us clamber out to survey the damage. The man has already flung his bicycle into the ditch by the side of the road and is anxious to assure us, "I fix it!" Lying prostrate in the squelching red mud underneath the vehicle, he clearly thinks it is merely a matter of slotting whatever has dislodged itself back into place with the aid of a single bicycle spanner and we will be on our way in no time. Oh that repairing a car was so simple!

Already a crowd of curious onlookers has materialised from the surrounding bush like spectres at a funereal feast. Barefoot children in ragged and tattered clothing, toothless and wrinkled old grandmothers and would-be car pushers looking to make a quick buck have all gathered to gawp at the 'mzungus' predicament.

Just our luck, when we have not seen a single vehicle since turning onto the Chilumba road, a truck now hoves into sight. Because of the awkward angle the heffalump remains slewed in, the truck driver is forced to pull up behind. Then a second vehicle appears in front.

"What is happening?" shouts one driver. "Why are you stopped here?"

"Don't you know you are blocking the road?" rails the other, shaking his fist at us. "Can't you shift this vehicle out of the way?"

"Me, I have to get to . . ." The driver of the truck behind names some unpronounceable village located the far side of Chilumba.

"Me, I have to get to Kitwe," claims the one in front. "In fact you are in my way."

In the midst of this mêlée, Mr Chalwe calmly proclaims, "The problem as I see it is . . ."

*The problem is, Mr Chalwe, if it hadn't been for you, we wouldn't be in this mess.*

By common consensus, the motley collection of would-be mechanics decides to jack up the vehicle in order to slot the bit that is out back in place once more.

"I can see it is the prop shaft," announces one of them knowledgeably.

"Is that a good thing?"

"It is better than the crankshaft . . . But it is still not good. However we will try to get it back in."

However the vehicle is too heavy. Each attempt to jack it up higher only results in it sinking ever deeper into the red mud, which by now is liberally splattering the clothing of all and sundry.

"What we must do is push the vehicle over to the side of the road so that other vehicles may pass," announces the driver of the truck. He is wearing a lime green T-shirt, red trousers and purple flip-flops. So far he is the only person present who has not got mud on his clothes or dirt on his hands. Yet he is exceedingly impatient to reach the place with the unpronounceable name.

They attempt to push the vehicle off to the side of the road. However, since the prop shaft drives the wheels, the wheels refuse to turn without its active participation. Time is ticking inexorably by. In Zambia, where darkness falls with monotonous regularity and help is not always at hand, time is of the essence.

"We need to phone for a towing truck to come out from Kitwe and tow us back there," I point out.

"In fact I don't think so," disagrees Mr Chalwe. "All that we need is to get this prop shaft back in its place so we can continue with our journey."

*Continue with the journey, surely he is joking?*

"That is supposing we can make the phone call," adds Faith. "For sure the nearest cell phone coverage to this place is ten kilometres away."

"You mean ten kilometres back towards Kitwe?" I am anxious for reassurance this is the case.

"No, in fact ten kilometres on in the direction we are travelling."

*"In the direction we were travelling!"* But this difference in tense escapes both Faith and Mr Chalwe. Yet short of pacing the entire length of the road from here back to Kitwe, we have no means of proving her right or wrong.

"What you are saying is that unless we can reach Chilumba, where we *were* heading and where the nearest cell phone coverage is, we have no hope of getting out of here at all?"

"Indeed!"

Eventually, thanks to the combined efforts of the entire project team, villagers, man on bicycle, and even truck driver in lime green T-shirt and to the accompaniment of children whooping in excitement and toothless old grannies ululating a noisy encouragement, the wounded vehicle slithers off onto the side of the road.

"This man says he will take us on to Chilumba," announces Faith. "Maybe there we can pick up a signal and phone for some assistance."

"Myself I will stay with the vehicle," announces Mr Chalwe.

"Correction," interjects Bob grimly, "*I* will stay with the vehicle!"

In the end they both stay, leaving me to travel on to Chilumba with Faith and Mr Mbai who so far has contributed little. Clearly he is suffering the after-effects of working till 4am on the proposed plans for Kafubu Baptist Church.

I climb up into the stiflingly hot cab of the truck while Mr Mbai and Faith clamber up into the open truck behind. We resume our slippery sliding progress, this time in a twenty ton truck with bald tyres and holes in the floor of the cab through which the muddy road surface visibly speeds by three feet below.

"Is this your first visit to Zambia?" shouts the driver above the din of protesting gears as he rams his way mercilessly up through them and into top gear causing the entire truck to vibrate.

"No, we have been here many times," I yell back.

"Many times?" he repeats incredulously. "Then what are you doing travelling on *this* road in *that* vehicle?" He shakes his head in disbelief.

"You remember the man back there, the one who stayed behind with the vehicle? *He* assured us the road was okay."

"Ah that one!" he says knowingly, though I can only presume he realises that I meant Mr Chalwe, and not Bob.

Ten kilometres further down the road, we reach Chilumba. The lorry driver dumps the three of us at the side of the road. He refuses any offer of payment and drives off.

"Will he come back for us?" I ask hopefully, because unless he does, I see no other way out of here.

"I don't think so," responds Faith.

"So how do we get back to where we've left the other two with the car?"

"That I don't know. Maybe we can get another lift."

It is now almost two hours since the car broke down. In that time there have only been two other vehicles on the road, one of them travelling in the wrong direction.

So now the three of us are here, while the other two are ten kilometres away with no means whatsoever of getting back to each other, nor of communicating one with the other. There is no public transport, no phone box and no rescue service. On either side a long red ribbon of dusty road stretches as far as the eye can see. Here and there figures are dotted along the road, yet not a single vehicle is in sight.

"So, shall we continue with our programme?" suggests Faith brightly.

"No Faith," I say firmly. "The purpose of coming on this far was to try to contact someone who can help us. For the moment the programme must wait. The priority is to contact Chep and get a tow truck here fast, preferably before dark. So, where can I pick up a signal?"

Faith looks disappointed, yet does not deny our pressing need to get help. "First you can try over by the pit toilets."

Cell-phone in one hand, I circle the crumbling block of pit toilets. Not a peep.

"Maybe you can try that anthill over there."

Keeping a wary eye out for hidden snakes, I scramble up the sides of the anthill. The phone shows emergency cover only. Dialling our partner organisation Chep produces no response.

"Then you must try walking up and down the road until you pick up a signal," suggests Faith.

I pace up and down the red dirt road weaving from side to side until eventually the familiar Celtel signal appears on the screen. I dial Chep where the Executive Director answers. Speaking rapidly lest the signal dies, I relate what has happened. But has the ED registered where we are? Chilumba is not a Chep project.

"You are at Kaputula then?" he asks.

"No, we are Chilumba."

"Chilumba, where exactly is that?" I suspected as much. Chilumba is twenty-five kilometres away from Kaputula as the crow flies and along an entirely different dirt road. The ED hasn't a clue where it is. Just then the signal fades . . .

"What now?" I ask the other two who have sought refuge from the hot midday sun in Chilumba's one classroom where Mr Mbai is dozing in the corner.

"Maybe I can try my colleague and friend Mr Chama." Mr Mbai regains consciousness sufficiently to make this suggestion. So Mr Mbai paces up and down the road trying to gain a signal. But Mr Chama has his cell-phone switched off.

"Who else's number do we have?" We find the number for Mrs Musungaila, head of accounts at Chep. I try her number. "Mrs Musungaila?"

"Ah Mrs Cooke," instantly she recognises the voice. "How are you?"

"I am fine Mrs Musungaila, how are you?" In Zambia observing greeting formalities remains important, however desperate the predicament.

"I also am fine. So, you are back from Kaputula?"

"No Mrs Musungaila, we are not back from Kaputula because we didn't go to Kaputula. We are stranded at Chilumba. Our vehicle has broken down."

"Ah, your vehicle has broken down, but you are not at Kaputula . . . so why is our ED sending a vehicle to Kaputula to fetch you back from there?"

It would be considered very bad taste, even when stranded in the middle of nowhere with your rescue party heading off in the opposite direction, to lose face and scream. Nevertheless the temptation is great. "He is sending it there because he thinks we are at Kaputula. He doesn't even know where Chilumba is."

"Is that so!" states Mrs Musungaila with typical Zambian phlegm which is rarely surprised even by the most unexpected of circumstances.

"Mrs Musungaila," I say as patiently as I can, "do you by any chance know where Chilumba is?"

"Ah but you have forgotten, Mrs Cooke!"

"Forgotten what, Mrs Musungaila?" I could weep with frustration.

"What I am telling you on the day we travelled to Kaputula and you indicated the road which led to Chilumba. Then I was telling you that in fact I am knowing that road very well because I was born near to that place."

Tears of despair turn to tears of relief. Mrs Musungaila knows *exactly* where we are. "Mrs Musungaila, please can you intercept the rescue vehicle and explain how to reach us here?"

Mrs Musungaila promises to do so without delay. Finally rescue is on the way.

"Good, so we may resume our programme?" proposes Faith with alacrity on hearing this good news.

I have little heart for speech making, yet agree to address the motley collection of villagers, orphans and orphan carers who have gathered here today. I thank them for coming. Word has spread about the fine school Starfish has constructed at Kaputula. Hopes are high that Starfish will do the same here for this deprived community.

It is becoming hotter. In the late rainy season heavy afternoon rain is not uncommon until the rains finally fade away in late April. Under the mistaken assumption that the truck or some other vehicle would return us to where Bob and the vehicle remain stranded, I left everything behind in the car. I haven't a drop of drinking water and only two packets of Sunmaid raisins to eat. To ask for a cup of water here is out of the question. Their water supply doubtless comes from the local stream or river. Even boiled it would be unsafe.

"Anywhere where I can buy a coke?" I try optimistically.

Faith looks at me as if I am mad. We sit sweltering in the now deserted classroom where flies buzz relentlessly around our heads and Mr Mbai struggles with his battle to stay awake.

"They are bringing us some food," announces Faith.

*Oh yummee!* There is no electricity, no running water, no sanitation and certainly no hygienic method of preparing food. *What will arrive for lunch?*

Two village women enter the classroom struggling under the weight of a large plastic washing up bowl filled with mealies (corn on the cob) as well as some indeterminate vegetable of the squash family. They kneel before us to present their offering.

"You will like it," says Faith encouragingly. "But first let us wash our hands."

*In a bowl containing local river water!* As the water trickles over my hands I pray silently and fervently, 'Lord, protect me from whatever is in this water, dysentery, cholera, typhoid, just to name some of the less pleasant possibilities!'

I eat a mealie freshly picked and cooked from the fields, as well as some squash which tastes like floury mashed potato and thank God for sustenance in *whatever* shape or form.

"I think it's really marvellous," Faith waves her half chewed mealie as she speaks, "that you can sit here as one of us and partake of our food. It is good, very good."

*'Oh Faith,'* I cry silently, *'if only you knew what traitorous thoughts are currently racing through my mind!'* Hopefully she cannot read my thoughts!

But God is listening after all. Just at that moment the man on the bicycle, still in his mud-splattered clothes, appears on the road weaving dangerously from side to side because his progress is severely hampered by the weight of the cool-box from the car. He is carrying it balanced precariously across the handlebars of his bicycle. Silently I thank the Lord and saint Bob, or whoever had the foresight to remember us in our hour of need.

The cool-box contains sodden sandwiches made earlier this morning as well as . . . bottled drinking water! Too late, I discover that in my haste this morning, I forgot to pack cups. As is the Zambian custom, because I have shared their food, now I share what I have with them. But how can we all drink from the same bottle with no cups?

"No problem," says Faith. "I am sure they have some cups which they can make available." They have indeed, red plastic ones, washed in the same river water and still ingrained with its muck. Prayer time yet again! 'Oh Lord, be merciful . . .'

"You will have noticed," says Faith, perhaps by way of a diversion to while away the long afternoon, "that many of the orphans have these sores on their legs."

"I noticed last time we were here."

"They get these sores in the rainy season. We think some insect attacks their bare legs when they are walking through the tall grass."

The sores are open weeping ulcers, which eat right through to the bone exposing it. "Can nothing be done about it?"

"Not much," answers Faith in that tone of Zambian resignation, which suggests: surely not without outside help. "The nearest clinic is six kilometres away from here. How can these children walk that far when they are lame? Indeed how can they afford the money for the medicine?"

I shake my head helpless against such insurmountable odds, yet reluctant to be drawn in further. The afternoon is drawing on. Over in the corner Mr Mbai still dozes fitfully, only stirring to swat at the persistent flies. Of the rescue vehicle there is still no sign. I seriously consider the very real prospect of having to spend the night here.

But what about Bob still stranded with the vehicle . . . and Mr Chalwe? How will Bob fare if we are all stuck here all night? At least the three of us are in the village where Faith and Mr Chalwe grew up. But where are they?

At 2pm I dial Mrs Musungaila's number once more, though already the phone is showing signs of discharging its power.

"Ah, Mrs Cooke, you are okay?"

"Mrs Musungaila, what is happening?"

"In fact Mrs Cooke, a Chep vehicle is preparing to leave right now."

"Right now, Mrs Musungaila?" I try not to scream. "But it's over two hours since I spoke to you. What has been happening?" I manage to add more calmly, "So we can hope to see them soon?"

"Indeed that is so, Mrs Cooke."

Even allowing for their best vehicle, it will be at least 3.30pm before they arrive here. Then there are the other two to collect, the vehicle to fix or tow . . . Time is ebbing away.

Almost one and a half hours later, a massive high clearance Chep 4x4 appears on the red ribbon of the road. Pim has accompanied the driver, sent by Mrs Musungaila because Pim also is of this area. And . . . Bob who after five hours by the roadside in the hot sun with no shade, no phone, no toilet and very little water is prepared to go anywhere rather than remain on the roadside for one minute longer.

"And the vehicle?" I ask him.

"Two mechanics from Chep are working on it with the proper tools. By the time we get back, they hope to have done a temporary repair which will get us back to Kitwe."

"And Mr Chalwe?"

Of Mr Chalwe there is no sign. We all clamber into the Chep vehicle and head back down the road only to meet . . . *Mr Chalwe driving towards us behind the wheel of our vehicle.*

"No problem," he greets us gleefully. "Your vehicle is working once more!"

*And the cost of the repair bill, Mr Chalwe?*

"Mr Chalwe, " I inform him frostily when rightful ownership of the vehicle has been restored and we are on the road back to Kitwe, "I have it on good authority that we should not have brought this vehicle along this road today?" In fact on the authority of the truck driver with the lime green T-shirt, but Mr Chalwe need not know that.

For once Mr Chalwe does not have an answer. He remains exceedingly quiet all the way back to Kitwe. Perhaps he also is thinking of the bill and his own responsibility towards today's disaster. In silence we limp back to Chep headquarters where at 6pm a veritable reception committee of Chep staff has remained behind after work to await our safe return.

"Welcome back!" They clap in delight at our reappearance. Apparently work halted for the entire afternoon given the state of emergency caused by the 'mzungus' breakdown in the bush and the urgent need to bring us back safely before dark.

"Ah but we must make plans!" exclaims the ED.

"Plans?" All we want to do is crawl back to base for a bath and bed.

"We must get the vehicle straight away into a garage tonight. Then we must arrange for you to borrow a Chep vehicle, so that tomorrow you can resume the programme you have been forced to abandon today."

"Oh no!" Realisation strikes us both. "We have omitted to pick up the sign-writer from Kaputula. We promised him faithfully he would only spend one night in the bush and we would be back today to pick him up."

Not forgetting a truck driver at Kafubu awaiting payment and fifteen pairs of orphans' shoes due for delivery today to Kaputula. Now they are suggesting we start all over again tomorrow.

But in Zambia tomorrow is always another day, another chance to redress the balance. Besides, do we even have any choice? In fact we don't, and so the next day the trips to Kafubu and Kaputula are successfully completed . . . but **not** to Chilumba.

Plans are also handed over to the Kafubu Baptist Church community and shoes to the orphans at Kaputula. Of the sign-writer there is no sign. Apparently he fell ill with malaria overnight and refused to stay at Kaputula. He was ferried on a moped to Kafubu where presumably he picked up a minibus back to Kitwe.

What we did not reckon on was that, following on from his day stranded in the bush, most of which was spent near a stream where he was copiously bitten by mosquitoes, Bob developed malaria some four weeks later back in the UK. Further the 'heffalump' was consigned to the scrap heap. Only one person survived unscathed . . . Mr Chalwe apparently suffered no ill effects whatsoever!

Original classrooms at Musonda School

Telling the Starfish story at
Musonda School

Tresford

Mr Banda's office

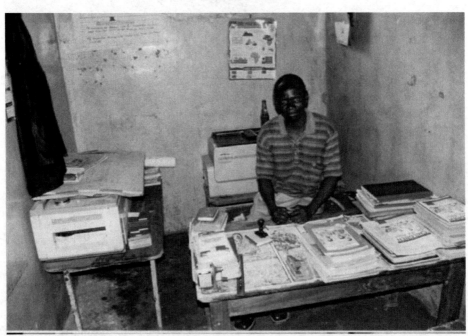

Twatasha pupils carrying chairs home

Delivering books at Fisenge School

Musonda pupils with shoes and bags

Old classrooms at Salem Centre

Moira with Augustine Mumba

Bob with Frederick Phiri

Salem new classroom blocks

Original church at Kafubu

Mr Chama with 'hummers' and 'gogolos'

Kafubu, the tale of a ball

Kafubu new church building

Chilumba Orphans' Centre as Dynass puts her question to Moira

Chilumba orphans receiving shoes

Chilumba grannies and orphan carers

Chilumba new classroom block

Chilumba orphans – Kennedy
(see also front cover)

Chilumba orphans –
Dynass October 2010

Roadside picnic with Messrs. Chalwe, Mbai and Chama

147

Simooya clinic before completion

Simooya clinic completed

Simooya nurse's house

St Andrew's Chibuluma

Kaputula brick kiln

Chalet at Chisoboyo Farm

# CHAPTER SIXTEEN: OF HUMMERS AND GOGOLOS
## ... and the tale of a ball.
*Tuesday July 25<sup>th</sup> and Wednesday August 9<sup>th</sup>, 2006*

Punctuality is a virtue greatly to be encouraged. Today we are meeting our Project Manager and Building Supervisor at Chep headquarters at 9am. Messrs Mbai and Chama are notorious timekeepers who rarely appear at the appointed hour. One or other of them is always late. Today neither of them is there on time.

"Ah, even Mbai is not yet here?" pants Mr Chama breathlessly, having run the hundred yards from his cubby-hole of an office to join us beside the car. Yet this is a dangerous position, with neither of them as yet safely closeted in the car.

"Mr and Mrs Cooke, I have to inform you, we need to buy 'hummers'," announces Mr Chama.

"What 'hummers'?" we ask. Our involvement in both Kaputula and Salem building projects has proved a steep learning curve, yet neither of us has to date encountered 'hummers'.

Mr Chama's astonishment would indicate he fears we no longer understand plain English. "You know, 'hummers'," he repeats. "One big 'hummer' and five small 'hummers' for the Kafubu project."

"But Mr Chama, we finalised the Kafubu budget last week," we remind him patiently. "There was no mention of 'hummers' then."

"Ah but 'hummers' are required for breaking up the large rocks which they have dug out of the foundation trenches. With the 'hummers' they can break these large rocks up into small stones, which can be used to fill in the footings. That way we won't have to pay so much for ferrying loads of stones."

At last Mr Chama is making sense. In a flash of inspiration I ask," Do you by any chance mean *hammers*?"

"Precisely, Mrs Cooke. We need, 'hummers!"

We concede an urgent need for 'hummers'.

Just at that moment Mr Mbai rolls up in a taxi. The morning is ticking away. Yet Mr Mbai also must turn his attention to the need for 'hummers'. Finally he concludes, "Mr Chama, you must set off now to the market in order to buy the 'hummers'."

I groan inwardly. "Surely it will be quicker if we all go in the car and wait for Mr Chama, then we can head off for Kafubu?"

"Ah no," points out Mr Chama. "If those guys at the market see 'mzungus' in the vehicle, they will double or even triple the price of the 'hummers'."

Reluctantly we hand over the money for the 'hummers' and prepare for a long wait. Time, which perhaps could have been more profitably filled. Now with Mr Chama gone to the market, Mr Mbai also vanishes. We phone Mr Chama to see if we can pick him up on his way back from the market with the 'hummers' thereby saving some valuable time.

"I am coming, right now," he assures us."

"Then let us meet along the road to save time?" we suggest.

"Unfortunately, Mrs Cooke, we cannot do that. I have left my bag at Chep. I will need to pick it up before we leave."

Eventually Mr Chama returns struggling under the weight of four five pound 'hummers'. He loads these into the back of the vehicle, before disappearing to fetch his bag. Before we can prevent it, Mr Mbai is running after him, waving the receipt and loudly protesting that he has paid too much for the 'hummers'.

"In fact it was because you paid with a fifty thousand kwacha note that those guys knew it was 'mzungu' money and overcharged you! Ba Chama, they have upped the price and ripped you off!"

"Mr Mbai . . . Mr Chama . . ." I call helplessly after their receding backs. "The time . . ."

"Don't worry, we are coming!"

It is ten o'clock. Already we are one hour late leaving. But at last we are off. Except . . . "There is still the ten pound 'hummer' which we must stop and buy on the way," announces Mr Chama from the back seat.

"But Mr Chama, you've just said if they see us in the vehicle, they'll up the price?"

"Ah no, here it doesn't matter if they see us because these guys know us. Here they can't change the price."

Finally we are off. Or are we? Just as we reach the roundabout by the Coca Cola bottling factory Mr Chama exclaims," Ah me, I am forgetting to purchase the 'gogolos'!"

He really has got us this time. Are 'gogolos' another type of 'hummer'? Maybe it's the name of a new fizzy drink, or even something from everyone's favourite bakery at Kalulushi?

"'Yes, 'gogolos'," continues Mr Chama blissfully unaware of our confusion. "We are needing ten pairs of safety 'gogolos' for those men who will be using the 'hummers'."

*How could we not have guessed?* He means safety goggles.

"But Mr Chama, why do we need to purchase ten pairs of 'gogolos' when we only bought five 'hummers'?"

"Bah, you know, these 'gogolos', they are always breaking."

Bob performs an about turn in order for Mr Chama to leap once more into the thick of the African market to purchase ten pairs of unsatisfactory safety 'gogolos'. At least the children at Kafubu will have fun with the broken ones.

It is almost eleven o'clock and, by Zambian standards, quite punctual really. "So, we are off?"

"If we can just stop by the bakery in Kalulushi," requests Mr Mbai. "This morning I am forgetting to have any breakfast."

This deviation via the bakery at Kalulushi has become routine for trips to Kaputula, Kafubu and Chilumba projects. Whereas we pass other bakeries en route, it is the considered opinion of both gentlemen that the meat pies, doughnuts and sausage rolls from Kalulushi bakery are vastly superior to those from other establishments.

Finally we are on our way . . .


Kafubu is a small town situated about five kilometres before Kaputula and along the same road. Life there focuses around the local sawmills, where those lucky enough to have employment work. The Kafubu Baptist Church community has observed with great interest work on the school at Kaputula. Some two years ago Mr Kauseni, who lives at Kaputula but worships at Kafubu, approached Starfish with a request to rebuild their church.

The original Baptist Church at Kafubu was built using timber from the local sawmills. However a first visit there in August 2005 verified the church community's claim that the wooden supports were being eaten by termites. In another one or two rainy seasons the church would surely collapse.

Initially Starfish expressed some reluctance to undertake this project. To date all our involvement had been with children and schools. Besides, we were already heavily committed with building work at both Kaputula and Salem. Eventually the UK committee decided to farm out the Kafubu community's request to local Baptist churches in the UK to see if any interest could be roused in funding this project.

To everyone's delight our nearest Baptist church responded positively. But this church was also one of the smallest ones in the area. How would a church of less than twenty people *ever* fund the rebuilding of a church for over three hundred worshippers?

But who were we to question the ways of God? It was agreed that Hockley Heath Baptist Church would fund the project, which Starfish was to manage.

Anxieties about this project were further exacerbated by the fact that Kafubu lies not five kilometres distant from Kaputula. Would this project also become bedevilled by the same problems as Kaputula?

Yet right from the start there was a different ethos at Kafubu. Maybe because it was a church project, or because, in Zambia, no two communities are ever the same!

On our first meeting the Kafubu community greeted us as honoured guests, seating us on wooden chairs like thrones at the front of the church. But also right from the start they could not do enough to assist us or to help themselves. However, fine words and promises don't build schools let alone churches. It was clear, this was going to be one big church.

Earlier this year in February 2006, we held a community meeting to decide the budget for this project. We had learnt a great deal from our experiences at Kaputula. This time there was to be a fixed budget. There were to be written contracts for skilled labour, while all unskilled labour was to be voluntarily supplied by church members. And all this was absolutely and totally non-negotiable. *Oh how fast we have learnt!*

Since this meeting took place at the height of the rainy season, there was only a certain amount they could achieve before our current visit. We therefore left them to source local free materials such as sand and chipped stones and also to mark out the footings so that work could begin in earnest as soon as the rains stopped.

Before we left in March we provided them with a wheelbarrow, two shovels, two picks, oil drums to fetch water and twenty pockets of cement so that work could commence making concrete blocks for the church. At this point the reality suddenly hit us . . .

"Heavens, this is already our third building project!"

"So where's it going to end?" But the answer to that, as ever, lies in greater hands than our own.

To our great delight and relief, so far this project has not been bedevilled by problems of labour and wages, nor by community disputes, which dogged the Kaputula project. Already it has amazed us how a community so close in distance to Kaputula, could be so far removed in temperament.

Today we arrive complete with 'hummers' and 'gogolos'. All is going well. In the past couple of days the Kafubu workforce has dug out all the trenches for the footings. These trenches stretch so wide and deep, the entire terracotta army might well fill them.

The need for 'hummers' is immediately apparent. While one end of the trenches consists of sand, the end near the proposed porch entrance to the church has revealed massive rocks and boulders. With the help of 'hummers' they can break up the rocks into stone chippings. These can then be used to strengthen the foundations at the sandy end of the church.

Everyone is eager to try out the 'hummers', especially the huge ten pound one. Bob, Mr Chama, Pastor Mweetwa, the entire male workforce wants to wield the immense brute of a hammer. Testosterone fuelled enthusiasm perhaps? The women standing shyly by are content merely to watch.

Sweat glistening like black pearls on his forehead, Pastor Mweetwa swings the 'hummer' high over his head, then brings it crashing down on top of the largest boulder as easily as if he was shelling walnuts. We declare him the easy winner, which he has been all along. As pastor of the church he has shown himself willing to lead by example. He is always on site, always working to capacity, yet never demanding any payment.

Now the women are eager to have a go, but with the small five pound hammers. These they swing with ease breaking up smaller rocks into stones. Certainly it is a reminder just how labour intensive the work is on these projects.

"Stop, wait a moment!" I call anxiously. "Mr Chama, you have forgotten something!"

He looks puzzled, before realisation dawns. "Indeed, we have forgotten to apply the 'gogolos'!"

Like a magician flourishing a rabbit out of his hat, Mr Chama produces the 'gogolos' from the back seat of the car and dangles them enticingly. The women wrinkle their noses. Smashing rocks is much more fun without these things. Reluctantly one agrees to try a pair. Pastor Mweetwa also dons one pair. They do not look impressed. Perhaps if one gets hit by a flying stone, then the others might see the point.

Progress is also rapid in other areas. Church members have started moulding 8" blocks for the slab retaining wall. Next to the site for the new church they have constructed a makeshift shelter. Already in a couple of days they have filled it with 990 blocks. How this community works, yet no-one receives any wages except for one skilled bricklayer and one carpenter.

"Please can you convey to them how fantastically they are doing?" we ask Mr Mbai.

To our surprise he shrieks, "Aieeh no!" Then he rolls the whites of his eyes heavenwards in dismay. "Whatever you do, don't encourage them!"

"Why ever not?" we ask bemused.

"Otherwise they will turn into reluctant workers, if they think they are doing too well."

*And we wouldn't want that, would we? Not after all the trials experienced at Kaputula.* Mr Mbai is project manager and as such we respect his advice. So we adopt expressions hopefully conveying the message . . . 'Hey, you guys, you really ought to put more effort into it!'

Gradually over time we establish a working relationship with the Kafubu community. It is always a delight to pass by there, especially after a trying day at Kaputula. Their enthusiasm, hard work and commitment to rebuilding their ramshackle church never cease to amaze us. In particular the women erupt onto the scene and greet each arrival of our vehicle with songs and clapping and ululating voices.

Of course as we slip into the ease of familiarity, other requests start to emerge. However with few qualms we readily respond to the request from one of the women for a football for the children of the Sunday School.

"Of which there are many," she assures us. Indeed a dozen or more are that very moment clamouring around her, or else writing with their fingers in the dust of our coming besmirching the sides of the vehicle. Barefoot and ragged, stomachs bulging from malnutrition, it is hard to resist their beseeching looks.

Bob therefore takes it upon himself to purchase the ball from 'Game' superstore during our next visit to Lusaka.

Granddaughter Thandi, on glimpsing the ball, demands, "I want that ball!"

"No," we tell her firmly. "This ball's not for you. You already have a ball. This ball is for children who have no ball to play with."

So we duly turn up on our next visit with the ball.

"You have remembered the ball?" asks one of the women almost immediately.

"Are you the one who asked for the ball?" It is important to ensure the ball ends up in the right hands. The woman who originally asked for it claimed to be a Sunday School teacher. The last thing we want is for the ball to end up in the wrong hands.

A lengthy debate ensues in Chibemba amongst the gaggle of women. "She is the one," they eventually decide, pushing the woman who addressed us upon our arrival to the fore.

"And these *are* the same children who were here the day she asked for it?" It is difficult to tell. Sadly one set of ragged children, of which Zambia has so many, looks much the same as the next.

Further debate ensues until a rag tag and bobtail group of children is assembled and they announce, "These are the ones."

Bob fetches the ball from the car and punches it high in the air. The children run squealing to catch it. They run off delighted with their ball, shouting and tossing it one to another while the women ululate in thanks and jubilation.

And there the story might well have ended with the gift of a ball to an impoverished community in Africa and people back in the UK happy to feel their money is used to good purpose. What an amazing difference the simple gift of a ball can make to such people!

Except that the story doesn't end there.

Soon older more athletic children, attracted by the shouts of delight coming from the younger ones, join in the game and take possession of the ball. The little ones, for whom the ball was intended, become sidelined. They stand forlornly by, their crestfallen expressions saying . . . 'Hey, what happened to our ball?'

Then along comes another group of three or four lads with a large outsize and once yellow ball bearing the markings of a tennis ball, but the size of a football. Balls of this ilk are also on sale in Game store, prompting me to mutter somewhat disgruntedly to Bob, "I thought the children in this community had no balls to play with?"

The Sunday school teacher notes our puzzled expressions and quickly intervenes. "Hey you ones go and play elsewhere. The men are wanting water for the work. Take yourselves off and fetch some water for the workers."

The Kafubu project has no on-site water supply. All water is fetched by bucket from a stream down the hill, carried back up the hill, then emptied into waiting barrels from which it is obtained by the workforce for mixing cement and block making. It was agreed in early discussions that the women would bear the load (no pun intended) of fetching water. It is time-consuming work. Hardly surprising they want to offload some of the task onto older children with nothing better to do than play ball.

No sooner are the older ones occupied elsewhere, and the younger ones repossessed of their ball, than they tire of it. So I mutter again, "Hey, I thought the need for a ball was something which would *really* make a difference to them? How come they tire of it after five minutes?"

The ball lies forgotten in the dust until one of the workers from the building project, passing by with a wheelbarrow load of cement, picks it up and gives it a tentative twirl. "Very nice football," he says twirling it professionally on the tip of his index finger.

Another worker joins him. He also takes possession of the ball and examines it minutely. "Number four ball," he pronounces like a true pro.

"Is that good?" we say.

"Oh the best!" is his reply. Clearly someone around here knows a thing or two about footballs, though it certainly isn't us. We can't tell one football from another and simply picked up the first ball in Game stores, which looked like a proper ball.

Slowly realisation dawns that in our efforts to ensure the children received a proper football, we merely ensured that is the last those who wanted the ball most, are likely to see of it. The ball is destined to become the much vaunted plaything not of the children, but of the workforce.

So what is the moral of this tale? That in Africa nothing is ever what it seems, not even the simple gift of a football. We acted with the best of intentions and, as has happened before, we are left wondering why such situations produce more questions than answers, more dilemmas than solutions and foster an on-going inability ever to comprehend fully the conundrum which is Africa today. We may well have spent the last four years doing this work, and in the process rediscovering our heart for Africa, yet we are still no closer to discovering any of the answers ourselves!

# CHAPTER SEVENTEEN: A WIFE FOR KUSHUKA...
*Saturday 5ᵗʰ May - > various dates, May 2007*

One important task each trip is checking up on loose ends left dangling from the previous trip. Little did we envisage however, that task would include checking on the progress of a goat.

In August 2006, on completion of the school at Kaputula, the grateful community presented us with a live goat. Their intention was that we would slaughter and eat it, the gift of a goat being the ultimate gift in Zambia. This we could not bring ourselves to do. Instead we donated a much distressed but very live goat to the Heart of Africa Mission located on the Kruger family farm some 15km from Kitwe. Returning to stay there in May 2007, it was clearly our duty to check on Kushuka's progress.

On Saturday May 5ᵗʰ, having the entire day free created the ideal opportunity. Unfortunately we didn't have Kumasamba Lodge to ourselves . . .

The previous evening, as we prepared to sit down to a peaceful dinner, and just at the moment Zesco cut the power supply, a rowdy white South African accompanied by three friends pitched up at Kumasamba for the weekend. With him he brought enough alcohol to put the neighbouring Kafue River into full flood even in the middle of the dry season. In no time Sid was handing round beers by the light of torches.

"So what are you folks doing out here?" Sid soon wanted to know.

When one white guy meets another in the heart of Africa, it is always a subject of conjecture as to what exactly the other might be doing there: mining, farming, fishing, setting up a company, or simply bumming around with a woman and a bottle in tow. It is arguably less curious why the woman tags along. Since Sid initially showed little interest in why I was there, maybe he presumed that like his two female companions, I was simply along for the sex.

No sooner had Bob explained the nature of our charitable works in

Zambia, than Sid began swearing himself a lifelong friend. "Man, I take my hat off to you!" Sid bent low, sweeping the ground in an exaggerated bow and spilling his beer in the process. "Man, what you're doing for these indigenous folk brings tears to my eyes. George, George!" He interrupted this litany of praise to bawl for George to fetch yet more beers.

George, if you recall, was reputedly an ex-High Court judge under Chiluba, now employed by the Kruger family as chef at Kumasamba Lodge. When George failed to materialise within seconds, Sid bawled once more. "George! Where the f*** are you!"

George appeared in his own time. Presumably he was reluctant to abandon cooking our food in order to traipse along the veranda to the bar overhanging the river to fetch yet more beers. George, generally so amenable, wore a face like thunder.

Sid grabbed the beers without so much as a please or thank you and carried on. "I tell you, man, I have contacts, people who might really help you guys."

"Really?" We doubted that was the case. However, since Sid was far too drunk to argue with, it was safer by far to humour him.

"You know who I am?" He waved his beer bottle our way. "I'm a warrior angel." He paused for effect just as the lights chose to come back on. I've never seen an angel, warrior or otherwise, but in the merciless glare of the electric light, unshaven and drunken Sid sure didn't match my perception of one.

"You don't believe me? Oh what the f***, I need a rum and coke." Sid delved deep into his cool box of drink in search of something stronger. There followed a few moments' silence while Sid passed rum and cokes all round. We politely refused. His companions, expected to keep pace, knew better.

Sid soon picked up where he'd left off. "What was your name . . . Bob? You know, Bob, I reckon I was destined to meet you. You and your good woman are angels sent to look after me this weekend."

Angels come in many guises, but for sure we're not numbered amongst them. However, at that moment George announced dinner was ready and we escaped hopefully to eat in peace.

But no, just as we were picking over the last of the fish bones, and as the lights failed once more, Sid and his companions appeared in the dining room. By now they'd downed several more rum and cokes. The others were more or less holding their own. Sid however was definitely the worse for drink. Ignoring a table for four in the corner, Sid joined us at our table.

He placed one hand on the shoulder of his newfound friend and guardian angel. "Bob, I want to tell you about the love of my life."

I sneaked a look at one of the two accompanying women who 'belonged' to Sid. Though the woman was still good looking, she had the air of someone who'd been around the block a few times. She caught my glance and smiled ruefully. Clearly she'd heard Sid's eulogy many times before.

"See that lovely woman there?" Speech slurring worse than a skier on the downward slopes, Sid raised his glass her direction. "The love of my life, she is. But I'm not married to her, the f*** I'm not. I'm married to someone else."

We murmured something between sympathy and veiled disapproval.

"So what does that make me, Bob? Can you tell me?" Mercifully Sid answered himself. "A sh** of a Christian!"

Perhaps his language also had something to do with it, but I kept such dangerous thoughts to myself as a tear rolled dejectedly down Sid's cheeks, narrowly missing his drink and landing with a plop on the tablecloth.

"But I trust you Bob!" He slapped Bob's shoulder. " 'Cos you're going to tell me what to do about it!"

"I'm not sure I'm . . ." Bob protested.

"Oh but you are!" exclaimed Sid. "You and that good wife . . . you are his wife aren't you?"

I nodded my head, not trusting myself to speak.

"You and that lovely wife of yours, you're my guardian angels!"

The time had come to put Sid right. "Sid, I'm afraid you've got it wrong, we're no angels!"

"Yesshh, you are!" Sid was verging on tears.

"Look!" I pointed over my shoulder. "See, no wings, we can't fly."

Sid surveyed us in disbelief, then shook his head and staggered off to join his friends.

Throughout this exchange, George had sat head in his hands over in the far corner of the dining room. George likes to clear up and slip away to the hole where he sleeps by 20.30. Tonight he clearly foresaw a long evening ahead.

Eventually we made our excuses and left to a final drunken wave from Sid. "See you in the morning," he slurred in farewell.

However, on Saturday morning we are up and away to check on our goat well before Sid stirs, glad of an excuse to escape. If in the cold light of day Sid still thinks us his guardian angels, it could prove an awkward weekend.

To reach the mission, where Kushuka is kept, entails walking one or two kilometres through virgin bush. A scary experience since pug marks along the way impress the track. Whether they belong to leopard, baboon or hyena, we're not knowledgeable enough to tell. And of course a straying hippo could also pose a danger by grazing away from the river.

The pastor at the mission is delighted to see us. More so his wife who was clearly hoping we would return. "Kushuka is very fine," she assures us.

Led out from his stall, Kushuka is indifferent to our reappearance. Maybe he recalls it was in our honour he was ignobly fettered and slung in the back of our vehicle. Like many male goats he may be of an unforgiving nature. Keeping our distance we admire his newly tufted billy-goat beard.

"He looks well," we tell the pastor and his wife.

She grins. "Every day we let him out to graze in a different spot."

"Like a lawn mower?" jokes Bob.

"Indeed! However he is needing a female goat to keep him happy."

We ponder the proposition of owning two goats. And presumably in due course a few kids also, maybe starting a farm in Africa. "Okay, but where would we get a female from?"

"Ah, that is no problem. One of the workers here knows someone who has a female goat for selling."

"But how much will it cost?"

"He will let us have it for K90 000."

About £10, which sounds reasonable enough. We agree to return on Wednesday when the man will also bring the female goat. If we like it, we will pay K90 000 for it.

"Then I will be very happy," announces the pastor's wife. "For sure soon I will have myself a whole flock of goats."

Goat check completed, we stroll back to the lodge keeping a wary eye for stray animals, then take books and swimming towels up to the swimming pool in the hope of avoiding any other unwanted company.

But no, the gate crashes open. "Man, I thought I'd find my guardian angels here!" Sid arrives and sits uninvited on the edge of Bob's towel. "You'd like a drink Bob, wouldn't you, and some food? Man, I need food in my stomach! How about some chicken platters? George! Where the f*** is he? Never f****** there when you want him!"

It's 11.30 am and the usual mammoth Kumasamba breakfast of sausage, bacon, egg, fried onions, tomatoes and toast is still lying like undigested lead. The last thing we want is fried chicken. We manage to convince Sid we want neither food nor alcohol at that time of the morning. Not so Sid's friends who are there to court Sid's wishes.

"So Bob, how are you today?"

Bob assures him he is fine.

"But not so fine you don't want a drink," Sid nudges him suggestively. "It's the drugs you know, f***** up my head good and proper. Now I can't stop the drinking either."

That would explain an awful lot, but unfortunately, not how best to deal with the situation.

"Say, Bob . . . uncle . . . how old would you say I am?"

Bob doesn't dare to hazard a guess. An error of judgement could prove disastrous.

"Uncle, I tell you, I'm thirty-six! What do you say to that, aunty?" Sid suddenly turns to me, for some bizarre reason best known to Sid, using the polite Zambian way of addressing an older person. We have no idea why, though maybe it's preferable to being called guardian angels.

I don't know what to say. Sid is the same age as our own children, yet he looks fifty-six. What a waste of a life! "I'd never have guessed," I respond cagily, hoping it sounds like a compliment.

Unable to tempt us with beer or chicken pieces, Sid eventually loses interest and wanders off with his friends in tow seeking other distractions.

In the middle of the afternoon we spot him shoes off and ankle deep in the fast flowing Kafue River. *Surely he knows there are crocs in there?* But Sid is waving yet another rum and coke in his hand and shouting, "You want me to cross it? Then I'll cross it. I mean it, I'm going across!" Then he rips off his shirt and stands bare-chested braving off the opposition, crocs and all.

His bimbo teeters towards him in white stiletto sandals. She is also drunk, though not as far gone as Sid. "You f****** b******, you go in there and I'll come in there after you!"

But the threat of losing the 'love of his life' sobers Sid up. He retreats from the river and spends the rest of the afternoon drinking with a group of Zambians. Every so often he bawls George out yet again. But as the afternoon progresses, he has to shout ever louder. George has inexplicably developed a case of congenital deafness. Which means, as Sid's shouts get louder, they become ever more offensive.

As night falls in the velvety enveloping blackness of Africa, peace finally reigns. Sid has passed out in his chalet. All efforts to rouse him have failed. His friends sit disconsolately by drinking soft drinks, ashamed perhaps of their betrayal in not also drinking themselves into oblivion.

On Saturday evening Zesco is once more up to its tricks. The lights flicker and fade only to resurge, then finally die for the rest of the evening. Zesco is load shedding, since there is not enough electricity to keep Zambia lit up. Though since they are reputedly still selling it to surrounding countries, this may be nearer to the true reason for shortages.

Load shedding however is not evenly distributed. Some areas of town, where people of influence or money live, suffer remarkably less power cuts than others. Hardest hit are the African compounds where sometimes the power remains off during the entire period of darkness. Located beyond the city limits and on the same grid as neighbouring compounds, the Kruger homestead has been hit hard. They have received bills topping K6 million. Perhaps in the belief that 'mzungus' can afford to pay bills of such magnitude, Zesco therefore threatens to cut them off entirely for non-payment.

In pitch darkness George pads along the veranda and knocks at the chalet door. In the light of our one candle, he looks anxious and stressed. "Excuse me, baas, madam, maybe it will be better to serve your food to your room. Unless I can persuade those other people to eat down by the bar, in which case I will serve your food in the dining room."

There is no need to ask to whom George is referring. He has had a day of it. He has been bawled at and insulted, yet has neither complained nor retaliated. "George, we are sorry about today."

"Myself also, I am sorry." George shakes his head. If he ever indeed was a High Court Judge, then I bet he would relish sending Sid down for a few years. Banishing Sid and his companions down by the bar, where they might just topple over drunk into the river and get eaten by a croc, is perhaps the next best thing. Ironically in black Zambia, yet working in a mostly white environment, George still feels unable to speak out freely for himself.

"George, does Mr Kruger or Venus have any idea what's gone on today?" I ask him.

"I have told the madam," he replies stoically.

"I also will say something. You shouldn't have to put up with this. These people shouldn't speak to you in this manner."

"Aaah, they are bad people," is all George will say.

But Venus and husband Jonathon are after all aware of the problem. Both appear in the dining room that night.

"Aachh, that man, he's trouble," says Jonathon. "But we have to be careful. If we throw him out and he spreads rumours about us, then we're

164

done for. We live on a knife edge here. Fall foul of the wrong white guy and a drunk to boot, is as bad as falling foul of anyone else here. It could cost us our livelihood."

So for various reasons we all keep quiet, praying that tomorrow will bring an end to the situation . . .

As ever we are off to church for a three hour marathon by 08.30. There is no sign of Sid and co. At breakfast George is sombre and uncommunicative. He looks as if he slept badly. However, when we return at lunchtime, there is a changed air about Kumasamba. Peace has been restored. Sid and company have departed.

"They left because I told them to go," announces George stiffly when he serves our lunch.

We can't believe this. Did the worm finally turn?

"I told them their presence was no longer required here."

"Good for you, George! There's no way you should have to put up with another day like yesterday."

Such solid support opens George up sufficiently to reveal all. "Ah, the things those people were saying, you would not believe it. Apart from the swearing, they were making references to my height, or rather to my lack of height."

George is barely five feet, but for them to have ridiculed this is unspeakable. "Ah sorry," we say.

"Even though they were apologetic this morning, I told them they were not to stay here. They were disrupting other clients and being rude and offensive. Also I informed them that I was so small because my God also is small."

*Also black*, I'm inclined to add, but say instead. "And they just left?"

"Indeed they left quietly and this time they will not return."

"So they have been here before?"

"Yes. Even that time that man was swearing, saying he would jump in the river, till Mr Jonathon told him to do so and welcome. He'd happily watch a crocodile make a meal of him. Even then he told them never to return."

"But how did they manage to come back?"

"They used the name of the other person who was with them, so that the madam and Mr Jonathon were not knowing it was them."

So much for the goings-on of a restful weekend in Kitwe, it almost rivals what goes on during the week. And there's still a wife to find for Kushuka . . .

165

By Wednesday evening the last thing on our minds is looking at a female goat. We have had a day of it at Kaputula. Only as we return tired and dusty to Kumasamba, do we remember the promise of a goat. But a promise is a promise so, as we enter the property, instead of heading for the chalet and George's welcome cup of tea, we turn right down the sandy track to the Heart of Africa Mission.

Surprise, surprise, there is no female goat.

"The man who is selling the goat is saying the price is K110 000," says the pastor acting as go-between.

No wonder Mr Mbai and Mr Chama always insist we remain secreted in the vehicle while they buy building supplies. Even the price of goats goes up when there is 'mzungu' involvement.

But we are not easily taken in. "Tell the man we will pay K90 000, or we go elsewhere," we tell him. Though actually we haven't a clue where to buy a goat in a country where goats roam freely along roadsides wherever we go.

Later we share our dilemma with Jonathon Kruger. "There's a white farmer up the road selling off his goats and sheep," he tells us. "He's sick and tired of Zambians stealing them from him. It costs him more to keep replacing them than what he's making off them."

"But that's terrible."

"Even one night he was stranded in his car. Heavy rain had flooded the road and he couldn't get through to his farm. What did they do? They broke in and stole ten goats that night."

On Friday we are due to travel down to Lusaka for the weekend. There is still no sign of a female goat at the right price at the mission. Either the seller is craftily hanging out for a higher price, or he has lost interest and sold elsewhere. We pass by the neighbouring farm to see if the owner will sell us a goat.

"Ach man, I'd sell you one if I could." The owner looks like a man at the end of his tether. "The truth is the goats I have here, or what's left of them, are all thoroughbreds. Yet the buggers round here pinch them for bloody rations! K400 000 kwachas a time I should sell them for, but they're gone before I can even get a sale. Man, I'm sick of it."

We concede these particular goats are not for us. That doesn't however solve the dilemma of where to get a female goat. In the end we confide our dilemma to our dear friend and project manager, Mr Mbai.

"You can ask the Kaputula community for a female goat," he responds.

That sounds rather too obvious, since the first goat came from there anyways. But also awkward, because in requesting a second goat, we would have to confess . . . we didn't eat the first goat!

*How can we possibly do that?*

"I think it will be okay," says Mr Mbai. "If you tell them that you want the female to breed with the male, maybe they will be delighted that you are putting their gift to such good use."

*Or maybe not, depending on which way they view our treachery!* But at this late stage we have no choice. Not only is it the end of the week, but also the end of our time in Kitwe and of another trip to Zambia. If Kushuka is to have a wife, it's this or nothing.

Later that day we face a circle of solemn black faces at Kaputula. "We have a request to make."

Mr Chipotyo, speaking for the community, spreads his hands face upwards indicating the go ahead to speak.

"It is about the goat which you gave us last year . . . "

"In fact the goat which we did not eat . . ."

"Aaahhh!" A long drawn out sigh escapes from the circle of bewildered faces. What will these 'mzungus' think of next to confound them?

"In fact the goat is alive and well . . . "

"On a mission station near where we are staying . . ."

"But what it now needs is a wife!"

Faces beam. Smiles break forth. "That's very good."

"But we don't know where to find a female goat . . ."

"So perhaps someone here would like to sell us one?"

Their faces become blank once more as they mutter amongst themselves.

*Goodness, how difficult can it be to obtain a goat in a country overrun with them!*

"There is a woman near here who lives in the forest. Maybe she has a goat to sell," offers one. However no-one seems certain whether she has one or not.

Then Mr Nyrongo pipes up. "Myself, I have a goat."

"And would you sell it to us?"

He shakes his head from side to side weighing up the issue. "Yes, I can sell it to you," he says. "I wasn't going to sell it, but I am happy to sell it to you."

*Could K90 000 have helped him make up his mind?*

In order to obtain the goat, we will have to go to his house to collect it. Today we are in a Chep vehicle. Our own is yet again in for repair for the tenth time in a month following the Chilumba breakdown. We clamber into the Chep vehicle along with John the bemused driver who has carried a goat for us before, but not actually accompanied us to buy one.

We bump off down a sandy track, which gets narrower and narrower. It is bordered by densely packed shoulder high grasses, which whip past the open windows scattering seeds and insects inside the vehicle. The seeds are itchy while the insects bite instantly without leaving time to swat them. Gradually the track peters out to nothing.

"We can leave the vehicle here," says Mr Nyrongo.

"Is the goat here?" I ask.

"From here we must walk to my house."

I was afraid of that. My favourite pastime is walking through shoulder high, snake-infested grasses, down paths with holes where a snake can lurk ready to strike.

It is a fair hike to the Nyrongo settlement. Like most of the Kaputula community, Mr Nyrongo is a subsistence farmer living on what he grows on the land and what small things he can sell. As we approach his group of huts, he whistles to summon the goats. A pair of young females appears along with an older female with two kids.

"You can have this one." Mr Nyrongo indicates one of the two young females.

"She looks very young," I hazard. "How old is she?"

"She is nine months."

"Is she old enough . . . I mean to put her in with the male goat?"

"She will be okay!" Mr Nyrongo is clearly more concerned about the prospect of money than the goat's tender feelings. He ties the goat's front legs to its back legs before slinging it unceremoniously over his shoulders for the long trek back to the car.

We resume the path back through the bush. On the way Mr Nyrongo snatches handfuls of sweet potato leaves, cassava leaves and husks of corn to keep the goat happy on the car journey back to Kitwe.

"Aieeh snake!" yells Mr Nyrongo suddenly.

We stop and peer dubiously at the snake. Mercifully it is dead, clubbed to death possibly by children who fear snakes even more than I do. Running barefoot through the bush, snakes are a common hazard for Zambian children many of whom get bitten.

The goat is slung in the back of the Chep vehicle from where it beseeches us pitifully with its sorrowful brown eyes. How should we console it? *Never mind, a night of unbridled passion lies ahead!*

Mr Chipotyo observes my quivering bottom lip with a wry grin.

"Bwanakula Thandi, I am thinking perhaps your sympathies for the goat are misplaced," he has the audacity to say. "After all Kushuka will be delighted!" he smirks knowingly.

I turn angrily. "Bah, you men are all the same! You get all the pleasure, while we females get all the pain!"

"Ah, but she will have her young ones," intervenes Mr Mbai. "And you also, your Zambian farm is already growing."

*Small consolation!*

"But for now, what will you call your new goat?" asks Mr Chipotyo.

Giving it a name really was the last thing on my mind.

"Perhaps you should call her 'Bwana Kushuka'," he suggests.

*Mrs Kushuka?* It's as good a name as any, though by the time we transport her back to Chep, transfer her into our vehicle back once more from the garage, clear up the urine in both ours and the Chep vehicle, I'm wishing this was one project we hadn't caught up with.

As we drop the goat off at the mission, she looks as if the last thing on her mind is a night of passion. Kushuka is going to have a lot of convincing to do, if he's to have his way with her. The pastor's wife tethers her close but not too close to Kushuka who immediately senses what all this is about. We leave them to it, praying he might be gentle with her.

Later that night the electricity is on the blink yet again. They can only have eleven light-bulbs on at any one time, Jonathon tells us. But whether that is some crazy Zesco ruling, or the failure of the Kumasamba generator, who knows. In Zambia anything is possible.

We dine in style on George's signature dish: T-bone steak and chips with a dab of coleslaw on the side. George is happy tonight because earlier Bob caught two barbell in the dam, which he gave to him for his supper.

We retire to bed content at the thought of another trip over and most of what we set out to achieve has been achieved. But what is that noise piercing the velvety blackness? Though it is some distance away, the hideous braying and piteous bleating are unmistakeable.

"Oh no!" I groan from under the bedclothes. "That's Bwana Kushuka! The ruddy male's got her on her first night there!"

But there's nothing we can do. This is Africa after all, by turns both savage and beautiful, and as ever bigger than both of us put together.

"Maybe there'll be some enjoyment in it for her," quips Bob.

Which is as typical a male comment as you can get! Tonight my heart goes out not just to Africa, but to poor reluctant Bwana Kushuka. And as to whether their union indeed produces any issue, this must await another visit, another chance to catch up on everything from sponsorship programmes to building projects, and not forgetting monitoring the occasional, very reluctant goat!

# CHAPTER EIGHTEEN: WHEN GETTING INSIDE PRISON PROVES HARDER THAN GETTING OUT ... *May 2007*

Starfish receives many requests for help. Some people appeal directly in Zambia; others send letters of appeal to the UK. Sadly many get sidelined. If you have read this far, then you will surely know . . . we CANNOT take on any more projects.

Prior to this trip, Starfish received a letter on behalf of an inmate of Kabwe Prison. This letter may well have headed straight into the filing system except, not wishing to abuse the decision making powers of the Wednesday House Group, we submitted it to them with the proviso, "Everyone gets these letters, but before filing it away, we thought we'd show it to you anyways."

"I quite like the sound of that," was Rachel's reaction.

"Me too," added Nick. "What's this guy inside for? Not that it matters anyway."

We shrugged non-committally. "Murder, robbery, assault, our guess is something serious given the length of the sentence."

The sentence was for twenty years. Secretly we had little doubt Frederick Phiri, the subject of the letter, was a murderer. But as Nick rightly pointed out, it didn't matter. We weren't being asked to judge him, merely requested by his physiotherapist to provide an electric wheelchair costing . . .

"One thousand pounds!"

"You have to be joking!"

"Some wheelchair that must be!" Such were the comments circulating our living room that Wednesday evening.

We agreed, then told the group about a man we often see about the streets of Kitwe. "He is paralysed from the waist down and rides around in wheelchair made from bicycle wheels and powered by means of his hands pedalling a bike chain. And that certainly didn't cost one thousand pounds!"

Nevertheless, though we might have sidelined such a request, or else sent a polite but firm refusal, the group agreed it should be investigated further. Besides, what is the point in having a decision-making group, if we don't abide by their decisions?

Thus Monday May 3rd 2007 finds us trying to locate Mr S R Banda, writer of the letter and physiotherapist in the University Teaching Hospital in Lusaka. In the letter he explained Frederick Phiri, an inmate of Kabwe Prison, was a patient of his. He had injured his back in prison and was in constant pain. Though a pair of crutches might assist him, it was Mr Banda's considered opinion that the real need was for an electric wheelchair costing the equivalent of £1000.

"I didn't even know you could get such things in Zambia," I mutter to Bob as we walk the corridors of UTH in search of the physiotherapy department. As ever we are the only white faces in the building. Each person we pass scrutinises us closely, speculating as to what two 'mzungus' are doing there. By now we are used to forever treading where others fear to tread.

"Nor did I," agrees Bob. "I wonder if this Banda person is trying it on?"

"Can I help you?" a polite voice interrupts these speculations.

"We're looking for a Mr S R Banda of the physiotherapy department."

The gentleman looks puzzled. "I don't know any Mr Banda . . ."

"He wrote to us about Frederick Phiri of Kabwe Prison who comes here for physiotherapy."

"Ah, Frederick Phiri," says the gentleman. "He is one of my patients. But there is no Mr Banda in this department. Perhaps I can help? My name is Peter Phiri, no relation to Frederick Phiri," he smiles wryly. "If you would like to follow me."

We troop along the corridor until our rescuer stops outside a door with MR PETER PHIRI, SENIOR PHYSIOTHERAPIST written on it. Presumably he is who he says he is, and equally no relation of Frederick Phiri. He ushers us inside. "How may I help?"

We explain about the letter from Mr S R Banda requesting assistance for Frederick Phiri, principally with regard to the purchase of an electric wheelchair.

Mr Phiri, *Peter*, steeples his fingers. "Firstly let me reiterate, there is no S R Banda here. I think maybe someone was writing on behalf of Frederick Phiri in order to gain something for himself. These things happen in Zambia."

172

We murmur something along the lines that we are quite aware of that, which is why we are verifying the situation for ourselves.

"Secondly, let me add that there is indeed a patient named Frederick Phiri who attends this hospital for physiotherapy. In fact he was here today."

"Today?" we can hardly contain our excitement.

"But he has gone back to Lusaka Prison where he stays when he comes here from Kabwe Prison for treatment."

"And in your opinion does he need a wheelchair?"

Mr Phiri, *Peter*, snorts derisively. "Not in the slightest! The man is in considerable pain; there is no doubt about that. But a wheelchair, no! What Frederick Phiri needs is a pair of adjustable crutches. The most vital thing is for him to remain mobile. If he were to resort to a wheelchair, he would soon lose what little mobility he has."

"And you can provide him with these crutches?"

"Sadly not us. He is only able to have the use of a pair while he is on the hospital premises. However, I can tell you where you may obtain a pair."

"For how much?" we ask guardedly, aware the price of crutches might well escalate to rival that of all-electric wheelchairs.

He tosses a figure into the air somewhere in the region of 5% of the cost of the £1000 wheelchair.

"But before you make up your mind what you will buy, why don't you meet Frederick Phiri for yourselves? Lusaka Prison is not five minutes away. It is just down the road from here."

"We can do that?" we ask. Never having been inside a prison before, we are not familiar with the formalities of prison visiting, Zambian or otherwise.

"For sure," he says. "Just present yourselves at the gate and tell them who you are wanting to visit and they will let you in."

*If only it were that simple!*

We exit UTH and retrieve our car from the car park. It may only be two hundred yards to Lusaka Prison, nevertheless, since I am carrying over K4million (about £500) in my handbag, I have no wish to get mugged en route. We are not currently in one of Lusaka's better districts.

From the outside Lusaka Prison, surrounded by a high brick wall with barbed wire on top, does not look welcoming. Set in the wall is a pair of heavy double iron gates. There is no other way in and equally no other way out. We bang on the gate not expecting any response.

To our surprise a small flap opens, from behind which peers a black face. "Yes?"

173

"We have come to see Frederick Phiri," we say. "We understand he is currently inside here."

"You can't come in here!" declares the voice belonging to the black face.

"But they sent us here from UTH where he goes for treatment," we try.

"Ah no," insists the disembodied voice. "For that you must get permission from Home Affairs."

We know instantly what that means, an application mired down in bureaucracy and with no chance of achieving our objective before we fly back to the UK.

Nevertheless we follow his directions to the Ministry of Home Affairs, located, we are told, along Independence Avenue where all the major offices lie including Government House, the High Court and Police Headquarters.

"I'm sure I've seen Home Affairs by Immigration," I say after we've searched unsuccessfully up one side of Independence and down the other.

We drive round the corner into Haile Selasse Avenue. Sure enough outside the Department of Immigration is a sign saying Home Affairs. However, three times around the parking lot and after finally squeezing into a space the size of a shoebox, we are told, "Sorry, the Ministry of Home Affairs is not in this building."

"So can you please tell us where it is," I plead with the uncooperative receptionist with the habitual soldier with an AK47 standing guard beside him. "We've been up and down Independence where they told us it was, but it's not. Then we came here where the sign says it is, only to be told it's not here either."

"It is in fact by the American Embassy," says the receptionist. We must look blank, because he adds for good measure. "Even it is by the British Embassy."

"Which is where?" we ask, not having a clue, even though our small granddaughter only last Sunday morning at 07.00 inadvertently rang the home phone number of the British High Commissioner on Mummy's cellphone by pressing all the wrong, or should that be the right, buttons.

"It is on Independence," says the guy.

We shake our heads in disbelief. But that is enough for today. If our daughter has the British High Commissioner's phone number in her cellphone memory, she must also know where the British Embassy is. Home Affairs must wait for another day.

Because we are up in Kitwe, it is almost two weeks before we resume our search for Home Affairs. Crawling along Independence at 5mph, we find every single Zambian ministry there is, but no Home Affairs. In the end we park at Foreign Affairs, an ugly greyish-white building rivalling Moscow's concrete wedding cakes from the Stalin era.

Inside the receptionist regards us as if we are crazed. By now we almost are. "Why, it is directly opposite you," she says. "It is the building you are looking at."

We glance across at a faded yellow building, which, if my memory serves me correctly, said Senate and Office of the President. I put this to her.

"That is so."

"What, it is the Senate and Office of the President, or it is the Ministry of Home Affairs?"

"It is all of them."

Once more we drive down Independence, round the roundabout, back up the other side and into the Senate cum Office of the President cum hopefully Ministry of Home Affairs. Every single parking space is taken. Either the president is in his office, or the Senate is sitting, or the Ministry of Home Affairs is busy, probably with all the other people trying to find it because they also want to get into Lusaka Prison. The only part of the car park where there is any space says restricted parking only.

"Can I help you?" Someone taps on the window of the vehicle.

"We can't find anywhere to park," we tell him.

"You can park by me," he says indicating a space which leaves us triple parked in the president's own car parking space, definitely a wheel clamping, if not a deportable offence.

*Or are we by any chance addressing the president?*

"We are looking for the Ministry of Home Affairs," we tell our helpmate.

He directs us to an office on the third floor of the building. I refuse to trust Zambian lifts so we climb three flights of stairs passing men in grey suits who appear to be conducting Zambian affairs of state in the stair well.

"Yes?" says the woman seated behind the desk, barely lifting her eyes our way.

"We have come to request a letter of permission to visit a prisoner in Lusaka Prison," we tell her.

"I cannot give permission for that," she responds.

"This is Home Affairs?" we ask.

"Yes, it is Home Affairs." She seems surprised we should even ask.

"And this is where permission is given for prison visits?"

"Indeed, but what I am saying is, I cannot give you permission to visit a prisoner."

"But why not?"

"For that you must go to Foreign Affairs."

"But we've just been *there* trying to find *here*!"

"And that is where you must go back in order to get permission."

"Whatever for?"

She finally deigns to look straight at us with a look of such withering contempt that reveals she fears we have finally lost the plot. "Because you are foreigners," she says in a tone resembling that of the lady behind the special bread counter in Shoprite, or Mrs Musungaila outraged that we are querying Chep meal allowances for K30 000. "You are foreigners," she repeats in case we do not understand English. "*Foreigners* must apply for permission via *Foreign* Affairs."

"And will they give us permission?" we hardly dare ask.

She shakes her head from side to side. "You can try them and you will see," she says non-committally.

Back to the vehicle, which mercifully has not been clamped or removed, and over the road once more to Foreign Affairs. "Ah, you are back," says the person in reception.

"Yes," we say wearily. "It appears we require Foreign Affairs after all."

"How may I help you?"

" We are trying to get permission to visit a prisoner in Lusaka Prison. It seems because we are foreigners, we must apply to Foreign Affairs and not Home Affairs."

"That may be so," she says which is not encouraging. "You can try in Room C5." She nods in the direction of a corridor piled high with discarded furniture.

We squeeze past dangerously wobbly piles and knock on the door of Room C5. "Yes?" calls a disinterested voice.

We enter and state our case. "No, it is not C5 you are wanting, it is C9."

Off we troop further down the ever narrowing corridor to knock on the door of room C9 where yet again we state our case. By now we know our little spiel off by heart. *Why then is it getting us nowhere?*

"It is not C9 you are wanting. You must apply in person to the Permanent Secretary in the Office of Protocol."

Back along the corridor and up three flights of stairs, climbing ever higher in the echelons of Foreign Affairs. Eventually we locate the aptly named Office of Protocol, apt because clearly we know zilch about the protocol of trying to get inside Lusaka Prison in order to hand over a pair of crutches. Yet again we run through our spiel to the person in reception.

"You may take a seat." She indicates a tatty velvet settee.

Then as suddenly as she told us to sit down, and without announcing our presence to anyone else, she declares, "You may go in." Maybe she just wanted us to further wear out the sofa, so that it could join the furniture downstairs to be replaced at great expense.

To our surprise the occupant of the Office of Protocol is a genial faced young man. He is the image of Adrian, a good friend of ours in the UK, except of course his face is black. Well, everyone has his double somewhere. We have found Adrian's in the Office of High Protocol. The young man is also trying very hard to look busy but failing dismally. Maybe our arrival will create some light relief. He listens avidly to our story punctuating any pauses with, "Okay, right, that's good!"

When we have finished he announces with great satisfaction, "What you must do is apply in writing for permission which the Permanent Secretary will approve . . ."

"That is good . . ."

"Permission is then faxed through to Home Affairs . . ."

"But we've just . . ."

"Which in turn responds to Foreign Affairs. Then Foreign Affairs will give you permission . . ."

"But you said . . ."

"No, Foreign Affairs will give you permission *after* it has received a fax back from Home Affairs, because you are . . . FOREIGNERS!"

Do I detect a note of triumph in his voice? I adopt a suitably obsequious tone and ask, "Please could you spare us a sheet of paper so that we can write out our application now?"

"I don't know . . ."

"You see all this is going to take time."

*Not that it hasn't taken enough time already!*

"Time which we haven't got. Tomorrow we travel up to Kitwe for one last week, then the following Thursday we fly back to the UK."

Our genial friend passes over one sheet of paper on which we write out a request to visit Frederick Phiri in Lusaka Prison. We slide the paper back across the desk towards him.

"Right, okay, that's good," he announces. "But it must be typed and signed."

I look at Bob who looks at me. We could scream. Instead we say, "I don't suppose someone here could type out the letter? We don't actually have access to a typewriter ourselves."

Our letter disappears off down to the corridor to C5, or is it C9. Five, ten, fifteen minutes tick by while we make polite conversation with the Adrian look alike. He continues to punctuate everything we say with, "Right, okay, that's good!" Even, "Right, okay, that's *very* good!" And all the while flicking a biro back and forth between his fingers, or else twiddling with a rubber band.

*Are we perhaps boring him?*

"Please don't let us keep you from your work," says Bob.

"Oh no problem," says our genial friend who then feels some explanation is due as to why he has nothing whatsoever to do anyways. "Mainly the office is very busy in the mornings, but in the afternoons, not so much." Which might perhaps explain why, at 3pm in the afternoon, there is no sign of the Permanent Secretary and one of his minions is in charge with not much to do other than twiddle his biro and talk to us.

Eventually our letter beautifully typed returns to us. We duly sign it and part company with it. "So . . ."

"You may return one week on Monday," says our genial friend, "when you can have the response of the Permanent Secretary."

"You went to the Office of the Permanent Secretary?" exclaims our daughter later. "Blimey, you believe in going high up!"

"We hadn't any choice," we tell her. "It's where we were sent."

"All the same, not many people here get to speak to Permanent Secretaries." Clearly she is impressed.

"Oh, we didn't see the Permanent Secretary," we tell her. "Since it was Friday afternoon, he or she had knocked off. All we saw was a minion."

"No surprises there then!"

Even less surprising when we return ten days later on Monday morning to find . . . "Sorry, we can't find your letter. Perhaps if you come back later . . ."

In anticipation of actually receiving a letter *later,* we set off to locate an organisation called DISACARE, which both makes and sells crutches. This gives the Office of Protocol time to produce the letter, which perhaps is not lost, but simply not yet dealt with. Doubtless our presence back in Lusaka and actively seeking that same letter, goes some way towards providing the motivation for them actually to produce it, rather than while we were 250 miles away in Kitwe.

After a morning spent driving around compounds behind the hospital we eventually have a pair of wooden adjustable crutches costing about £15, certainly a lot less than an all-electric wheelchair.

But what will Frederick Phiri the erstwhile recipient of the crutches think of them? Somewhere in all the shenanigans of obtaining permission to visit him, we seem to have lost sight of the fact that *he* is what all this is about. Also that we've never actually met him, nor anyone of his ilk, given that we are fairly convinced he is in prison for committing murder.

It is 2 o'clock on Tuesday before we *finally* hold in our hands two letters both miraculously saying the same thing . . . we have permission to visit Frederick Phiri inside Lusaka Prison. One letter is from Foreign Affairs and one is from Home Affairs, which proves it is possible to get things done in Zambia if you are persistent enough.

We drive to Lusaka Prison and knock on the gate. The same black face peers out the same hole and demands, "Yes?"

"We have come to visit Frederick Phiri," we tell him.

"I'm sorry but you can't . . ."

"Ah but we have permission."

"From Foreign Affairs . . ."

"And Home Affairs."

"Wait here!" he orders. The disembodied black face disappears.

Outside the full force of the tropical sun is bouncing off the white-washed walls of the prison entrance. It is blisteringly hot. There is no shade in which to seek relief.

Eventually a prison officer in uniform appears and steps outside the gate. He requests our letters of permission. We hand them over reluctantly. They are all the proof we have that we are entitled to enter here. He scrutinises them minutely. "Wait here!" he barks before also disappearing along with our letters.

"I hope that's not the last we see of him," I say.

"Or our letters," adds Bob who is clearly thinking along the same lines as I am. The precious letters we have struggled so hard to get . . . *have just vanished from our grasp.*

We wait and wait. Over the past couple of days I've developed a stinking cold. Standing around sweltering in the hot tropical sun is unbearable. Just as we reach the point where I can stand it no longer, the iron door swings open. "You may come in," says the guard.

Inside another guard stands behind a desk. "Do you have a mobile phone?" he asks.

Reluctantly we hand over our Zambian cell-phone praying that's not the last we see of it. Though why he wants our phone puzzles us.

It would seem more logical to ask whether we are carrying knives or screwdrivers.

"You have another phone?" he asks.

"I hand over my UK phone. "It will be safe?" I feel impelled to ask.

"It will be locked away during the time you are here," he assures me.

"Follow me," says the first guard.

We follow him along a long corridor feeling more like prisoners ourselves with each passing minute. He leads us into a pokey office containing a couple of rickety chairs and a small table covered with a piece of dirty 'chitenge' material. *Home from home then, is it?*

We sit nervously on the edge of the chairs. This is it, the moment we have waited for. What will our murderer be like?

Frederick Phiri, led by two guards, hobbles in supported on one crutch. He is a thin man with a soft face from which the light has gone out. He peers uncertainly into the room, unsure what to expect. Then he catches sight of us. Instantly his face lights up as if he cannot believe what he is seeing.

We are at a loss what to say, not having conversed with any supposed murderers. His response to our opening gambits is slow and hesitant, then, as he gathers confidence, his speech also gathers pace. "How is Rachel Boer?" he wants to know.

We are puzzled by his question, then we recall Rachel was designated to write and let him know Starfish was taking up his case. "She is well and sends her regards."

We learn that he is forty years old and in prison for ten and not twenty years for manslaughter. We're not sure how deeply we should probe, yet Frederick seems willing enough to share his story. "How did the crime come about?" we ask gently.

"It was the drink," he tells us shaking his head sorrowfully. "Both I and my nephew had been drinking before we got into a fight. In the course of the fight I kicked this young man in his kidneys."

"Ah, sorry," we say which is the Zambian way of expressing regret, sorrow, anything really.

"Me also, I am sorry. He died the following morning and I was arrested."

"So what will happen now?"

Frederick shrugs with typical Zambian fatalism. "Maybe with good behaviour in here, I can appeal to the president to release me after six years."

This is not very likely. He could well rot for a long time in prison before anyone does anything about it. "How long have you served?" we ask.

"So far three years, so maybe, maybe . . ." his voice trails away.

"And what will you do when you leave prison? Will you go back to your village?" Not that he would be all that welcome there, we imagine.

"When my treatment finishes here, I must return to Kabwe Prison. There is a priest there, Father Benny Bohan, who will get me a place at the Good Samaritan Centre which trains prisoners after their release from prison."

"And what would you train as?" We imagine the openings for ex-prisoners are somewhat limited in Zambia.

"I would like to train as a tailor," he says with something like pride entering his voice for the first time.

"And your injury?" we ask. "Would you like to tell us how it happened?"

"It happened while I was in prison working as a carpenter. I fell from a ladder injuring my back and leg and breaking my arm." Frederick's voice has become increasingly quiet and difficult to understand. This information is only extracted with several repetitions of both questions and responses. Certainly he is in a lot of pain. Apparently he was left for a long time after the fall before being taken to hospital. He shakes his head at the futility of it all. "I doubt I can ever be as I was before my fall . . ."

"But we have something here for you," we say bringing forth the brand new pair of crutches. "Maybe these will help you to become more mobile."

Frederick's eyes become watery with tears. He clasps and shakes both our hands over and over again as if he will never let them go. "God bless you!" he murmurs over and over again.

We are equally filled with emotion. "Is there anything else you need?" we ask, though seriously questioning our ability *ever* to get inside the prison a second time. Yet maybe we could get stuff to him somehow.

"Toiletries . . . maybe some clothes," he says. He is wearing a vest and what looks like a pair of pyjama bottoms. Can this be all he possesses?

We leave him with the promise we will do what we can which may not be a lot. Though somewhere along the line we have acquired an email address for Father Benny Bohan so all may not be in vain.

We watch Frederick Phiri hobble off along the corridor bizarrely on his one prison crutch and carrying his new crutches under his arm. Maybe he wants to adjust them first before trying them out.

During the time he spent with us, two guards sat discreetly to one side observing what was going on, clearly intrigued that a couple of 'mzungus' took the time to visit a prisoner and bring something for him. Bizarrely they now thank us for what we are doing.

"He is well looked after here?" we ask.

"Oh very well," they assure us. We have no means of verifying what they say.

We return to reception and collect our two mobile phones before being let outside once more into the big wide world.

"Well, in spite of all the effort," I say, "I'm glad we did it."

"I wouldn't have missed it for anything," says Bob. "But was he what you expected?"

I cast aside any preconceptions of murderers, or man-slaughterers as in this case. "No, I have to admit, he wasn't in the least what I expected. He was too . . . gentle."

"Well, maybe a pair of 'mzungu' do-gooders wasn't what Frederick Phiri expected either!" says Bob. "After all, we weren't asked to pass judgement on him, merely to provide . . ."

"An all electric wheelchair costing one thousand pounds!"

"Which wasn't what he got, so you could say . . ."

"Neither of us got what we expected!"

## CHAPTER NINETEEN: THIRD TIME LUCKY, as Faith dreams of Bunsen burners . . . *Thursday May 10th, 2007*

Today for the third time we are attempting the impossible. Third time lucky, who knows, *but we're not superstitious anyway!* Yet again we are trying to combine visits to Chilumba, Kaputula and Kafubu all in one day. That we have tried twice already and failed, could mean somebody is trying to tell us something. However it doesn't deter us.

First stop is to pick up Faith Lyena, director of Faith Orphanage Foundation, which administers the Chilumba project. Her office is located up five steep flights of steps inside the Post Office building in town. However, unwilling to face the climb today, we wait outside in the car and phone to say we are there.

As we wait, we reflect that time has not yet drawn us any closer to reaching a decision whether to commence building at Chilumba. Indeed, in July last year we quite clearly stated that Starfish was *not* in a position to consider building there. Only to be told . . . they have started clearing the ground for the new school.

*Whoops, did somebody get their wires crossed?*

Yet, in spite of breakdowns and to date very little evidence that the Chilumba community might build anything, let alone an entire school, something keeps drawing us back there. As for the orchard fencing . . . it's still not completed!

Today Faith has abandoned her usual style of dress à la Nigerian mode with bustled posterior and puffed sleeves and is clad in a more rural style. Someone once warned us to be wary of Zambian women in fancy clothes and claiming to do good works. Not that there is any reason to be wary of Faith, who is certainly doing good works in and around Kitwe.

Nevertheless we continue to feel uneasy about building at Chilumba. Not only because of the extreme poverty of the community, but also because of Mr Chalwe, who clearly would be closely involved in the project. To date encounters with him have often ended less than satisfactorily, and none more so than in the construction of orchard fencing.

Today however, like a chameleon changing colour to match its surroundings, Faith has sloughed off her fancy clothes in favour of a rural 'chitenge' wrapped around her ample waist. Maybe she's dressed for a day not 'in the field', but in the *fields* . . . hoeing and planting?

"So, we can go?" With Mr Mbai also on board we are off . . .

Not quite! First there are twenty-two pairs of shoes to purchase from Bata shoe shop in the second class trading area, this time for the Chilumba orphans. Since last year, the number of orphans at the centre being sponsored by people in the UK has grown from nine to twenty-two. This trip their sponsorship money is being used to purchase shoes for each orphan.

"You have the names and shoe sizes?" I check with Faith.

"Indeed yes," she passes over the list with a pained expression as if to say, 'These are orphans' shoes we are dealing with, not orchard fences!'

I glance down the list of twenty-two names and shoe sizes ranging from size 11 to size 7. In the shop we ask for Mathilda, the assistant manageress who has dealt with us before in the complicated matter of buying orphans' shoes.

"You remember us?" I ask her.

"Yes, I remember you." Her guarded reply reveals little other than since not many 'mzungus' frequent her establishment, we must be the awkward pair who expect a receipt. She's right!

"We want more shoes," I tell her. "Twenty-two pairs."

"Twenty-two pairs?" she repeats. "Then let me see the list." Mathilda makes to grasp the list, but I hang on tight. Lose that and we're done for.

"I think we can do this more quickly if I have the list," she persists.

Reluctantly I hand over the list. Mathilda disappears behind the curtain and begins fetching out shoes several pairs at a time. With the assistance of the shop manager, we soon have a pile of twenty-two boxed pairs of shoes lying on the shop floor.

"We need to check these carefully." We count out each pair of shoes in turn, checking there is a left and right one of the same size in each box and that the shoe size matches the shoe size on the box. It's a long way back from Chilumba if even one size is wrong.

Eventually Bob and I are satisfied we have the right shoes in the right boxes. "So, we can go?"

Not quite! First, we must stop off at everyone's favourite bakery in Kalulushi. Today I also clamber out of the vehicle and follow Faith and Mr

184

Mbai into the bakery. This trip the food at the lodge where we are staying has steadily deteriorated from bad to diabolical. This morning on checking the contents of our packed lunch, I found chicken pies of dubious origin. What is for sale in an African bakery can't be that much worse, so I buy a Cornish pasty. Since it certainly hasn't originated from Cornwall, time alone will tell whether it tastes like one.

Back in the vehicle once more, we soon turn off onto the Chilumba road, scene of our disastrous breakdown. "The road is okay now?" I ask.

"It is not so bad," responds Faith.

This doesn't encourage us at all. The rainy season is only one month ended. Though the heavy rains have stopped, there is no guarantee the road will have improved. Nor has it. Deep ruts and vast swathes of still drying mud bear the evidence of serious rainy season damage.

As we pass the place of our breakdown, Bob is keen to indicate the exact spot where he spent five long hours and subsequently went down with malaria. Today however, all is well. With a wing and a prayer we reach Chilumba without mishap. But even in the blue skies and sunshine, the former tavern built of burnt red bricks and standing amidst its shabby surroundings still looks as decrepit as ever.

"There is no doubt about it, they really do need a new school," I mutter to Bob.

"But dare we take on such a commitment with a community even more impoverished than Kaputula?" Bob has a point. Due to the effects of the Aids crisis combined with population movement towards the towns, there is a chronic shortage of both men and skilled labour. The community is almost entirely made up of women, grandparents and children. Worse, the road here is virtually impassable for five months of the year. The same thought is in both our minds as we clamber from the vehicle . . . how would we ever make a project here work?

A skinny and frazzled lady comes out to greet us. She looks as if she carries the cares of the world on her shoulders and is dressed like the village women in a wrap-around 'chitenge' with a cloth to bind her hair.

"This is Josephine, our new centre manager," Faith informs us.

We greet Josephine in the traditional manner with a handshake palms, thumbs, palms in one fluid movement. "You are from these parts, Josephine?" I ask.

"No, I am not from here." Josephine's reply does not give much away and certainly not where she does hail from.

"She has come here from the Skills Training Centre," says Faith. "She

185

was trained there in farming, tailoring and education so she will be a great help to the people here."

"So you are an orphan?" I ask.

"I am an orphan and also I am a widow." Certainly Josephine's careworn face reveals life has treated her harshly.

Mentally I speculate as to Josephine's age. But it's hard to tell. Her features could be young going on old, or equally old going on young. "Are you staying here?" I ask.

"Yes, I am staying here."

The implication of the question clearly puzzles her. Maybe she misunderstood what I meant by 'staying' and thought that I implied she might only stay awhile then do a sudden flit. "I mean are you living here?"

"Yes, I am living here."

"With the children who stay here?"

"Yes." Goodness, making conversation with Josephine is harder than getting blood out of a dried up vein and her face hasn't even cracked into a smile as yet. Maybe Josephine is unused to conversation with 'mzungus'.

However as we make a tour of inspection, Josephine begins to thaw. Soon she is pointing out how she has encouraged the women to plant an area with beans, which can be used to feed the orphans who stay on site. She also has plans to raise chickens, not on the scale of Salem, but enough to feed those who stay on site. Could Josephine prove an asset to this impoverished community after all?

She agrees to show us her sleeping quarters. Unfortunately there is little by way of accommodation in the two room former tavern apart from two storerooms to the rear of the building. Because Josephine now sleeps in one storeroom, the back part of one classroom has had to be sectioned off with a ragged curtain to provide sleeping accommodation for the girls who used to sleep in the store.

By now we are surrounded with orphans. Word of our arrival has spread to the older ones who attend government school nearby and who soon start appearing in dribs and drabs. One of the first is Dynass, the child whose request for me to be her mother has led to the setting up of the sponsorship scheme here.

"Shouldn't Dynass be in school?" I ask Faith.

"She should, but since her 'mother' is here, she will not stay away."

Time to give out the shoes before emotion overwhelms. Seventeen of the twenty-two sponsored orphans are now on site so we begin distributing shoes. As Faith calls out each orphan's name, the child comes forward to receive a pair of shoes.

All goes well until the last of those orphans present receives their shoes. Suddenly a heart-rending wailing and howling breaks out over by the school. It sounds more like a wounded animal in pain than any noise a human would make. "What is that?"

"That is Kennedy," says Faith. Over on the veranda stands a boy in ragged shorts and a torn and faded red top, howling and wailing like a banshee. His face is buried in his arms. "He is crying because he did not receive any shoes," continues Faith.

I glance quickly down the list of names. "But there's no Kennedy on the list." If ever a child looked vulnerable and in need of support, it is Kennedy. "So why isn't he on the list?"

"Because he does not belong here."

"You mean he doesn't live here?"

"Yes, he lives here, but he doesn't belong here. He is deaf and dumb. We have no facilities to cope with him here."

"And he's crying because he doesn't have a pair of shoes?" On the ground in front of me are five pairs of unclaimed shoes. "Why can't Kennedy have one of these pairs," I say to Faith.

"Maybe he can have a pair," she concedes. She calls out, "Iwe!" and beckons Kennedy over. However, since he is deaf he can't hear her and since his face remains buried in his dirty arms, he can't see her either. Eventually one of the wrinkly grandmothers takes hold of his arm and gently steers him over.

We select a pair of shoes, which appear his size and hand them over. Suddenly Kennedy's face lights up with joy, as brilliant as the sun emerging from behind a cloud. "Huh huh!" he manages which may be thank-you, but then may not.

"What will I do about the boy who now has no shoes?" asks Faith.

"For goodness sake," I tell her, "we'll give you the money for another pair when we get back. You can bring them out next time you come"

"What's more to the point," Bob wants to know, "what will happen to Kennedy?"

"Ah, that I don't know," says Faith. "Maybe he needs to go to a school for deaf and dumb children . . ." Her voice trails away as if that is an impossible dream, which is beyond her ability to turn into reality.

Unfortunately there is no time to pursue that today because, after photographs are taken, it's time to drive on to Kaputula. To reach Kaputula entails returning along the worst part of the Chilumba road as far as the police post and there picking up the Kaputula road.

As we go, we munch our various pies and pasties. We long since learnt, it is not possible to eat packed lunches in front of people who only have one meal a day, or who may not have eaten at all. Sometimes we stop along the road from Chilumba where a fast flowing stream flows under the road, though in the rainy season it more often flows over it. Today, since time is pressing, we eat in the car as we go.

Needless to say, the Cornish pasty from Kalulushi bakery does not live up to expectations. After the first few bites its taste begins to pall, though it still looks better than the chicken pie that Bob sticks with, at the same time praying the consequences won't prove too disastrous.

Ah Kaputula, how many visits have we paid here? In truth only a fraction of the total number were ever recounted in 'Bwanakula Thandi.' By May 2007 and the time of this visit, the new school has been open and operational for almost one year. Certainly our connection with the school has not come to an end. We visit there at least once every trip to Zambia, partly to continue Starfish support for orphan carers there, but also to see how the school is faring . . .

And the answer is not well! *Well, what did you expect? Everything in the Kaputula garden would come up roses?*

The community is *still* at loggerheads. There are maintenance issues with the building. The head teacher, Mrs Tembo, is *still* absenting herself. There is a chronic shortage of staff and pupil numbers have dropped alarmingly because of all the problems. *Oh joy!*

Still, we have informed them we are coming with a visitor today and so community members are out in force. Mr Chipotyo is there still sporting his outsize glasses, Messrs Chanda and Nyrongo in their Wellington boots, old grey haired Mr Chapuswike the interpreter, Mr and Mrs Kauseni who have taken time off from the Kafubu Baptist Church project, all have come to greet us like the loyal friends they are. Bizarrely members of the newly formed PTA are also there, though of Mrs Tembo there is no sign. Even more strange, and in spite of reports to the contrary, they appear to be united as one.

"Ah that woman, she is never here," begins one community member.

"Always absenting herself, saying she is sick," takes up another.

"When she is not sick, she is attending one refresher course after another at Chep!"

All of which may well be true, because only this morning when we were leaving Chep, who should we encounter but Head Teacher Mrs Tembo dressed in fine new clothes and looking not the slightest bit sick. *Did someone mention incentive allowances for attending courses?*

However this morning at Kaputula, standing out under the hot tropical sun, her absence seems to have achieved the impossible, she has united the Kaputula community as one . . . against herself! *Who would have thought that was possible?*

"Ah, but this is a beautiful school!" exclaims Faith in raptures and totally oblivious to the barbed comments flying around her like arrows seeking a home.

"Indeed," we agree while declining to reveal its underlying issues of which she remains blissfully unaware.

"And I am thinking you will build one just like it for us at Chilumba!"

"Er . . . will we?" Faith, unaware both of our thoughts and of the undercurrents as ever at play at Kaputula, is content to dream of a world in which schools appear as if by magic like rabbits out of a magician's hat.

"We are wanting to show you what has been achieved with the pit toilets," announces Mr Chipotyo by way of a diversion.

"You have made progress?"

"Yes," he responds with a pained expression implying how could we ever doubt the work would be done? Or maybe he recalls that Starfish pulled the plug on them in the final run up to completion at Kaputula when the pit toilet budget was appropriated for finishes.

We stroll over to the area to the left and rear of the school designated for the pit toilets. Three pit toilets are being constructed each with a double drop eighteen feet deep.

"As you can see, we have one team working on each toilet in order to complete."

But who said this? "Ah, Mr Nkhoma!" Mr Nkhoma was one of the newly elected PTA. Last thing we heard, he was still at loggerheads with members of the building committee and the former PTA.

"We are wanting you to appreciate that now we are working as one people," continues Mr Nkhoma. "This community is no longer divided and so now we are wondering when you will start building houses for the teachers here?"

"Er, we're not quite in a position . . ." Bob and I look desperately at each other. Take on another Kaputula building project? Surely we'd never be so crazy as to even consider it? But what is the alternative, a struggle of equally gigantic proportions at Chilumba?

"Maybe this needs looking into," which is as good an answer as we can come up with.

"Aaah, it is truly amazing what has been achieved here," Faith drools on, still totally oblivious of the eddying undercurrents threatening to suck all of us under and maybe even drown us. "Me, I am hoping you will do the same for us at Chilumba, and soon, even with proper pit toilets also."

I think of the stinking hole which currently passes for a pit toilet at Chilumba. Maybe that for one isn't such a bad idea. However, lest we are tempted, I suggest weakly before the dangerous undertow currently eddying around us takes it toll, "Maybe it's time pass on to Kafubu?"

The Kafubu Baptist Church project started less than a year ago, yet has already far outstripped Kaputula in terms of achievement. During our long absence since last year, they have already completed the immense foundation slab for the new church.

Earlier this visit they received the first injection of materials for several months. Yet in less than a week they are putting these funds to good use. An area has been cleared to one side of the church and a temporary shelter erected. Underneath it they have begun making blocks for the church walls. A few hundred blocks already stand maturing for use. Now we make our way five kilometres back along the road with Faith to show her what has been achieved by this community which has proved so very different to the Kaputula one.

"But this also is truly amazing!" As Faith clambers out of the car, her eyes grow round with the wonder of it. Certainly the size of the church is daunting. "Oh, I can see you people will build us a *very* fine school!" she says with tremendous feeling.

Did we hear correctly? "Well, we haven't actually said . . ."

"And the school which you build for us must be very big, even up to grade seven or even grade nine. Then also we must have a library and science labs with Bunsen burners."

I think she just said it again. "Er, I don't think . . ."

"Just wait till I tell the people back there what you are going to achieve for them!" Are those tears of emotion moistening Faith's eyes?

*Faith, read our lips, we have not as yet expressed any intention of commencing a building project at Chilumba!* Does one of us actually utter this aloud? Or in the emotion does it remain unsaid? Which in Zambia is a dangerous thing to do. Things left unsaid can lead to all sorts of things . . . schools, churches, sponsorship programmes . . .

I glance at Faith. As far as it is possible for the unreadable dark chocolate pools of her eyes so to do, hers have grown green with envy. Could it be the light reflected from a hundred Bunsen burners sparkling in the science labs of her dreams?

"Maybe we will see . . . one day," I manage to say. Which in the Zambian scheme of things undoubtedly is an *exceedingly* dangerous way to leave things, because as yet we haven't any inkling at all how we might go about it.

# CHAPTER TWENTY: AND GOD SENT MILDEN . . .
## *Thursday November 1ˢᵗ, 2007*

We first met Milden's wife at a coffee morning in Alcester held in aid of Starfish. Catherine was a Zambian nurse living in the UK and working in a care home. Not long after, phone calls started coming from Catherine's husband, Milden. Presumably Catherine had told him about Starfish.

It soon became apparent Milden was not easily put off. He would ring up at all hours, generally as we were about to eat or sit down to watch television or go to bed. Did Milden perhaps work shifts, given the odd timing of some of his calls?

The phone calls continued for a year, maybe longer. On and on would ramble this Zambian at the other end of the phone. "I have started a clinic project . . ." He would begin.

"Sorry, we don't do clinics," we would respond discouragingly.

"It is in the Choma area . . ."

"Sorry, we don't do Choma either. All our work is based on the Copperbelt." *Four hundred miles away we might well have added!*

"But you see I have built it with my own money . . ."

"Then you can't really need our help!"

"But right now the money has run out."

*So, no surprises there!*

"So I am asking if the Starfish Fund would be willing to undertake the completion of this project."

"Sorry, but Starfish is really only a very small organisation . . ."

"It would mean so much to me and to the people of Simooya."

"I'm afraid we're already quite heavily committed to completing a school project at Kaputula, also a Baptist Church at Kafubu . . ."

"If you would at least visit my project next time you are in Zambia?"

"Choma is a bit out of our way. We really can't promise anything . . ."

"At least let me send through a proposal so that you can read about my project?" Clearly Milden had little intention of his project becoming another starfish stranded on the beach.

Thus a well drawn up document entitled: A DREAM FOR SIMOOYA landed through our letterbox. It brought tears to our eyes. Our interest was roused, as was the interest of the Starfish committee. We agreed to visit Simooya and assess what needed doing.

"Nothing more!" we emphasised, hoping at least this promise might stop all the phone calls. "In visiting your project, we are making no commitment whatsoever."

"For sure, there is no commitment," Milden agreed before adding, "I will book myself on the same flight to Zambia."

*So no pressure then!* Milden booked to fly out and be in Choma at the same time as us. "You realise we can only make one quick overnight visit?" We made one last valiant effort to forestall the inevitable.

"That is no problem. Myself, I need to be there at that time."

So one hot and thundery Thursday afternoon in November finds us sitting under the shade of a mopani tree, next to a half completed clinic project in the middle of nowhere and silently asking God yet again just what He has in mind this time?

We picked up Milden this morning at 9am outside the Holiday Inn in Lusaka. Though we've never met before, Milden isn't difficult to spot standing with his brother-in-law outside the British Airways office. Each carries a rucksack on his back. They look like Zambian backpackers. Except you never see Zambian backpackers, so it has to be Milden and brother.

After shaking hands and introducing ourselves we ask, "Are you both travelling with us?" We have been warned to be careful who we let into our vehicle. People tell such stories . . .

"Myself I will travel with you so that we may enjoy the opportunity to talk. He will travel with my brother-in-law who is also coming."

Brother, brother-in-law, Milden, us? Already we are quite a party. We say nothing as Milden settles himself in the rear of the vehicle. It is 280km to Choma, time for *plenty* of talking.

Choma lies to the south-west of Lusaka on the road to Livingstone and the Victoria Falls. We have barely left Lusaka before Milden launches forth on himself, his life history, how he came to build the clinic. Barely pausing for breath, he fills in every last detail of background information.

Then he turns his attention to the road we are travelling. Back in the 1970s it was single strip tarred road pretty much all the way from Lusaka to

Livingstone. Each time a vehicle came from the opposite direction, drivers drove two wheels on, two wheels off the tarmac.

The area used to be one of the most highly developed agricultural areas of Zambia. However droughts in the past few years have currently brought agriculture pretty much to a standstill. Maize is no longer a viable crop for this area. Towns that were once bustling hives of activity now sleep away the days under a hot and merciless sun. Grain stores stand empty.

Milden expands on the controversy surrounding the wide scale sale of tribal lands to an Australian company in order to mine nickel. Then there is the leasing of vast tracts of tribal land to white ex-Zimbabwean farmers to grow tobacco and farm cattle, both of which are more resistant to the lack of rain. Would this information overload ever end? Maybe if we over-dosed him on sugar then, like our dear friend Mr Chama, he might fall asleep?

However Milden considers it more important to stock us up. We stop at Mazabuka to pick up rations for which he insists on paying. "No, no, you must not pay for anything," he insists, heaping the supermarket basket full of apples, drinks, biscuits, crisps and sandwiches and only stopping long enough to make yet another call on his cell-phone.

"Can he afford all this stuff?" I mutter to Bob.

"Search me," he responds, "but he seems to want to do it."

"You are making a lot of phone calls," I hazard.

Milden regards me enigmatically. "That is because there are still other people who wish to be present at our meeting this afternoon."

We stop at a lay-by to pick up a Mr Sandford Mweeni, the local village project co-ordinator, then again at a district health office in Batoka to pick up a vehicle, a driver and two health officials. Now we are nine. Just how many more are set to join us today . . .

"It is important that these people from the health office accompany us," says Milden.

"Why is that?" we ask guardedly. We have always had as little as possible to do with government departments in Zambia. Word has it that money which passes through their hands often mysteriously disappears down a black hole, never to surface again. Though we have no proof, we prefer to remain cautious.

"When the clinic is completed, they have agreed to staff it with a nurse or nursing couple . . ."

"That's good . . ."

"Of course the nurse will need a house, which I have plans for . . ."

"Milden, we agreed to visit an uncompleted clinic, nothing more," we remind him. "What is far more important, are essential items for the clinic."

"For that there is no problem. The Health Department will also provide basic furniture, as well as supply the drugs the nurse will be needing."

The white Health Department Landrover is ahead of us as we near Choma. Milden has assured us they know the way to the clinic. But this makes us more uneasy. *How difficult can this clinic be to find?*

At the 20km peg the Landrover turns off onto a dirt road. We follow at a discreet distance, not wanting to travel continually in the dust of its passing.

"The road to the clinic is okay?" asks Bob.

"It is a good road," Milden assures him.

*Now where have we heard that before?*

"Also I am knowing the way."

"I thought the people in front knew the way?"

"I also know the way because it is my village. I was brought up there."

Who are we to doubt Milden's word? Besides, we overheard him discussing the route with the health officials. Take the dirt road as far as the white ex-Zimbabwean farmer's farm, cross the dam wall and you're there. Simple . . .

"Ah, they are not going the right way!" Milden leans forward agitatedly from the back seat.

We have reached a fork in the road. The white Landrover continues to bat along at high speed along the dirt road to the left, while Milden points to the right fork. "It is this way, I think."

"You don't know?"

"Yes, it is this way . . . " His voice trails away uncertainly.

We turn off to the right. In a matter of minutes we face a baffling array of tracks criss-crossing newly ploughed fields planted with tobacco. All seem to lead anywhere but to a clinic project.

"It is this way, I think," Milden offers yet again. "Or maybe this way."

"Milden, surely these are just farm tracks?" I suggest.

"So we can use them," he responds. "But look, we can ask this person."

This person is a woman who, when asked, merely waves us onwards. Either she doesn't know, or she doesn't want to be bothered by a couple of 'mzungus' in a 4x4, even if they are accompanied by a Zambian who, by his manner and dress and way of speaking, clearly knows better days than she can ever imagine on what she scrapes by.

In the middle of a field in which the ex-Zimbabwean farmer is attempting to grow tobacco on land granted to him by the local chief, we encounter another woman. She is wearing a bright red dress and carrying most of a tree across the back of her shoulders. A lengthy conversation ensues in Tonga between Milden and the woman.

"We can go!" Milden waves us on.

"But which way did she say?"

"She doesn't know. She is not from these parts."

*So what is she doing in the middle of a field in a red dress and carrying half a tree on her shoulders?* Sometimes in Africa, it's best not to ask too many questions.

A man riding on a motor scooter appears from nowhere heading our way. "Maybe we can ask him," says Milden.

Another lengthy conversation ensues before Milden announces, "He also is not from these parts."

For the middle of nowhere and in the midst of newly ploughed tobacco fields, there is an amazing abundance of people not from these parts who don't know where the place we are looking for actually is.

We take a right, a left and a right again, then suddenly we are back on track, driving past the ex-Zimbabwean farmer's farmhouse where the gatekeeper assures us a white Landrover bearing a driver and two other men has not long passed through. He indicates the tyre tracks, the only ones to pass this way all day. Clearly *they* knew the way after all.

Just past the farm we meet the farmer himself zipping along on his little motorbike. He is brown-faced and wizened from long days spent in the burning sun trying to scratch a living from this merciless land. His accent dispels any remaining doubts as to his origins.

Milden asks if he also will be joining this afternoon's meeting. After all everyone else is.

"Ach no, man," responds the farmer in that achingly familiar accent which rouses so many vivid memories. "I'm too busy today." He zooms off to plant yet more tobacco.

"That man, Clive Wixley, is very interested in the project," Milden informs us.

"Why would that be?"

"Because workers on the farm will also benefit from a clinic in this area."

"How come?"

"At the moment if a worker falls sick then, like the people from the village, he must walk twenty kilometres to the nearest clinic and back again. He loses one, maybe two days away from his work."

"And if he can't walk to the clinic?"

Milden shrugs. "Then Mr Wixley or one of his drivers must take him to the clinic. Then two people are away from their work."

"Hmmm!" We allow this new information to sink in.

We turned left at the farm and are now heading across yet more fields. The tracks have become even narrower. In the distance farm workers are taking an early afternoon break, maybe the first food they have eaten all day. They stop and stare in bemusement at the second vehicle to pass them in one day. Now we are bumping up hillocks and grinding down hollows, over bumps and potholes till we come to a dam wall built of earth. One dirt road leads up over the dam, another track down into the valley where the stream was dammed.

"We go this way."

My heart sinks as Milden points to the track over the dam wall. It is barely the width of the vehicle's wheels. On one side is the dam of unknown depth, while on the other side the bank rolls steeply downwards into the valley far below. One wheel wrong and we are done for.

"I'm not sure we could ever find the way out here by ourselves," I tell Milden uncertainly.

"That is not a problem as long as someone is with you," he responds.

"Or get a truck laden with building supplies out here," I add even less convinced.

"That also is not a problem," responds Milden, the eternal optimist.

Now we are following mere sandy tracks, though there are still signs of the Health Department vehicle's passing. "Are we nearly there?" I ask.

"We are nearly there."

And then we are there. A half built clinic literally in the middle of nowhere stands before us. It is a red brick building constructed of fired anthill clay bricks as yet un-plastered. There is no roof on it, no doors and no windows. Initial views from the side are not impressive.

"Welcome to Simooya!" announces Milden as we ease aching limbs from the vehicle and follow him round to the front of the building. Here the building looks more impressive. Along the front is a wide veranda running almost the whole length of the building.

"This will be used as a waiting area for patients who sometimes wait all day to be seen," says Milden before leading the way inside, easy enough since there is no door to the building. We step into a reception area. Behind is a doctor's room for the doctor who will come maybe once or twice a month.

"What happens to people who are really sick?" we ask. "They surely can't wait a month until the doctor comes?"

"The nurse will arrange for them to be taken to the hospital in Choma," says Milden.

"In fact that is where we come in," interposes one of the health workers. "If the nurse contacts us that there is a patient in need of admission to hospital, then we send a vehicle out for them."

"As long as the cell phone is working . . ."

"Or the radio . . . "

"Or the roads are okay for the vehicle to pass," adds each health worker in turn.

"But then sometimes, maybe in a thunderstorm, none of them will be working."

It all sounds very hit and miss. But this is not only Zambia, but also a particularly impoverished and difficult rural area to reach. Any medical help is surely better than no medical help.

Just off the doctor's room is a storeroom. "This will be for storing the drugs," says the first health worker.

"It will be necessary to put a lock on it," adds the second. They are beginning to sound like a slick double act.

At either end of the clinic and running the full width of the clinic are two larger rooms. "These will each become six bed wards," announces Milden proudly. Clearly he saved the best till last.

We allow a suitably impressed "Aaah!" to escape.

"One will be for males and one for females. The latter will mainly be used as a labour ward."

This is progress, a place for Zambian women to stay when they give birth instead of immediately returning to work in the fields or around the village.

"I think now we may start our meeting." Milden indicates the ubiquitous line of 'best' chairs waiting in the paltry shade of a lone mopani tree located to one side of the clinic.

Some forty or fifty villagers have gathered to hear what is said. They are Tonga people, a tribe we have never worked with before. We are not sure what to expect. "For sure they are glad to see you," someone says.

"Why is that?" we ask, not yet having agreed to anything.

"Because you are the first white people ever to come to their village." Which is a daunting prospect. Responsibility weighs heavily. We don't want to let them down.

It is hot and thundery in the mid-afternoon sun. Already clouds are massing ominously with the promise of early rains, though hopefully not this afternoon. We don't fancy weaving our way back through that maze of tracks or crossing the perilous dam wall in a tropical thunderstorm.

Milden makes the first speech welcoming us to Simooya. He is followed by a health official, whose speech follows the lines of the fine clinic we are to complete for the people here.

Then we are invited to speak which creates the challenge of pronouncing fine words which don't actually promise anything, yet which don't fill the villagers with despair. Finally the chairman of the village project makes his speech. By this time we accept there is not that much difference between the Tonga in south-west Zambia and the Bemba and Lamba up on the Copperbelt . . . they both like speeches.

Afterwards we head back towards the clinic. It is time to ask more searching questions. Who will be in charge of the project? What contribution will the villagers make? What locally sourced materials are available? How will they be brought to the site? How will materials purchased in Choma reach the site? What skilled labour is available?

Our impression is that the villagers know what they are doing. More importantly, they appear committed to the task. There is little doubt the completion of the clinic will make a huge difference. The thing is . . . *are we the right people for the task?*

What is amazing is that the clinic has stood here un-completed for almost nine years. No-one has picked up the project or done anything about it. Apparently Milden began the project over nine years ago in memory of his parents who had recently died. At that time he was living and working in Choma and earning reasonable money and bought a bit here and a bit there to get the project underway. However when his wife Catherine announced she was applying for a job as a nurse in the UK, Milden came with her, only to find his skills were not so much in demand in the UK as in Zambia. Money ran out and the project ground to halt.

Back to the chairs once more and time for yet more speeches. By now it is late afternoon. The air has grown oppressive. The weight of responsibility hangs ever heavier. How can we walk away? But equally, where would we get the money from to fund the project?

Maybe the community senses our weakening resolve. Their speeches now express their greatest wish that we will undertake the completion of the clinic. The heat is making us light-headed. I have a raging thirst and not enough water to quench it. Drinking the water here is unthinkable. Thoughts run riot in my head . . :

*Why us Lord? Haven't we taken on enough? We are old, we are tired, we are weary, please let someone else do this instead of us . . .*

In the confusion, do we actually say yes or simply omit to say no?

"We must discuss our findings with our committee back in the UK," we tell them. This is always our fail-safe option until such time as a decision is reached, or Starfish has enough money to take on another project.

Actually at this time we have our own project waiting for us back in Suffolk, a house in need of modernisation. Not to mention sitting on our veranda in the sun, buying fish and chips or Suffolk cream teas after a stroll along the beach or a swim in the sea. *Why land ourselves with a near impossible project in the middle of nowhere?*

Yet we both know in our hearts, we will not walk away and leave them. So we concede, "Maybe if we received a proposed Bill of Quantities for the completion of the clinic?"

"And also one for the nurse's house," suggests Milden hopefully.

"I would like to make these generous people a gift!" A man from the village clad in cropped denim trousers and with a mobile phone dangling from the waistband leaps to his feet. "I want to give them a sheep."

Oh no, I groan inwardly and turn to Milden, "Isn't he a bit premature? We haven't done anything yet."

"No, but he senses that you will."

"But we can't take a live sheep back to the lodge we're staying in tonight." Imagine it grazing all night in some grassy corner then pooing all the way to Lusaka tomorrow, only to be let loose beside our daughter's house where it will at some point be slaughtered and we'll all feast happily ever after . . . *on mutton!*

Fortunately Milden has his head screwed on. Or has lived long enough in England to know there are some things the English don't take to so readily. Transporting a live sheep two hundred miles in their car being one of them. "Leave it with me," he advises, "but for the moment you must thank him."

I thank the gentleman in the cropped trousers most profusely for his kind offer, assuring him we are absolutely bowled over, because it's not every day in England that you are offered a live sheep. Privately I suggest to Milden, "Next time we come, perhaps . . ."

Next time, already we are talking about next time. Oh well, our vegetarian daughter will no doubt be delighted at the future prospect of whole sheep dead or otherwise cluttering up her freezer or chewing her lawn.

We say our goodbyes and drive off into the sunset retracing our route to reach the Choma road. Fortunately the white Landrover is once more in front, so we cannot lose our way back to the main road.

That evening within the sanctuary of our accommodation, a strange thought occurs. We have always recognised a day will dawn when we personally, through age or illness or whatever, will no longer be able to continue the work of Starfish. We have prayed that, when that day finally comes, there will be someone to take over the work of Starfish for us.

In our imagination we envisaged a fit and active thirty or forty year old with a heart in the right place, or at least with an experience of Africa in general, or of Zambia in particular to qualify them for the job. Not forgetting that, both the heart and the experience, would need to be great enough to cope with all the flack and frustrations that go with the rescuing of stranded starfish here.

So far our prayers have not been answered. But then God answers prayers in strange ways. Maybe God has sent not the white ex-VSO we anticipated, but an able-bodied Zambian by the name of Milden, who doesn't like UK all that much, but possesses a heart as big as ours for Zambia. Combine that with a willingness to come back and forth here as many times a year as we might be inclined to send him.

And God sent Milden . . . now there's a thought! The only problem is . . . the clinic project still lies four hundred miles away from the rest of Starfish work, while Milden and his generous heart, like us, lives six thousand miles away in the UK. A problem of logistics then? You bet! And quite how we might set about resolving it, is not at this point at all clear. Suggestions on a postcard, please . . .

# CHAPTER TWENTY-ONE: MR CHIPOTYO
# DISAPPEARS IN SUSPICIOUS CIRCUMSTANCES . . .
## November 13th -> 21st, 2007

Returning to Zambia after several months' absence always proves difficult. What will we find at projects we left behind? Will our partners have squandered materials, or made a mess of the building work? Will they even have abandoned projects entirely? Yet no return visits are more fraught with anxiety than those to Kaputula, especially when news of there is not good. However there is still an Orphan Carers' Support Programme to run there, so any thoughts of not going back are not an option.

"Then we must arrive when they are not expecting us," suggests Mr Mbai. "That way you will see things as they really are."

So this trip, totally unannounced, we make our way to Kaputula. It is approaching midday when we arrive there. At least today Mrs Tembo is on site, though her disconcerted expression, combined with the absence of both the workforce and the PTA, suggests they were indeed not expecting us.

"We thought we would pay you a surprise visit." Since she clearly is surprised, maybe there is no need to say this. "Also we wanted to assess the school's current position."

"Our most urgent need is teachers' housing," deputy head teacher Mr Nkoma informs us when we are all seated inside Mrs Tembo's office. "This would greatly improve security on site and also encourage teachers to live here. All four teachers are currently renting accommodation at Chati or Kafubu Depot, which is causing a problem with punctuality."

"What, theirs or the children's?" we are quick to ask.

To our surprise he answers, "Theirs, since they are not here when school commences because either they must walk or cycle to get here. Even when it is raining, sometimes they cannot come."

"Punctuality is an issue which must be addressed." Donning his school inspector's hat, Bob glares at Mrs Tembo, before demanding, "How many children are currently on roll? Isn't it true that many pupils are not attending the school?"

"Some children have gone elsewhere, to Chati or the Depot."

"Because of the punctuality issue, or other reasons?"

"Maybe because of all the arguments," Mrs Tembo shrugs non-committally. "Also some people have been spreading a rumour that I am leaving."

"And are you leaving?" But Mrs Tembo's expression remains as featureless as a blank sheet of black sugar paper.

"I am not leaving," she says stubbornly.

Silently I reflect that if she were, this might well solve many of Kaputula's problems. Instead I say, "I think now it's time to look around."

We begin with the first classroom blocks constructed under the phase one building programme. These blocks are barely three years old, yet already the classrooms show signs of wear and tear. Plaster is missing in chunks from windowsills, while floors are pitted and pockmarked like a badly erupting case of the pox. What is more disturbing is that only three of the five classrooms show evidence of having been in use today.

We head over to the last block built during phase two, where sadly things are no better. In two classrooms the blackboards are as unblemished as the day they were first installed, thus indicating these particular rooms have never even been used.

"And the pit toilets?" I pray these might prove today's one redeeming grace. "Are they operational yet?"

Mrs Tembo leads the way down the track behind the school. "The pit toilets are completed, but they are locked and we do not have the keys to open them," explains Mrs Tembo. Then adds the astounding news that to date the building committee has *refused* to hand over the keys.

*Are we dense or simply missing something?*

I spin round to confront Mr Nkoma. "And you expect us to build teachers' houses? First you and the rest of the community must get *this* house in order!"

"And we'll be back!" we call out one final warning, before driving off, hearts weighing heavy with disappointment.

We return on Friday of the same week, before they have time to gather their wits. Again we plan to arrive before the expected time, except we bargain without our two notorious timekeepers. When neither has appeared by the appointed hour, I phone Mr Chama.

"Mrs Cooke, you are already there?" comes his perplexed response.

"But where are you, Mr Chama?"

"I am coming. And Mbai also is not there?"

"No, he is not here," I say as patiently as I can.

"Then he also is coming," says Mr Chama and rings off.

When eventually they are both safely in the car, I point out to Mr Mbai, who has recently been offered a place at Lancaster University to study project management, "You really will have to improve your time-keeping before you come to the UK."

"Why is that, Mrs Cooke?" As ever, he is bemused by all things British.

"Because lectures, meetings, all will start without you. Even buses and trains leave if you're not there on time."

"Ah me, how will I manage? This living in the UK is going to prove very hard. There are so many things I must learn."

While Bob concentrates on the road to Kaputula, the rest of us sink deep into our own thoughts. The main purpose of this trip was to assess what might become Starfish's next building project. Over the past few days, Bob and I have discussed a possible recommendation to the UK committee. So far we have visited Milden's project at Simooya. Attractive as it is, it remains four hundred miles away from our other projects, thus posing considerable logistical problems. Chilumba, as ever, still presents as a non-starter because of the chronic labour and transport problems inherent in commencing any project there. Kaputula, with its urgent need for teachers' housing, therefore should be in pole position. Yet after our visit the other day, it's been relegated to last position. Unless by some miracle maintenance work is done, pupil numbers pick up once more and the DEB'S office provides more staff.

*So, no small decision then deciding between these three!*

At Kaputula Mrs Tembo emerges from her office to greet us. She looks more herself today. Maybe she had a bad hair day the other day, because today her hair is once more wired up into tiny plaits sticking out like unruly sprigs all over her head. She is accompanied by Mr Nkhoma, deputy chairman of the PTA. Not to be confused with Mr Nkoma, deputy head teacher, who is *not* there today. Nor are any members of the community or of the building committee even though they were asked to come for 10.00.

"Ha, but then we came early to see how things are," we tell her.

We follow her around to the rear of the school where about forty children are busy hoeing, digging and planting a plot of ground stretching the whole length of the three classroom block. By now the first community members and members of the building committee have begun to trickle in. They all shake hands and greet us, yet no-one greets Mrs Tembo.

"Mulishane!" Hands are shaken, palm, thumb, palm, all in one fluid movement.

"Bwino mulishane!" comes the response.

One person however is missing. Our larger than life friend, Mr Chipotyo, is not here.

"He is in Kabwe, on a course," they tell us.

The little old interpreter, Mr Chapuswike is also absent, apparently in hospital. Then Mrs Kauseni is away at Kafubu. The list of absentees grows steadily longer. So who *is* here? Even two of the teachers, and one of them the deputy head, Mr Nkoma, are not here, which is strange, since he was the one pushing so hard for teachers' houses, even requesting one for himself. Yet he has missed an important meeting to discuss the matter.

Our depleted number gathers in one classroom, ourselves, Messrs Mbai and Chama, Mrs Tembo, the two remaining teachers and a handful of community members. Mrs Tembo means business and immediately chalks up an agenda on the blackboard.

"Ahem!" A scruffily clad man at the back of the room teeters unsteadily to his feet, belches, then loudly clears his throat. "I am wanting know what is this . . . A O B?" He sinks down with a heavy thump, drunk and incapable of standing.

"Sssshh!" hisses someone loudly.

But the man will not be hushed and bawls, "Is no-one going to tell me what this AOB means?" This time he has breached etiquette by not rising to his feet.

"Order!" calls someone. "He must not be allowed to disrupt in this way. This is a serious meeting!"

*Is any meeting at Kaputula ever anything else? Oh for a light-hearted one for a change!*

Finally Mrs Chanda, overwhelmed with embarrassment, rises to her feet and unceremoniously removes the man from the meeting. Mr Chanda remains where he is, stony-faced and staring steadfastly forward.

"That man is their son," whispers Mr Mbai. "Maybe Mr Chanda prefers to disown him."

At least now the meeting can commence. Mrs Tembo has grandly entitled the main item on the agenda 'school development.' We take that to mean: *what next is Starfish going to build for them?*

Mr Sichamba, Area Chairman, rises to his feet. "What we are now needing are teachers' houses and also a borehole."

*Actually, Mr Sichamba, it's not quite that simple.* So we say, "First things first! There is the matter of maintenance of the school building, and also the issues of staffing and falling school numbers which matters must be addressed. We cannot commit to building anything further here when the school roll is falling."

"Unfortunately, we cannot get teachers to stay here, nor pupils to attend, unless the issue of teachers' housing is addressed," we are told.

*Catch 22 perhaps?*

"Perhaps if the community showed willing by making bricks for the teachers' houses, then we might reconsider our position," we toss this idea into the arena. Yet this proposal is received with great surprise . . . *do something for themselves, and without receiving any payment?*

"But how can we make blocks if we have no block mould?" asks one.

"Mr Chipotyo began making bricks for the rebuilding of the SDA church," we remind them. "How did he make his bricks? Maybe he has a block mould which you can use?"

"Ah no, he borrowed that mould," says one.

"If we are to do this job, we must have one of our own."

"How can we fire bricks without a kiln?"

"Or indeed an expert to show us how to construct a kiln?"

We look despairingly at each other till suddenly telepathy kicks in: let's present the community with a challenge. "If we were to provide a couple of block moulds from the orphan carers' allocation for this trip, then you could mould anthill clay bricks off your own initiative."

"Instead of being paid to do so?" the speaker is shocked. A long drawn out sigh susurrates round the room, allowing time for the outrageous idea to sink in that they do something to help themselves.

With nothing left to say, it is time to wind up the meeting. There is no AOB and the drunk has slunk away to sleep off his hangover. All that remains is to settle the Kaputula Orphan Carers' allowance. Since the rains have not yet arrived and food is scarce, they request an allocation of roller meal and cooking oil for each family caring for orphans.

We climb wearily into the vehicle along with Messrs Mbai and Chama. Without a by-your-leave Mr Kauseni climbs in the back. But as one of the most hard-working and loyal members of both this and the Kafubu project, he deserves a lift.

After the weekend we return, yet again attempting to arrive before the Kaputula community expects us. Except this time purchasing bags of roller meal from Olympic Milling in Kitwe and bottles of cooking oil from the African market holds us up. Fortunately Mr Chama is travelling in a lorry with extra cement for the Kafubu Church project and can transport this load for us. Mr Mbai travels with us.

"Maybe we can pass by the District Office," he proposes out of the blue, when we have him safely in the vehicle. "Then you can share some thoughts about Kaputula with someone there who is a good friend of mine."

Community schools have now passed somewhat loosely under government control and, as funding partner, we are unsure what authority we now have, so we concur and present ourselves at the District Office in Kalulushi, only to be told frustratingly, "Mr Matesi is busy, but he will see you in a few minutes." Will it be worth a possibly lengthy wait?

Inside Mr Matesi's office is luxuriously furnished: leather suite, drinks tray, radio murmuring in the background. *Oh how the other half lives!*

Mr Matesi listens politely to our catalogue of issues concerning Kaputula. We spare him nothing, though secretly doubting his authority to do anything.

"For sure he will do something," Mr Mbai assures us when we are outside once more. "He is my brother."

"But he looks nothing like you," I say bewildered.

"No, he is my brother in the close way we have worked together in the past," he explains. "Also he is the District Commissioner *himself*," he adds proudly.

*Whoops!* Hopefully a Zambian as important as Mr Matesi won't hold against us the fact that we almost didn't hang around long enough to see him today when he kept us waiting for almost twenty minutes!

We pass by Kafubu on the way to Kaputula to find the church project racing ahead. Already the workforce has started making extra blocks for beam filling. Rows of freshly made blocks lie maturing on the floor of the church. *How can a community so close to Kaputula in distance, be so far apart in ethos?*

At Kaputula however, nothing has changed. They have had an entire weekend to start maintenance work, yet not a single thing has been started. So we make a list classroom by classroom of all the things which need setting to rights: broken windows, chipped windowsills, holes in walls, pitted floors, dust and cobwebs festooning the roof timbers, one room being used as a storage barn. Then we summon together head teacher Mrs Tembo, deputy head Mr Nkoma, his namesake, Mr Nkhoma of the PTA, as well as Messrs Chanda and Nyrongo of the building committee.

Of Mr Chipotyo, strangely and worryingly, there is still no sign. Where can he be? Is he sick? Has he suffered an accident? But there is no opportunity to investigate his absence right now. Mr Mbai joins us in one classroom where we prepare to read out the list.

"So, there will be no more money until these issues are dealt with?" asks one of them as soon as I finish reading.

"How can we put these things right, when we have no money to do so?" demands another one.

"Nor any materials," chips in another.

"In fact if the cement mix had been right in the first place, we would not be needing to do these things now," Mr Nkoma tosses into the arena.

"Ah him!" Mr Nyrongo in his Wellington boots leaps angrily to his feet, sparks flying. "What can he as a teacher know about cement mixes?

A spark of conflagration is easily fanned by such words.

*Time for us to leave perhaps?*

"Look, the time for blaming others has ended," I tell them. "You are getting no more funding."

"Either you start pulling together as a community, or there can be no further building work done here," adds Bob.

A heart for Africa? Yet again the Kaputula community is straining our hearts to breaking point. Unfortunately, since we have to wait for Mr Chama to turn up with the roller meal and cooking oil for the orphan carers, we can't drive straight off. Instead we must sit under a tree, munching sandwiches and gazing in despair at what is threatening to become the biggest white elephant ever constructed in the African bush.

Yet as we eat and wait, there is time to ponder yet another conundrum .. . Mr Chiptyo is again conspicuous by his absence. Where is he? Eventually Mr Kauseni and Mr Chapuswike, now restored to health, pluck up enough courage to saunter over and join us.

"So, still no Mr Chipotyo?" we say by way of an opener to take the edge off what has just been said at the recent meeting.

"Ah no, we think he went to Kabwe for a course, or maybe it was a conference."

"Or was it a seminar?"

"Even a workshop perhaps, but he has still not returned."

"We think maybe something has happened to him," they concur.

"Perhaps you can contact him?" suggests Mr Kauseni hopefully. "At least to check that he is still okay?"

We confirm the cell-phone number for Mr Chipotyo and promise to contact him when we get back to Kitwe. Which problem slightly takes our mind off the sadness of this particular leave-taking. If we are not destined to build here again, then will we ever see Kaputula again?

Later that evening I try repeatedly to raise someone on Mr Chipotyo's number. At first no-one answers, then later someone repeatedly pages us. Finally we get through . . . "Hello, is that Mr Chipotyo?"

"Yes . . ." The voice sounds strangely unlike his. Has he been mugged and someone else is using his phone? Yet usually the first thing thieves do, is change the sim card.

"This is Mrs Cooke, from the Starfish Fund," I try.

"Ah, you are from the UK?"

"Yes, we have been to Kaputula, but you weren't there."

"For sure I am there!" exclaims the voice most indignantly.

"But we were told you were in Kabwe?"

"That is my father. I am Chipotyo junior . . . but he has told me all about you!" *Oh yes, and what exactly might that entail!*

"So, is your father still in Kabwe?"

"I think maybe he is stranded there and can't get back. The person who was running his course ran off to South Africa with the transport money and my father cannot get back from Kabwe until this person returns to give him the money."

*Another familiar Zambian tale of woe! But what is to do about it?*

Then I have a brainwave. "Look, we are travelling to Lusaka on Wednesday. Tell your father to be outside the Hungry Lion in Kabwe between 11.00 and 12.00 on Wednesday. We will see what we can do . . ."

At that moment the line goes dead. Has the son grasped the message? Despite our best efforts we fail to raise him again that evening.

The next evening, after another gruelling trip to Chilumba, strange text messages start arriving on our phone. Mr Chipotyo junior has contacted someone in Kabwe and is passing on a phone number for us to contact his father. With some trepidation I ring the number, praying at least Mr Chip himself will answer. "Can I speak to Mr Chipotyo please?"

"He is not here." Which voice yet again is not Mr Chip's.

"When will he be here, I mean, there?"

"Who is calling?" demands the voice.

"This is Mrs Cooke. I am from the UK."

" A 'mzungu' woman? From the UK? Calling for Mr Chipotyo?" Good, he has at last put two and two together and made . . . *whoops, not four but five and thinks I'm Mr Chip's bit of white stuff on the side!*

"Look, I . . . we are passing through Kabwe between 11.00 and 12.00 tomorrow. Will you please tell him to be outside the Hungry Lion in the main street at that time?"

"You want to meet with him there?" Clearly my audacity astounds him.

"Yes, I . . .we want to meet him there, so will you tell him, please?"

"I will tell him." And the phone goes dead.

As I write this up later that evening, I reflect that, if I didn't write it all down, nobody would believe the half of what goes on. Now some man in Kabwe clearly thinks I'm Mr Chip's 'bit on the side'.

Meanwhile we pray that this does turn out to be a genuine emergency. Should we arrive in Kabwe to find Mr Chip perfectly well and happy and enjoying a jolly away from home while his wife is left behind in Kaputula, boy, are our faces going to be red!

On Wednesday we crawl through the centre of Kabwe, partly because it has a speed limit of 25mph, but also because, if Mr Chip is there, we don't want to miss him.

He is there! But is this the Mr Chip we know, or a sad apology for him? If it wasn't for his familiar outsize glasses and lop-sided smile, we would hardly have recognised him. He is wearing a strange red velveteen shirt, which looks borrowed from someone several sizes larger. Or has our dear friend shrunk? Hmmm, maybe he has suffered an ordeal after all.

We squeeze Mr Chipotyo into the back of the vehicle along with all our baggage and drive one hundred yards down the road to the Total garage where there is a passable café. Since the café sells little other than sausage rolls, meat pies and beef samosas and Mr Chipotyo, unusually for a Zambian is vegetarian, we buy him Fanta orange and two scones.

"You look as if you need those," I say when he is seated.

"For sure, Bwanakula Thandi, I am in need of these."

As he eats he outlines the story of what happened. He went originally on a one night course on bee-keeping in Solwezi. The course organiser then suggested he travel on with him to see a farm project at Kalulushi.

"But at that point, you weren't far from home?" I say.

"Indeed, Bwanakula Thandi, and if I had had any inkling of what was to befall me, even I would have walked to my home from there."

"So what happened then?"

"That man was saying first we must go here, then we must go there until eventually we ended up here in Kabwe."

"But Kabwe is three hundred kilometres from your home! Where have you been staying? How have you survived?"

"When it became clear the person who had access to the funding for my return fare had left for South Africa and no-one else had the authority to do so, I was forced to throw myself on the mercy of some people here in Kabwe."

"And have they been feeding you?"

"They gave me some food," he says guardedly which we take to mean the odd bowl of 'nshima', once a day if he was lucky, and not a lot else.

"And you couldn't get the money for your fare from anyone else either here or at Kaputula?"

"Ah no, there is no-one," he says with true African fatalism.

"And will this person return to give you the money?"

"That I don't know."

It is unbelievable that someone can be so easily stranded three hundred kilometres from their home in modern day Zambia with no means whatsoever of getting back there. Had it been anyone else, we would have taken the story with a pinch of salt. But Mr Chipotyo is one of the most resourceful Zambians we know.

At least now the cavalry has arrived. He has been here an incredible three weeks. That is quite long enough. I reach into my purse and give him K70 000 (about £10). "Will that cover your return fare?"

"How can I ever thank you?" His eyes mist over with emotion.

"Go home to your wife, Mr Chipotyo," I say patting his hand gently, "she will be missing you."

"And my farm also is missing me. It is the planting season and my crops are falling behind."

With heavy hearts we reveal to him the ultimatum left behind with the community, only too painfully aware of how much this one man's vision has driven the community through both phases of the building work and how much he still aches to see more accomplished there.

"Bwanakula Thandi, we will strive to do what the Starfish has set us to do." And he genuinely means it. If the Kaputula community consisted solely of Mr Chipotyos, then things quite possibly would get done.

But unfortunately it doesn't, and so we are still left with a dilemma. There is currently enough money in the Starfish coffers to undertake another building project. But should it be at Chilumba with its chronic problems of manpower and accessibility? Or at far distant Simooya, thus entailing round trips of 800 miles or more as we race from one end of Zambia to the other? Or should we start up again at Kaputula where, even if they do make the bricks, because of disputes and delays, the whole process could crumble before it even begins?

# CHAPTER TWENTY-TWO: A LAUNCH CEREMONY TO REMEMBER and a familiar figure comes back to haunt us!
## Sunday, September 14ᵗʰ, 2008

One of the earliest lessons learnt with Kafubu Baptist Church project was that, whether a day, a week, a month or a year passed between visits, we invariably returned to find all work accomplished. In fact, the real problem was keeping money coming in fast enough to match the speed at which the Church community got work done.

*Oh that the same could be said of Kaputula community!*

The request to rebuild Kafubu Baptist Church originally came from Mr Kauseni, a committed member of the Kaputula workforce. He and his wife lived in Kaputula, but worshipped at Kafubu Baptist Church. Every Sunday he would don his best but rather tatty suit, while his wife put on the distinctive red and white uniform of the Baptist ladies. Then, along with their family, they pedalled or walked four kilometres to the Baptist Church.

In 2004 we put Mr Kauseni's appeal for a new church to the Starfish committee. Starfish was not at that time flush with money, being at the height of both Salem and Kaputula projects. A request for funding was therefore circulated to local Baptist churches in the West Midlands. Ironically the one with possibly the smallest congregation responded. But how would a congregation of barely twenty faithful souls ever fund the building of a church numbering over three hundred and still growing?

"I foresee us taking about seven years to raise the funding," announced Derrick Hancock, church secretary of Hockley Heath Baptist Church, on an early visit.

Our hearts sank. Seven years was a long time. Would we still be around in seven years' time, let alone still doing Starfish work? Nevertheless, since no-one else had offered, we went along with it.

Now, in less than two years, the church is completed, though it is September 2008 before we finally see the finished building.

"Wow, it is big!" The sheer size dwarfs the adjacent Catholic Church. In the initial planning stages, Mr Kauseni joked that the Baptists wanted a bigger church than the Catholics. His wish has been spectacularly granted.

"So now we must arrange a launch ceremony," proposes Mr Mbai, Project Manager of both Kaputula and Kafubu projects.

"We hear you are preachers?" queries old Mr Kauseni expectantly.

"Ah, that would be my wife," Bob interposes quickly.

But Mr Kauseni is not easily duped. "No, if we are to have a launch ceremony, then both Mr and Mrs Cooke must preach."

And so, the launch ceremony is fixed for the coming Sunday. "Only four days to prepare," I groan to Bob as we head for the car.

"And I've *never* preached before!" he responds despondently.

But what will we preach about? I don't wish to rub it in too heavily, but we are in a pickle. We have no study aids, no preaching or teaching resources, annotated study Bibles, the internet, nothing. All we have is one leather bound travel Bible and a prayer for the Holy Spirit to move us.

One other problem augments our worries. Due to the combination of a restricted diet somewhat lacking in fresh fruit and vegetables and possibly an infection as well, as the weekend approaches, both our guts break out into open rebellion. This does not bode well for Sunday, since Kafubu does not possess a usable toilet. The nearest usable toilets are the brand new pit toilets at Kaputula . . . locked and four kilometres distant!

On our first visit to Kafubu, I tried their one pit toilet, only to escape gagging and unable to remain inside long enough to perform. Ever since I have done without there. Yet necessity may dictate otherwise on Sunday. Given the state of our unstable guts, plus the fact that the average church service in Zambia lasts three hours, *and* includes a sermon of at least one hour, one of us is sure to feel an urgent need to go. *And then what?*

Saturday should have seen us polishing our talks. Sermon is far too grand a word for what we propose to deliver tomorrow. Normally the peaceful lodge where we stay affords ample opportunity for quiet reflection, secreted in one of numerous nooks and crannies: down by the fast flowing river, out on the island in the dam, or on a fishing platform watching a resident croc watching us and wondering if we'd be good to eat.

Unfortunately, from Friday afternoon onwards, peace has deserted the entire location, where Jonathon Kruger, like his father, is an ex judo

214

champion. He runs a kids' judo club in a specially constructed hall on the property and this weekend has organised a judo championship there. Peace is shattered as kids roam freely and all available accommodation has been snapped up by organisers and trainers.

Normally we are in bed by 10pm. Not a sound breaks the silence until George or the night guard starts clattering about at 06.00. Last night we were kept awake till after 11pm by voices droning in the adjoining chalet. Since the walls are paper thin, every sound could be heard. Unbelievably they started up again at 4am this morning.

At 4.30am, torch in hand and braving the ferocious guard dog which roams freely during the hours of darkness, I padded along the veranda to knock at the chalet next door. All its lights were ablaze as if it was 4pm not 4am. An overweight Zambian in boxer shorts answered the door. Behind him a further two huge Zambians were crowded into a room designed for two persons. Yet he didn't seem fazed by a 'mzungu' woman knocking at his door at 4am. Maybe he thought his lucky number had come up.

"Excuse me, could you make less noise? We're trying to sleep next door."

"Oh sorry," said the man and shut the door in my face.

Over breakfast we mention to Jonathon we were disturbed during the night.

"Really?" he responds. "Only that was the Chairman of the Zambia Judo Association as well as a superintendent of police next door to you."

*Whoops! And we told them to shut up!*

During the day a run through our talks is further scotched by the constant stream of kids in judo kit traipsing across the dam and along the veranda in search of cokes from the bar, or else heading for the communal showers. Later a voluble representation from the Japanese Embassy in Lusaka also turns up. *Just as well, I didn't ask them to shut up!*

In the end we give up the effort and instead make the short walk to check up on the progress of Kushuka and Bwana Kushuka, the two goats left in the care of the Pastor and his wife at the Heart of Africa Mission. It is some months since we last saw them. Hopefully there will be news of a 'happy event.'

The mission and its surroundings are very quiet, so quiet that we have difficulty raising either the pastor or his wife. They don't look too happy to see us. "So, how are the two goats?" we ask.

A nervous glance passes from one to another. "Ah sorry," manages the pastor, "they did not survive."

"What, neither of them?"

"In fact we lost both of them."

"Do you mean lost as in wandered off, or simply eaten by a crocodile?"

"They both died."

This is not good news. How do we tell the Kaputula community who also had a vested interest in the well-being of the two goats? "Were both goats sick then?"

"The male goat was the first to die. We think it ate some plastic which was lying around and the plastic became stuck in its gut."

I shake my head in disbelief. "Don't you know goats will eat anything? Why did you let it near something which would certainly kill it if swallowed?"

"And the female?" asks Bob.

"Not long afterwards sadly she also died. We think she ate some poisonous frogs."

This sounds bizarre enough to be true. Nevertheless, the niggling doubt remains that the pastor and his wife simply slaughtered and ate the goats. Even if their story were true, we doubt they simply left the carcasses to rot!

"So, no happy outcome?"

"Well, no and yes. Before she died, the female gave birth to a young one."

Could this be the issue from Bwana Kushuka's wedding night? We follow the pastor round to the back of his house. A pitiful bleating greets us from a shed. Staring suspiciously out, is a young male goat bearing the unmistakeable markings of its late parents.

"At least one good thing has come from it!"

"But what will this one do for a wife?" The pastor's wife who, up until now, has said very little, sidles up to join us.

But we're not prepared to go down that route. If she is genuinely interested in rearing a flock of goats, it's up to her to locate a young female, then guard the pair of them from harm.

Later, as we sit on the veranda in front of our chalet trying one final run through and as the sun sinks in glorious splendour, the owner joins us. He also is an ex judo champion. Today he's enjoyed a field day, judo from early morning until sunset and he *still* wants to talk about it.

"Do you know anything about judo?" he asks me.

"Nothing at all."

"A woman like you should, you know."

*Really!*

"A woman should always know the basic moves. If you like I could teach you a few."

"No thanks. I'm really not into this whole martial arts thing." Though clearly he is.

"You never know when you might need a skill like that," he persists.

"True . . ."

"Then I'll show you a few moves." He edges closer.

I neatly side-step. "I'll just trust my faith will protect me if I get in any dodgy situations."

"Heck, even Christian women get raped!" he snaps perhaps angered at my lack of enthusiasm. "Look, I'll just show you." Before Bob can dodge out of his way, he has him in an arm-lock guaranteed to stop any further antics.

"Sorry, but you really must excuse us." We escape before Bob ends up with a broken arm and I'm wrestled to the floor and forced to submit. Clearly there's only one thing worse than a judo champion . . . an ex judo champion still imagining himself in the league.

Tonight neither of us can do justice to George's offering. We retire to bed doped on Immodium and Lomotil. All does not bode well for the morrow. We are under-prepared and on the run!

At 07.30 on Sunday morning George knocks at our door. "I'm sorry madam, but your breakfast will be late."

"But it *cannot* be late!" I tell him. "Today we are preaching at Kafubu."

"Then I will see what I can do." George waddles back along the veranda as fast as his little legs will carry him.

"And no cooked breakfast!" I call after his receding back. The last thing either of us wants this morning is one of George's mammoth fry-ups.

This morning we are picking up Mr Mbai and Mr Chama at 09.00 at the Post Office building in town. Since Mr Mbai is missing his regular Pentecostal Church in favour of Kafubu and since Mr Chama, a Jehovah's Witness, has agreed to attend a Christian church, we dare not be late.

At Kafubu everyone is there to greet us: Pastor Mweetwa, church deacons and deaconesses, the church secretary, the Kausenis, the deputy mayor, Mr Amon Kafwali, even Mr and Mrs Chipotyo have made the journey from Kaputula. Mr Chipotyo looks dapper in his Sunday waistcoat, or should that be *Saturday* waistcoat since he is a Seventh Day Adventist and their Sabbath is on a Saturday? Mrs Chipotyo also looks glamorous and every bit the charming lady our dear friend deserves.

Today the power is on. Mr Kauseni junior, head teacher in a local community school and also Kafubu Baptist Church Secretary, has set up a sound system capable of deafening people as far away as Kitwe.

He hands us a neatly written programme of events with the timing of each scheduled item. We note it includes 'MASSAGE FROM MRS COOKE', also 'SPEECH FROM MR AND MRS COOKE'. We point out I shan't be doing *massages* today, but will attempt to deliver the *message*. Mr Cooke will do the same.

The church is packed to capacity. Yet people are still trying to squeeze in. At the back they are hastily fixing up additional seating made of sawn off planks and wood off-cuts. We wait patiently trying to quell our nerves and our guts. They invite us to test out the sound system, but the amplifier is so huge it merely booms and crackles out over the expectant congregation.

In honour of the occasion, three choirs are on hand, the usual church choir, a children's choir plus a choir that has travelled all the way from Ndola. The programme begins with much singing from all three choirs in order to get the Spirit moving. Then there is much praying on the part of the pastor and various church deacons.

Finally we are invited to speak. Everything we say has to be translated into Lamba, the local language, for the benefit of people present who don't understand much English. This is a time-consuming exercise, but at least it reduced the length of what needed to be prepared.

Bob kicks off first with the parable of The Sower and the Seed. His message is that the seed of an idea for the church fell into fertile ground and geminated which is why we are able to celebrate its launch today. He is amazed when he sits down to find it has taken over half an hour to deliver.

My address is based on the theme of what constitutes a House of God, that we have come here today to celebrate not simply the building of a church, for a church is more than a building. I take as my text three passages. Firstly the account of Moses and the Tent of Meeting and how, even in the early days, it was a special place where people gathered to meet with God.

The second passage outlines the construction of the Temple in Jerusalem, how it was not David but his son Solomon, chosen by God to accomplish this task. Thus God's work is achieved in His timing and not our own.

The third passage from Acts describes the early Christian church, how it was a place of sharing and caring for others. "My hope today being that for all of you, this building will become a special place of worship, a place blessed by the Lord and a place where those in need of care will find a place to come."

Stunned silence fills the church for the first few moments after we finish. Was it what they expected? Then Mr Kafwali rises and pumps our hands up and down vigorously. Thus encouraged, the congregation claps, which in turn rouses the women to ululate their appreciation.

It is now Mr Kafwali's turn. Though not preaching today, he is obviously a man of many words. His thanks extend to a few dozen then a few hundred and even a thousand words. While he is in full flow, one of the ladies approaches on bended knee to place bottles of cold drink and Eet-sum-mor biscuits in front of us. Goodness knows where she unearthed them from, but she also produces two long stemmed wine glasses from which to drink.

Task over, we ease into euphoria . . .

"And so it is time for us to show our appreciation for the Cookes and for the Starfish and what they have done for us." Mr Kafwali is nearing the end of his extended thank-you.

*Appreciation?* Suddenly alarm bells are ringing. *Where have we heard those words before?* My heart skips a beat. Surely it can't be? Yet no tell-tale bleating has betrayed . . . All the same, do I feel another goat moment coming on?

Sure enough, yet another well-hung goat, its front and back legs tied with rope, is dragged into the church and slung before us. The goat lies there utterly distraught, feebly attempting to struggle up onto its feet. Each effort brings it crashing once more to its tethered knees.

*How do we get out of this? Kushuka, resurrected more surely than Lazarus from the dead and come back to haunt us!* Worse, the goat's appearance has produced exactly the same reaction as last time . . . this beautiful animal cannot die for our sakes. By now its flanks are heaving in distress, as it emits ever more painful bleats of terror.

And if this is not enough, in come women holding by the feet two very live village chickens. Finally come two pictures wrapped up in gold wrapping paper and tied with white ribbon and streamers. One is made of hammered copper engraved with a Bible verse. The other is a collage picture by a local artist. Kafubu Baptists have done us proud. Such generosity from people who have so little is truly overwhelming.

*But what to do with the goat?* Given the tragic fate of the two goats at the mission, donating another one there is out of the question. We watch dumbstruck as yet another live and kicking dilemma is loaded unceremoniously into the back of our vehicle.

Time to depart, though the goodbyes are long in saying. But where are

Messrs Mbai and Chama? We discover them round the back of the church, tucking into food intended for invited guests.

"We're off now," we warn them, "if you want a lift back to Kitwe."

"But what about my 'nshima'?" wails Mr Chama.

Since he is clearly peckish after the rigours of a 'proper' church service, we offer to wait. "But no, I am coming," he says and leaps into the back of the truck clutching pieces of village chicken and village polony to munch en route.

We travel back to Kitwe with the smell of their food pervading the car. Meanwhile the distressed goat and chickens pass the journey pooing liberally in the back under the cover of the tarpaulin, thus adding their own unique stench.

"What can we do with it? We simply can't hand another goat over to the mission."

"You could just let the goat go by the side of the road," comes Mr Chama's uninspired suggestion.

"But what if it wanders back to Kafubu to its owner?"

"Ah, you have a point," he concedes between bites of polony. "Though it is a long walk back."

I recall we have seen goats at the Faith Orphanage Skills Training Centre in Kitwe. I ring up director Faith Lyena to ask if that is so.

"In fact we do," she replies cagily, perhaps puzzled at receiving such a strange question on a Sunday afternoon.

"Then would you like an extra one?"

So midway through Sunday afternoon, we pass by the Skills Training Centre to drop off one distressed goat to Judith, the bemused centre manager, who clearly was not expecting its arrival. There are three other goats on the site. Soon Kushuka II is bleating his introduction to them. They seem less than impressed. Worse, since one of the other three is also a male, a power struggle is set to develop.

"For sure this goat is not for eating," we tell Judith.

"Sure!" she responds, yet her words lack conviction. Kushsuka II may have escaped our cooking pot, but for Judith it's sheer manna from heaven. What matters the fate of a goat two daft 'mzungus' drop off on a Sunday afternoon!

That still leaves two chickens. Judith also has her eye on them, but they're not destined for her. We transport them back to the lodge where George cleans them and freezes them down. George is happy. From the chickens he receives the wings, neck, giblets, feet and sausages or . . . intestines.

"Tonight I am rich!" he crows.

*Ah George, if only that were so!* But then maybe George is rich in ways, which the rest of us have long forgotten.

On Thursday of the following week we pass via Kafubu to take one last picture of the church for the album, this time without the throng of people present last Sunday.

One of the workmen on site comes up and pumps our hands up and down. "We are still talking about the sermon on Sunday!"

"Really?" Which makes us feel decidedly humble.

Back in Kitwe, we pass by the Skills Training Centre to check whether Kushuka II has settled in . . .

"You've *lost* him!" We can't believe we are hearing this. "How can you lose a goat?" Though I fear it is all too easy.

"We think someone left the gate open and it wandered out and was lost," says Judith none too convincingly.

*Eaten more like!* Yet how can we prove it?

On our return to the lodge there is no power. No sooner has Bob wandered off for an evening stroll, than the owner appears once more. "I see there's no power again." I pray this opener might forestall any further arm-locks and half nelsons.

"Bah, these guys! If they ever set foot on my property, I'll shoot the beggars! Cutting off our electricity like this! What a way to run a country!"

Does he mean Zesco or the government? Either way, not perhaps the wisest of sentiments if he wants to survive in a country where, like it or not, both government and electricity are nowadays run by *them*.

Today the lodge has been without power since 5am, a total of fifteen hours. There is no sign of the power coming back on. How long can people like the owners here survive running lodges in conditions like this?

Apparently South Africa has ceased supplying Zambia with electricity, while for some bizarre reason Zesco has shut off the main connector at Kariba power station with the Zimbabwean side. The roadsides are thick with people selling charcoal and primitive braziers. The sale of generators, for those who can afford them, has rocketed.

We sit by candlelight sipping coffee and camomile tea. "So would you say the sermons went down well?" I put to Bob.

"They certainly seem to have given them something to talk about," he responds.

"But were they what they wanted or indeed expected?" I persist.

"That we may never know. However, since they don't have much to entertain them out there, I'd say we were probably better than Zambian TV any day," pronounces Bob.

Which may not as yet make us rivals of the likes of Billy Graham or T D Jakes, but for two erstwhile preachers and over the hill charity workers, providing the entertainment factor is probably about as good as it gets!

# CHAPTER TWENTY-THREE: MR AND MRS COOKE GO 'THAT SIDE' TO DISCOVER HEAVEN ON EARTH
## ...*September 9ᵗʰ, 16ᵗʰ, 23ʳᵈ & 25ᵗʰ, 2008*

Zambia is floating adrift, like a rudderless ship. Three weeks ago President Levy Mwanawasa died of a stroke. Currently diabetes, strokes and heart disease are killing off hundreds of Zambians every year, as better-off ones swap traditional food for a western diet of fat-saturated and sugar-laden fast food and drink.

Following President Mwanawasa's funeral last week, the country has entered three weeks of mourning. No parties, no drinking, no large gatherings for twenty-one days. Woe and betide any bar or restaurant owner who contravenes the edict.

But does this apply to large community gatherings such as those held at Chilumba, Simooya or Kaputula? We pray not because, following a decision made by the UK committee, this trip we are finally tackling the impossible . . . the commencement of a building project at Chilumba Orphans' Centre.

"We understand the settings have been done and trenches dug?" we put to Messrs Mbai and Chama on our first day back on the job. It has been ten long months since our last visit. However, because a partnership already exists with the Faith Orphanage Foundation, money has been sent through from the UK to get the foundations underway.

"Indeed, Mr Chalwe has been most effective in motivating the community to get the task done," responds Mr Mbai.

"Ah, that man is becoming the driving force behind the Chilumba project!" enthuses Mr Chama.

"Nevertheless, one or two problems have arisen regarding transporting the stones and building sand, also the accessing of funding," adds Mr Mbai.

*When all is not plain sailing, it's time for a visit!*

The following day we set off for Chilumba. Mr Chalwe wants to deviate around Kalulushi, but is reminded of the need to pass by everyone's favourite bakery. Sadly both Mr Chalwe and Mr Chama emerge carrying foods laden with fat and sugar.

"Bah, those foods are bad for you," I remind them. "You really must reduce your fat, sugar and salt intake." I hesitate to add . . . *unless you want to end up like your late president!*

"What, even salt also?" Mr Chama is scandalised.

"Even salt, it's very bad for your blood pressure."

"But what must I do when a restaurant puts a salt cellar on the table?"

"Then you must resist the temptation to put salt on your food." However I fear such drastic health warnings fall on Mr Chama's suddenly deaf ears.

Soon we are passing the rural police post where last time the lone police officer begged for food. "Ah that one!" exclaims Mr Chama, recalling the event. "He has shot a man!" Which fact rather belies the fallacy that Zambian police carry guns but no bullets.

"What happened?"

"A mob had gathered there and tried to take possession of his gun. That one was drunk and opened fire killing a man. Later he was arrested for the shooting."

Today however, we pass unchallenged, though noting evidence of the former police post now razed to the ground by the rioting mob.

At Chilumba the usual raggle-taggle collection of orphans and carers awaits us, but with one marked difference . . . their faces are smiling. Is this the difference the reality of a project has made to them?

Already at 10.30 the temperature has risen to thirty-four degrees. A hot wind is blowing which dries the skin like dessicated coconut. We head out into the bush behind the current school to where the new three classroom block is underway. Already a well-worn track leads over there.

And it's looking good! The trenches are dug and awaiting the pouring in of concrete for the footings next week. Mr Chalwe is to arrange for a thirty ton truck to come out from Kitwe on Thursday. The driver will stay overnight in order to spend two days ferrying stones, building sand and block-mix from a site seven or eight kilometres away where they can be dug for free.

It is too hot out in the full sun to stand around for long. Yet these workers labour from 07.00 until 15.00 in full sun. The women and older children are also playing their part. Originally water for making concrete was to come from a stream, but they have deemed it too far. Now they are ferrying it in buckets and bowls from a neighbouring pump. Since it's still a long hike, they toss around plans for constructing a pipe. However this is a non-starter, so they must continue ferrying endless buckets of water on their heads.

Time for the speeches. We head back to the school to sit at desks carried out under the sparse shade of straggly trees. Hopefully we're not breaking the rules about large gatherings.

Mr Chalwe kicks off with a long, rambling dissertation about the reasons for the long absence of . . . "these people sent from God . . . who have a real heart for us and our children."

*Who, us?* Nevertheless, his flattering words contain so many inaccuracies as to why we finally decided to build a school for them, that I feel duty bound to set the record straight. "In fact, because the community failed to look after the orchard by not constructing the fence around it, Starfish very nearly didn't build here at all. Only Dynass's heart-rending request finally decided us that either we did build here, or . . ."

*Or what, left them to it?* Maybe that's too harsh and best left unsaid. Though we certainly said this to each other, and shared it with the committee back in the UK. However, instead of leaving them to it, Starfish has since reconsidered and has now taken the momentous decision to build here.

*And at Simooya!*

*While still keeping Kaputula on the back burner, mad or what!*

Next it's Bob's turn to speak about 'faith' with a small 'f', not to be confused with Faith with a capital letter, who supposedly runs this project, but is conspicuous today by her absence.

Finally Mr Chalwe picks up once more, mobilising the community to yet greater effort and revealing a different side to his character. Next he'll be standing as an MP. "There must be sufficient men on both this site and the digging sites for when the truck comes," he berates them. "But the good news is, there is no work of unloading. This kind of truck will do it for you."

For a man of so many words, Mr Chalwe is nevertheless eager to return to Kitwe. We drive off and park where the stream flows under the road through an enormous pipe, there to eat our packed lunches.

A woman is doing her washing in the none too clean water, at the same time holding a conversation at full throttle with another woman some distance away. She gazes bemused at these 'mzungus with a heart for Africa' currently polishing off their lunch in her laundry spot.

Eventually curiosity gets the better of her. She summons the other woman and they sidle up hands outstretched. We extract a couple of slices of bread from George's doorstep sandwiches and hand them over with sachets of salt and tomato ketchup. The two women wolf down the bread, then stand sucking out the salt and ketchup through gaps in their teeth, as if sucking succulent crab from delicate claws.

Later we ponder how Mr Chalwe has lately risen in our estimation. Certainly he is far more a man of the community than we previously gave him credit for and even now is taking the lead. But will he stay the course? *Let's hope he's not leading us up the garden, or still unfenced orchard path!*

A week later we return to Chilumba. For our part we have been back and forth to Kaputula twice, also to Kafubu and including the launch ceremony where we preached. We have also passed via the District Education Office in relation to the worsening situation at Kaputula and caught up with the ex-Musonda pupils along with Evelyn. *So, a nice relaxing time!*

But what has Mr Chalwe been up to? Today is the day for making the stone and concrete mix for the footings.

"I regret to inform you that the lorry which was to transport the materials did not reach 'that side' until yesterday," announces Mr Chalwe as he settles into the rear of the vehicle along with Messrs Mbai and Chama.

"But it was supposed to be there last week?"

"So you are saying that the materials are not there waiting for us today?" Mr Mbai's question like a well-aimed arrow penetrates right to the point.

"In fact no," mumbles Mr Chalwe, plummeting in our estimation.

Worse, in a last ditch attempt to remedy the situation, we arrive to find almost every member of the workforce has travelled 'that side' in the lorry to shovel sand and block-mix and to enjoy free rides. Even if we had the materials, there are not enough people left to do the task.

"So where is 'that side'?" we ask.

"Seven, maybe eight kilometres that way." Mr Chalwe points vaguely into the bush. "Maybe a bit further." Clearly his sense of distance and direction are challenged.

But the day must not be wasted. Messrs Mbai and Chama immediately set the remaining workforce to work making blocks for the foundation wall for which there are sufficient materials currently on site. To do this, building sand has to be mixed with block-mix, shovelful by shovelful, sifting it three times until the mix is correct.

In the meantime the women and older children walk two hundred yards backwards and forwards to the pump fetching and carrying water in buckets and bowls. The water is mixed in with the sand and block-mix, turning and turning with a spade until it is the right consistency.

"It's like making a cake," I say to Mr Chama.

"Indeed!" he agrees, though I doubt he's ever mixed a cake in his life.

When he is satisfied the mix is correct, it is filled into the block mould, compacted down, before being turned out onto the ground . . . one brick made!

For mid-September, it is hotter than ever in the sun today. We retreat to the shade, pondering what else to do with a wasted day.

"So, let us visit the site where they are collecting the sand and stones?" proposes Mr Mbai.

"In fact yes!" exclaims Mr Chama enthusiastically. "You will see, it is like heaven on earth! Even like God provided all our needs in one place! Sand, stones . . ."

"All our *building* needs you mean?" Since Mr Chama is a builder, he would think like that. Nevertheless we are intrigued and agree to go 'that side'.

We travel further on along the road before veering off onto a smaller road, which wends its way through vast eucalyptus plantations. We pass a fifty hectares farm where Mr Chalwe's father lives, then past the Chief's palace before taking a yet smaller track. On and on we travel, praying they know where they are going, because we certainly don't.

"We are here!" exclaims Mr Chama.

We clamber out, eager to see this 'heaven on earth'. All we can see is an immense truck standing idle and the men, equally idle, enjoying a lunch break. Though to be fair, they had no idea we were coming.

The truck is simply immense and they are a long way away from filling it. We pointed out to Mr Chalwe only last week that it was false economy to hire a larger truck costing more money, which would take all day to fill, than a smaller one costing less, but which could be filled over and over again. Besides, the stones have not been ready prepared, so they are wasting valuable time digging the stones then loading and all in intense heat.

*Oh dear, Mr Chalwe, you didn't get this one right at all!*

We leave the men to their lunch and retreat to sit on a fallen log under some scrubby trees to eat our own lunch. Today, in response to a request for less meat, we discover vegetarian pies. However one glance reveals . . . "Oh no, they've got mushrooms in!" To which I'm allergic, so it's nuts and crisps and fruit for me.

However it's not long before one, then two, then three pairs of curious eyes are peering around an adjacent tree. *Bet they don't see many 'mzungus' picnicking around here!*

Bob approaches the three boys and hands over the leftover pie along with sachets of salt and tomato ketchup. They hide behind the tree to enjoy their feast. Next along come a couple of women with babies who follow every morsel of orange as it disappears into my mouth. This is becoming painful. In the end I hand over the remains of a packet of biscuits and indicate, "NO MORE!"

Mr Chama has found a nearby stream and waves us over to see the tiny fish teeming in it. It is wonderfully peaceful, here in the very heart of the African bush. The immense arc of blue sky overhead and not a sound apart from the crickets whirring and the yak-yak of the women. But there's always something to disturb the peace . . .

"Maybe you can say something to the workforce," suggests Mr Chalwe, then proceeds to address them himself. On and on, until I remind him . . .

"Mr Chalwe, you've left nothing for us to say!"

We say what we can to rouse the workforce to ever greater efforts, even though the sun is scorching, they're not getting paid, they haven't had much lunch, some of them are not even from Chilumba anyways and finally, that ruddy great truck is going to take forever to fill.

Back at Chilumba, they have made all of thirty blocks with one bag of cement in our two hours' absence . . . *how long will they take to make sufficient blocks for an entire school?*

Someone hands over a baby for me to hold. "Is it a boy or a girl?" I ask. The fact that it is wearing blue is not necessarily a clue in Zambia.

"It is a girl, her name is Ned."

"But I thought you said . . ."

"No, her name is Nellie." Suddenly they change their minds.

Nellie may be a niece or distant cousin of Dynass. No-one seems sure to whom Nellie belongs. For one brief moment I'm tempted to do a Madonna and claim Nellie for my own. But is that wise for a granny pushing sixty-four? Reluctantly I hand Nellie back to whatever fate has in store for her.

It's time to return to Kitwe, travel on to Lusaka, then down to Choma. Then what? With projects running at opposite ends of Zambia, both now need our attention. Should we therefore stay down in Choma, or head over five hundred miles back up here again? Certainly Chilumba is pulling us back . . .

A week later we return to find they STILL have not got enough sand and stones on site. *Oh that we had heeded the still uncompleted orchard fencing as dire warning of things to come!*

Mr Chalwe therefore is to travel with a lorry from the Skills Training Centre in Kitwe in order to ferry yet more loads from 'heaven on earth' back to the building site at Chilumba. Meanwhile we depart with Mr Chama and Faith Lyena, director of the Faith Orphanage projects. Today again Faith is dressed in 'field' attire wearing a brightly patterned 'chitenge' wrapped around her waist. With her she carries a sandwich box full of sandwiches, made by her maid in Ndola, which she intends to share amongst five of us.

At Chilumba it is already hot. The children have abandoned the classroom and are helping the women to fetch and carry water, all ably mobilised by Josephine who now greets us like long lost friends.

Over on the building site the men have laboured hard in the week's absence and have filled in one long trench of the footings. However, two long ones still remain to be filled, plus all the shorter intersecting ones. Quite a task, since every wheelbarrow of cement has to be mixed by hand before transporting to the trenches.

It is too hot to stand watching in the full sun. However the half a dozen men working today carry on regardless, goaded by Mr Chama to greater effort until another of the two long trenches is filled in.

"If they stop for lunch, there will be no getting them back to work this afternoon," he declares. What a taskmaster! Sweat pours down his face, neck and arms, as he urges them on to ever greater effort.

Meanwhile, over in the sparse shade by the schoolroom, we set about photographing orphans currently sponsored by people in the UK. Each trip the list is updated as we add more names or replace those who have left, or sometimes sadly have died. These children suffer poor health and also are highly mobile. If the family can no longer cope, they get passed on from one relative to another.

When the list is updated, each orphan is photographed for the record, then a copy is sent to their UK sponsor. We now have twenty-five names on the list. It takes some time to photograph and record each one. Infuriatingly we sometimes call a name only to receive the response, "She is not around."

What does Josephine or Faith mean by not around? How do we tell a sponsor back in the UK, *'Sorry, your orphan was not around!'*

However Faith explains that pupils in grade four and above are not 'around' because they attend Basic School, which is three kilometres distant. Since they also must pay fees to attend Basic School, this also explains why the sponsorship money for older pupils covers school fees and not a lot else.

Bob clicks away with the camera. Unfortunately when editing and downloading, his digital camera annoyingly jiggles the order in which the orphans are photographed. Thus I need to record exactly what rags and tatters each orphan is wearing. Then we have to get them to smile . . .

Today Josephine persuades us to add another seven orphans onto the list, even though some still have no UK sponsor. Maybe people in Suffolk will come up trumps!

The whole process takes until lunchtime. Just as Bob thinks he's done and wanders off to see how the men are doing, in wanders another orphan and he's called back again. Even as we sit under an 'nsaka' for lunch, orphans are still wandering in to have their photos taken.

Faith produces her huge box of sandwiches for sharing. We also share our own plus oranges and biscuits as Josephine also joins us for lunch. Meanwhile the women at the centre, mainly widows and grandmothers, have made an enormous pot of 'nshima' for the men and children to share. I pray it's like the magic porridge pot and will keep filling and refilling itself until everyone receives their share. Today is the nearest one could get to a party or festive atmosphere in a place as deprived as Chilumba and we relish our good fortune in being part of it.

After lunch orphans are still turning up for photographs. Like the magician pulling a rabbit out of a hat, Faith produces lollipops and sweeties for the children, but is almost crushed in the stampede to get one.

"Stand back!" she pleads. "There is enough for everyone!" She plays with them, hiding sweeties under her 'chitenge' and waving the empty packets at them. But she fails abysmally to fool them and is almost knocked to the ground as they push and shove for their treats. One woman even yanks her baby off her engorged breast to thrust its hand forward for a lollipop. Grown women are walking around with lollipops stuck in their mouths.

By now Mr Chalwe has arrived and joined Mr Chama on site, but they are the last to eat. While the workmen retire to eat 'nshima', Messrs Chalwe and Chama opt for the last sandwiches washed down with gallons of squash and water, almost drinking the entire bottled supply.

"The problem is their 'nshima' here is like concrete," jokes Mr Chalwe.

*More's the pity! Since the women produced more this morning than was needed, they could have poured it into the trenches instead of the concrete which shovelful by shovelful is STILL taking forever to make!*

It is time to depart. Still one more orphan wanders onto site. "Ah, it is Titi!" Bob recognises the orphan he sponsors. Titi also is photographed before finally, hot, dusty and tired we drive off back to Kitwe.

*Bushed?* Yes, but nevertheless more than satisfied at the way today has gone.

One problem remains as we near the end of yet another trip, and that is leaving Chilumba with enough money and materials to achieve what needs doing before the rains start in late November. Since what we have always done with Kaputula was to pay travellers' cheques into the Chep account, we have also signed over travellers' cheques to the Faith Orphanage account for a designated amount of work. *All receipts next time please!*

But we bargain without the bad news . . . "Sorry the bank will not allow us to deposit the cheques into the Faith Orphanage account."

"There must be some mistake," we tell Mr Chalwe who breaks the news. Perhaps they would prefer cash instead, but cash is easier to lose track of, so we send him back to the bank to try again.

Faith phones later to say, "The bank manager is saying there is a freeze on cashing travellers' cheques at this present time."

We agree to accompany them to the bank. Nearing the end of six weeks in Zambia and with an almost total block on world news, we do not realise that the world's financial markets have just entered meltdown. Thus in ignorance of the true state of affairs, we prepare to confront any bank manager who tries to mess with us.

But first, there's another day at Chilumba to face. Today's travelling subjects include liturgy in the Church of England, women Bishops, homosexual priests as well as the forthcoming Presidential by-election which, since the period of mourning has now officially ended, is dominating each evening's live television programmes.

"So why is it a presidential by-election and not a presidential election?" we ask our travelling companions.

"It is because the person elected will not serve a full term in office, but only the time which was remaining for this term, had our late president not died," we are told.

"So what will happen when that term runs out?"

"Then we will have a full presidential election!" Which makes as much sense as all things Zambian! Just as well Zambians like elections as much as speeches.

Today there is a full complement of the workforce on site at Chilumba . . . all ten of them! However we are impressed. They have filled in all remaining footings and made at least thirty more 8" blocks for the foundation wall. There is not a lot to say other than, "Well done!"

"It is your continued presence here and your heart for our people which is really inspiring them," explains Mr Chalwe.

Pity then, that this is our last day in Kitwe till goodness knows when. How will they motivate themselves during our long absence? But all in all, they are coping better than we imagined they would. And if they still don't realise the economics of using a smaller lorry which can run more trips, against the false economy of a larger one which takes till doomsday to fill, then they have a few months in which to work that out.

For the moment we have a date at the bank with Faith. As we park in front of the Post Office building, the usual gaggle of street kids descends like vultures at the feast, jostling to guard the vehicle, spying out something to snatch while the door is ajar . . .

"Get your hand out the car!" Bob yells suddenly at one of them.

I turn on him, "Are you trying to start an incident, or what?"

He shrugs and we make for the bank. Only when we reach there does Mr Chama exclaim, "Oh no, my phone, I left it on the back seat of the vehicle!"

Which explains the street kid with his hand in the back of the car. Bob and Mr Chama race back to the car. Mercifully his phone is still there, but then spotting the same street kid still lurking there, Mr Chama picks him up by the collar and pins him against the side of the vehicle, "If you're still here when I get back, I'll have the police on you!"

Back in the bank we present ourselves at the Bank Manager's office. He is a she, and an encouraging sign of the increasing empowerment of Zambian women. A woman for president though? Not for a while yet, I think!

"I'm sorry but there is a freeze on accepting these," she explains. "You can return them to your bank in the UK."

"Unfortunately, we have already signed them over," I explain to her. "Technically speaking, they no longer belong to us, but to the person we signed them over to."

"Let me see what I can do." She picks up the phone and puts through a call, presumably to a higher authority than herself. All the while she shuffles and reshuffles several hundred pounds worth of travellers' cheques as if she was shuffling a deck of cards. Then she examines and re-examines the names, dates and passport numbers on the back.

*How high does one have to go in Zambia simply to pay a travellers' cheque into a bank account?*

Finally she replaces the phone. "I have permission on this one occasion, since you are clearly the people who gave this person the travellers' cheques." She glares at Faith for her complicity in accepting them.

232

"How long will it take for the money to come through?" We are aware we are racing against the advancing rainy season, but is she?

"Thirty, maybe sixty days."

This is not good news. It could well rain before the money comes through, washing away all the foundation work in the process. But as ever there is nothing to do but hope and pray . . . pray that the money comes through, that Faith has some in reserve to keep going for the moment, that the foundation slab will get done before the rains start and that God in His grace will grant us the time, energy and commitment to return and see the impossible finished.

As for the presidential election? Well that must run its course. With luck we'll be long gone before that shindig fully gets underway. Since we currently have our hands full coping with the logistics of running projects at opposite ends of Zambia, the election of a new president is one dilemma Zambians are welcome to sort out for themselves!

# CHAPTER TWENTY-FOUR: WHISPERS FROM THE PAST AT KAPUTULA . . . *September 10th – 18th, 2008*

Already we have been in Zambia for one week. At first five weeks seemed like a long time away from home. Now Zambia feels like home and Suffolk could be a million miles away.

Today should be Kafubu day, yet given its proximity to Kaputula, it may well be Kaputula which dominates the agenda. We find both Mr and Mrs Kauseni on site at Kafubu and indeed, once the beautiful church building has been admired, the conversation inevitably turns to Kaputula.

"Ah, you will see," Mr Kauseni shakes his toothless head. "Nothing there has changed. Mrs Tembo is still in charge, but also she is still absenting herself. Worse, no-one is knowing what she does with the funding she receives from the government or from the Global Fund."

"And the maintenance work?" we ask. "Has anything been done?"

"Nothing at all! Worse, the children are either not attending school, or their parents have moved them elsewhere. If they do come, there is rioting and fighting, because there is only one teacher to control them."

"What about bricks for the teachers' houses?" Last trip we left the community with the challenge of making blocks for the teachers' houses. So, has anything been achieved?

"They have made some." Mrs Kauseni says guardedly.

"How many are 'some'?"

"One, maybe two thousand."

Yet each house would need at least four thousand bricks. Just as well the committee made the decision to forestall work at Kaputula in favour of proceeding at Chilumba and Simooya.

"And that woman has elected yet another PTA committee." Mr Kauseni adds gloomily. "This time people from her own church who cannot even read or write. People are saying she is taking the money for the school and spending it on her church."

*Can this get any worse? At Kaputula, it always can!*

"Also we fear our dear friend Mr Chipotyo has become 'disturbed.'"

That's it! We decide not to venture near Kaputula today and instead drive back to Kitwe via the District Education Board office in Kalulushi, this time to put the deteriorating situation into higher hands than our own.

"Please, Mr and Mrs Cooke," beseeches Mr Kauseni as we say our goodbyes, "please do something on our behalf!"

The DEB's office is a typical relic of the colonial era made up of straggling one-storey offices set in a dusty compound. A few scattered euphorbias and cannas fail dismally to brighten the place up. This dreary place needs a good lick of paint and some life injected into it.

Inside we are directed to the office of the Staff Relations Officer who is a vision of loveliness in striking red and black and who reveals that today she is celebrating her fiftieth birthday.

"Congratulations!" we mutter fearing that with such news, the conversation is not set to go well. "Perhaps you are aware of the situation at Kaputula?" we try for openers.

"I have been there," she concedes.

"Then you know Mrs Tembo?"

"She comes often to this office."

*To complain of her treatment perhaps?*

"Then you will know also know the community has concerns about her, and also that the community has requested Starfish to build teachers' houses there? However, we wanted you to know that with the present situation, we cannot consider commencing any further building work there."

The Staff Relations Officer pauses for this to sink in. In building a school at Kaputula, Starfish has largely done the job of the Education Board for them. The same would apply with teachers' housing. Perhaps she senses a need to salvage the situation?

"You must speak with the District Education Officer herself," she concludes. And so an appointment is made for Monday next at 2pm.

But first it's time for the overdue visit to Kaputula. Yet again we plan to arrive unannounced, this time bringing the troops along for support: Messrs Mbai and Chama, as well as Evelyn Lumba representing Chep, whose management is now fully aware of matters at Kaputula.

We are just leaving everyone's favourite bakery when we receive a phone call from Mr Chipotyo. He has heard we are on the road and will we pick him up outside Kalulushi Post office. *So much for arriving unannounced!*

Even Mrs Tembo exclaims in feigned surprise, "I heard you were in the country." And the Kaputula workforce has reappeared on site today, further fuelling speculation that we were on the way, since no-one has seen sight nor sound of them for months.

We begin an inspection of the school. Yesterday the director of Chep gave us a lengthy document entitled: Guidance for Community Schools. This document confirmed our rights as funding partners to inspect the school. Little has changed since our last visit. No maintenance work has been done. Some rooms still remain unused, others are locked and the key 'unavailable'.

"The problem is we are only two teachers on site," excuses Mrs Tembo feebly, "myself and Mr Nkoma." Community schools are entitled to employ suitable unqualified staff from amongst the community, yet we have been told Mrs Tembo persistently refuses to do this.

Inside the school we find pupils grouped between four or five classrooms with only two people in control. As soon as the teacher leaves one room for another, discipline breaks down in the room they have just left.

Hearts plummeting as far as our boots, we head over to where a makeshift kiln is under construction for firing blocks for the teachers' houses. Mr Chama carries out a rough count and estimates about two thousand blocks have been made. "However they are of very poor quality." He chips one against another to prove how friable they are. "Even they were just made yesterday or today, while the work on the kiln is no more than one day's work."

Messrs Chanda and Nyrongo in their vests and Wellington boots shift uneasily from one foot to another. *No fooling the 'mzungus' when they bring such experts with them!*

We retire to Mrs Tembo's office to meet with her and Mr Nkoma. There is no point in inviting any community members to attend, since they and Mrs Tembo are still not on speaking terms. Besides, what we have to say is best said in private. Mrs Tembo appears subdued, leaving all the talking to Mr Nkoma. Nevertheless . . .

"Mrs Tembo," we ask gently for we are treading on eggshells, "do you feel your position here has perhaps become untenable?"

"There is much opposition to me from the community," she concedes.

"So do you think you can stay?"

"I think for me, it would be a blessing to go." Surreptitiously she wipes a tear from her eye. "However, both the chieftainess and the DEB's officer continue to support me here."

Which revelation suggests . . . *she is set to remain more firmly embedded here than a concrete block on the bottom of the sea!*

"Mrs Tembo, is it possible that you have been passing money to the DEB's officer in order for her to keep you here?"

Evelyn's bold question startles everyone, not least Mrs Tembo who gazes in undisguised pain at her former friend and ally. "How can that be?" she asks.

As we leave I take Mrs Tembo to one side. "I will pray for you, Mrs Tembo," I tell her. "I will pray that, whatever the outcome, it will be the best for both you and the school."

We retire to eat lunch, sharing around George's doorstep sandwiches made with white doughy bread and slices of plastic cheese since Evelyn, Mr Mbai and Katongo, who all travelled in the Chep vehicle, have brought none,.

Afterwards it's time to meet with Messrs Chanda, Nyrongo and Chipotyo. But in what capacity since, "The 'madam' has relieved us of our former positions on either the PTA or Building Committee," Mr Chanda informs us stiffly.

"Then let us say we are unofficial representatives of the community," suggests Mr Chipotyo treating us to his quirky grin. Which role must suffice, since no other community members are present, though we are also aware they are the ringleaders of the 'get rid of Mrs Tembo' faction. What they have to say, however, as ever is a catalogue of grievances against the 'madam'.

All we can respond with is, "The matter is now out of our hands. We are meeting with the DEB's officer on Monday."

"Our ED also wishes to be present at this meeting." Evelyn suddenly imparts this unexpected but welcome news. "Even he may be willing to take the matter to regional or parliamentary level."

"And will that work?" we ask dubiously.

"It can work," they all assure us. "Since the presidential election is coming up, the candidates do not want any trouble at grass-roots level and will deal with such matters promptly."

So even the late president's untimely demise may work in Kaputula's favour. But have we done enough to resolve issues here, or too much? Maybe we shall never know the full story behind the conflict between Mrs Tembo and this difficult community.

We mull over these thoughts later, as we stroll along the riverbank at the lodge just outside Kitwe where we are once again staying this trip.

Suddenly an almighty black face surfaces with a sploof mid-stream and watches us intently.

"A hippo!" I squeak in fear. Justifiably, since hippos kill more people in Africa than lions or elephants. They will attack boats in the water or, when on land, will not hesitate to charge at anyone foolish enough to get between them and the water.

We beat a hasty retreat to the rickety platform at the bar overlooking the river, there to watch its antics. This is our first clear sighting of hippo in the Kafue River, perhaps because the power cuts and ban on public drinking, mean less people but more hippos are making their way out to the lodge these days.

The next day we pass via Chep to confirm what passed the day before at Kaputula.

"Sadly I am also now of the opinion Mrs Tembo must go," agrees Evelyn. "However I also think Mr Chipotyo must assume a lower profile there."

I ask her wryly, "And who will break this news, since Mr Chipotyo is the last person to adopt a 'low profile'?"

"Even they are saying that side, there may be past history between Mrs Tembo and Mr Chipotyo." *Surely Evelyn isn't suggesting what we think she is?*

Later that same afternoon we moot this outrageous idea with Mr Mbai who to our utter amazement confesses, "I also have heard it said that side!" *Do they all know something we don't know?*

We can hardly credit this astounding suggestion. But then someone with something to gain from the situation could be rumour-mongering in the hope of creating a vacancy. Ah, the machinations of a rural community in Zambia, they would rival even those of a presidential by-election!

At 13.30 on Monday, in company with Alick Nyrenda, Executive Director of Chep, we travel to the District Education Board office in Kalulushi to see what can be done re the worsening situation at Kaputula, though the real issue remains the fate of head teacher, Mrs Tembo. An unpleasant task, yet continuing antipathy towards her, plus the way it is adversely affecting the running of the school, have left us no choice. Messrs Chipotyo and Kauseni join us as representatives of the community, while the District Education Officer invites her Educational Standards Officer and Planning Officer to join us also. We are a large group squeezed into the confines of her office.

First impressions are not good. The DEB's officer, who from her bulk clearly enjoys a lifestyle unknown to most Zambians and who rudely breaks off conversations to answer her cell-phone, immediately wrong foots us by saying, "So, we are pleased that your organisation is to build teachers' houses at Kaputula."

*Did we hear correctly?*

"The problem of persuading teachers to stay that side will be largely resolved once there is accommodation there. And have no fear," she settles into her stride, "our department will happily handle the funding for this project for you."

"Can we make one thing . . ." I start.

"Maybe more than one thing clear . . ." interjects Bob.

"At the present time Starfish has no intention of committing to any further building work at Kaputula . . ."

"Or of putting money through any government department . . ."

"At least until certain vital issues there have been resolved."

"Mainly the issue of management, which we understand is within the capacity of the DEB's office to do something about?"

*Between us have we made ourselves clear?*

Apparently not, because one hour later we are still skating like fledgling ice-skaters round and round the same issue . . . what the DEB's office is willing to do about it? At one point I scribble on my notepad and surreptitiously slide it across for Bob to read, "WE ARE GETTING NOWHERE!"

Perhaps also bored with getting nowhere, the DEB's officer suddenly turns on the two community members, one of whom, Mr Chipotyo, has dared to mutter, "Please madam, if I may . . ."

"Who are these people?" she demands, forgetting that the formalities of introduction made perfectly clear who everyone was. So, with patience wearing ever thinner, I repeat this information for her.

"Ah, these people," she sighs impatiently, as if Messrs Chipotyo and Kauseni weren't in the room. "They don't even recognise the value of education. Always they are saying they want schools, then they want houses for the teachers, but they don't understand what education is all about. When the planting season comes around, what do they do, huh?" She doesn't wait for a response but continues to plough her own furrow regardless. "They keep their children away from school!"

Barely able to contain my anger, I address her icily, "Mr Chipotyo is a former union shop steward on the mines. As for Mr Kauseni, his son is a head teacher of a Community School in Lufwanyama. You can hardly accuse these two gentlemen of not understanding the value of education."

So far Alick Nyrenda has remained very quiet. Yet he has kept his quiver full of arrows waiting for the right moment to fire one. Now he releases one, aiming unerringly for the bulls-eye.

"As I recall, we once had a similar problem with another head of a community school." Quietly and with exact aim, he fires another arrow at the target. "And when they failed to resolve it, if you remember, I took the matter to regional level."

Suddenly the demeanour of the DEB's officer changes, perhaps fearing that somebody higher might start examining her affairs. "I think maybe there is something we can work out between us to resolve this issue of management." Her simpering grin smacks of a devil sick of sin.

*Did we indeed hear correctly?*

"Of course, you must realise this will be very difficult for me to achieve."

*And just how difficult would that be?*

"There are many reasons why it is hard for me to get rid of a head teacher," she prevaricates. "In the first place, how can I sack her?" Eyebrows raised ceiling-wards for greater effect.

*You could try telling her!*

"Or even demote her? Even I must be sure that this is her wish."

*Which, to us, she has already stated it is!*

"So then what I must do is move her to another school . . ."

*Surely not, to carry on in the same way elsewhere?*

"Supposing that there is another school with a vacancy for a head teacher . . ." She splays her hands wide apart, pink palms uppermost, at the sheer impossibility of it all. *Who is she kidding?* In Zambia teachers are still dying of Aids and Aids related illnesses faster than they can be replaced. There are more vacancies than teachers to fill them!

Three long hours later, the meeting ends. Was it a success? Will Alick's quietly confident reminder that he is willing to go to a higher authority win the day?

It is 17.00 and our bladders are full to bursting point. Yet we still have to drive back to Chep, then make the half hour trip out to the lodge. And what about the community members who must wait for a minibus back to Kafubu Depot, then walk the four kilometres back to Kaputula?

"That is supposing they have the money for the minibus," suggests Alick as Bob starts up the vehicle.

"You don't think they have any money?"

"I don't think so."

So we crawl along the broken up road bumping over the unnecessary speed humps until we catch up with Messrs Chipotyo and Kauseni then hand over money for the minibus fare.

"And if you have something for us to eat, we would be grateful," says Mr Chipotyo sheepishly. "Only we have not yet eaten today." So I also hand over cool drinks and biscuits to see them through till they reach their homes, long after dark has fallen.

Today was our youngest granddaughter's birthday. Later we put a call through to UK to say Happy Birthday! Apparently she loves the Peppa Pig train set we bought her. We reflect on how she, like our other three granddaughters, has so much.

Then we think of Noami Kabwe walking up to three hours each day to and from school, and Messrs Chipotyo and Kauseni swallowing considerable pride to request food because they haven't eaten all day.

In contrast there is the District Officer for Education, whose heart earlier today appeared so unmoved by what we were saying, that good, kind, gentle Mr Kauseni finally exploded saying, "Madam, you are killing our children!"

Oh that by all the unpleasantness of today, we may have done something to stem that same slaughter!

It may have been politic not to show our faces at Kaputula again this trip. However the orphan carers' allocation still has to be dealt with. The planting season is rapidly approaching with the arrival of the first rains and they have again requested grain, fertiliser and top dressing.

It is not until late morning that we set off for Kaputula. Thankfully Messrs Mbai and Chama have so dramatically improved their timekeeping this trip that I feel emboldened to say, "I swear you are both turning into 'mzungus'!"

Just as we are on the road, Mr Chipotyo rings to find out where we are. "We are coming!" we tell him, which is such a very Zambian response, that I reflect maybe the opposite is true and . . . *we are turning into Zambians!*

Doubtless Messrs Chipotyo and Kauseni will have already given their version of what transpired in the DEB's office meeting. Nevertheless, from their expressions, it is clear the community would like to hear our version also. However, we are here to deal with the orphan carers' fund, NOT more argy-bargy.

But first, the list of orphans and carers must be revised to allow for those who have moved away, or whose circumstances have changed. Their poverty level may have worsened; some may even have died. Not surprisingly, this visit the list of names is revised downwards as a result of orphans being driven away by management and staffing issues at the school.

Mrs Tembo not surprisingly asks, "I have heard you were at the DEB's office?"

We can hardly deny it, since she has her spies amongst the community.

"Myself also, I intend to go there," she informs us. "And also to speak further with people at Chep."

We remind her that Chep management is fully aware of what is going on at Kaputula and that the ED was present at the meeting.

"Even Mr Nkoma also is thinking of applying for a transfer," she retorts.

To which there really is no response, because that would leave the school with no teachers and no pupils, so they might as well close the place down. Is this set to become the tragic last act of this long running farce . . . *one hell of a white elephant standing unused in the midst of the African bush!*

We say our goodbyes since we shan't be out there again this trip. Instead we are heading four hundred miles south to Choma in order to kick-start the Simooya clinic project down there. But is there anything we can say that might leave things here on a more positive note? Mr Chipotyo has angled for some words of comfort or encouragement all day. "And what about the teachers' houses?" he finally asks.

Not wanting to put him down too unkindly, we say, "Maybe when there are twelve thousand blocks made . . ." But twelve thousand bricks are a lot of bricks, enough to construct three teachers' houses for a school with no teachers and no pupils.

We drive a mile down the road and park under a tree to share a picnic lunch with Messrs Mbai and Chama. We fold down the back of the truck and share last night's cold chicken, bread from breakfast, cokes and apples.

"Ah, you Cookes are a real inspiration to us!" enthuses Mr Chama.

"And those people today were wanting you to keep talking and talking!" adds Mr Mbai. "Just to give them something to hope for!"

"That makes us feel humble," I respond. Though more accurately, guilty because, with our hearts so heavy with the sorrow of it all, all we really wanted to do was to get today over and done with before the long drive south.

As he eats, Mr Chama liberally tosses bones, apple cores, tissues, juice cartons out into the surrounding bush. "No, no!" I chastise him. "You must pick up your rubbish."

So he picks up every last bit of rubbish and ties it up in a red and yellow Shoprite bag. "So this is what we must do," he says, preparing to toss that also out into the bushes.

"No, no!" I yell just in time. "You must take your rubbish home with you."

But the reasoning behind that, as with the use of too much salt, the timing of trains and the state of the church in the UK, all are far beyond Mr Chama. He is as ever totally bemused by the antics of 'mzungus'.

As frustrated perhaps, as we remain, by the machinations of the Kaputula community, which yet again we are leaving, our hearts heavy with disappointment. Mutual understanding between two cultures? I wish!

# CHAPTER TWENTY-FIVE: A DREAM FINALLY BECOMES REALITY FOR SIMOOYA and Bob the builder willingly lends a hand
*September 27th - > October 3rd, 2008*

In the last week of this trip we leave the trials of Kitwe behind, hoping for an easier ride kick-starting Simooya Clinic project near Choma. Surely it can't prove any more exacting? Let's hope we're not forced to eat our words since Simooya has no clear budget, we have no clear idea how to get to it, other than, 'Turn off at the 20km peg outside Choma!' And we have supposedly been offered accommodation with a white ex-Zimbabwean farmer whom we've only met once, though Milden remains vague on this last one.

On Saturday afternoon we meet up with Milden who has just flown in from the UK to lend muscle to the completion of the rural health clinic near his former village. The three of us sit on the veranda of Lusaka's Holiday Inn, sipping cold drinks and overlooking a water feature where baby crocs sun themselves for the benefit of rich tourists who fly in and out, never touching the reality of Zambia's many problems.

"So on Monday, we can price up the smaller materials in Lusaka, then transport these in two vehicles." As before Milden unveils a bewildering array of contacts willing to lend vehicles and assistance to this project. However as yet, one dilemma remains unresolved, that of finalising our accommodation arrangements.

"Maybe it will be better if you stay in Choma," suggests Milden. "Since on Thursday we will be doing the bulk of the purchasing in town."

So, the delights of staying on the farm of an ex-Zimbabwean farmer must await another trip. Yet Milden's proposal gives rise to another conundrum . . . "If we're pricing up in Lusaka on Monday," I say to Bob later, "then buying in Choma on Thursday, what is happening in between? Driving to Choma certainly doesn't take two days!"

"Didn't Milden mention something about getting a visa for his son who's studying in South Africa?"

"Ha! While we could be down in Choma getting on with the job! Maybe Milden doesn't realise it's not Starfish practice simply to buy materials, dump them on a project then leave. Besides, we've only got till Friday there anyway."

So first thing on Monday we ring Milden up and announce, "Change of plan, Milden, we're travelling down to Choma tomorrow, not Thursday."

"Ah well, myself, I am at this moment in the Passport office sorting out my son's passport," is his only response.

"Right, Milden, half an hour," we respond not too generously, "then we meet up in the second class area to buy the materials."

But Milden has an atrocious sense of direction, He sends us in totally the wrong direction down Lumumba Road, which runs parallel to Cairo Road, Lusaka's main road, and dissects the second class trading area in two. Since Lumumba Road is constantly snarled up with traffic, few white people drive there. Today is no exception as we traverse it first in one direction, then the other, before finally spotting MICMAR SUPPLIERS on the opposite side of the road to where Milden claimed they were located.

Blessing number one, Milden is there. Blessing number two, Micmar sells everything we need and at a good price. Blessing number three, the helpful Asian manager takes us under his wing like a mother hen and in no time produces an itemised bill, even giving a discount.

A Zambian worker then locates the materials and piles them up ready for loading. Unfortunately our materials don't arrive all at once but in dribs and drabs, as do everyone else's. Soon there is a confusing array of paints, brushes, thinners, nails and tools littering the available floor space. Just in time I spot a fat Zambian swapping an inferior lock from his order for a better one from ours. Next his hand hovers desirous over our box of nails. From that point I stand guard over our purchases, only deserting them to complete payment. Even so, it takes all our efforts combined with those of Milden, his son and a supervisor to ensure our purchases arrive intact at our vehicle.

"So, we'll see you tomorrow?" I say as we leave Milden to continue sorting out his son's passport dilemma.

"I hope so," he responds somewhat dubiously. "Anyway my friend Mr Sima . . . will meet you at the African market near Batoka Clinic." But his friend's name is beyond us, so we can only hope Mr Sima-whatever is better at spotting out two 'mzungus' en route than we are at pronouncing his name, because if he's not, we're sunk!

On Tuesday we set off for Choma with £800 of materials in the back of the pickup, minus Milden but hoping to meet a Mr Sima . . . at Batoka Health Post. When we reach Pemba, Bob phones to tell him we are nearly there.

"Ah but your wife told me you were coming at 3 o'clock?" he responds.

"No Mr Sima . . . my wife said *in three hours*."

"Okay, you will find me at the African market." By which he means the roadside sellers of tomatoes, onions, squash, oranges, bananas, sweet potatoes and whatever else is in season. As soon as the vehicle pulls up, the sellers, mainly women, all think we want to buy *their* vegetables and that if they shout loudly enough or push hard enough or even climb in the vehicle with us, then for sure we will buy from them.

Mercifully Mr Sima . . . appears. Immediately we sense he is not happy, but whether because he thinks we gave him the wrong time, or because we still cannot pronounce his name the same way twice, who knows! At least he is there to guide us to Clive Wixley's farm where the materials will be stored in a secure lock-up. Without him we'd never find it ourselves, since Milden got us so hopelessly lost on our first visit. Fortunately Mr Simasiku follows a more direct route. I record the directions for future reference, should we ever have to find our own way there alone . . . *Right fork after the third cattle grid . . . cross the dam wall . . . don't look down! Ah, too late!*

We reach CHISOBOYO FARM at 12.30. There is no sign of Clive Wixley, who is out in the fields planting tobacco, even though outside the vehicle it is a searing forty degrees and hotter than Hades. We set off along a farm track following the power-line cable to locate Clive Wixley.

In the middle of a field, a line of African workers are planting tobacco by hand, while a massive ZAMSWIPE irrigator relentlessly sweeps round and round watering in the plants. Beside his battered blue truck stands a small wiry man. Clive Wixley greets us, shaking our hands with weather-beaten palms. His bare feet in sandals are equally weather-beaten while his face and lips are leathered from prolonged exposure to the sun.

We about-turn and follow him back to the farm. Someone has turned the thermostat up another two degrees as we stand watching his men off-loading the materials into a shed with a secure lock on it. I pray security here is better than that for the thoroughbred goats we tried to buy from the farm up in Kitwe.

A cool drink, a pee and a sit-down in some shade would be welcome. Yet Clive Wixley is off to plant yet more tobacco in the midday sun and we have yet to reach our accommodation in Choma. But what about our friend, Mr Simasiku? We ask where we can drop him, praying he doesn't say 40km back up the road at Batoka Health Post. But Mr Simasiku has other plans.

"I am needing to fix up the transport for the cement with the Choma Health Clinic," he says. *Wasn't he supposed to have done that already?* "And I am thinking we could begin pricing timber and other materials this afternoon?"

We remind him we have been on the road since 08.00 and instead drop him off at the Choma Health Clinic, telling him we will see him tomorrow when Milden hopefully also will have arrived. We're sorry if he anticipated an afternoon's entertainment, but right now we need to rest . . .

"We are not expecting you," a surprised receptionist tells us at Kozo Lodge. "How many nights are you wanting to stay?"

"Two or three, maybe four." The length of our stay largely depends on how soon Milden appears and . . . *how long it takes to get things done!*

They allocate us the same chalet as last time, the one with the front door that sticks, the bathroom door that won't unlock from inside and the curtain which falls off the rails when you draw it. Though they bizarrely agree the same discount as last time and not the higher price quoted by email. Confused? So are we, and also dehydrated, even though we have drunk our way through four days' supply of bottled water in one day. As the sun sinks, mercifully the blistering heat moderates allowing us to sit outside and watch a herd of impala which have strayed into the grounds and are grazing nearby.

Suddenly the phone rings. "Milden, how are things? Have you finished in Lusaka?"

Milden sounds agitated. "I have got the passport," he reveals. "However, I assigned the driver of the borrowed truck to collect the doors in my place and unfortunately in doing so he . . ."

"Don't tell me, he lost *our* doors?" I visualise the doors disappearing on the back of a clapped out truck belching smoke, to be lost forever in the warren of Lusaka compounds.

"No, he has not lost the doors, only the receipt," Milden assures us, as if that makes everything all right. "He has left the receipt locked in his office. But Mrs Cooke, it is all right because I am thinking that when you return to Lusaka at the weekend you can collect the receipt from this man."

We point out that since Milden got it wrong, perhaps it is his responsibility to rectify matters by collecting the receipt and posting it on to us when he returns to the UK. *As long as he has the doors?*

"I have the doors, Mrs Cooke," he says meekly.

So now we face up to four nights in a chalet where nothing works. Did I forget the tap, which swivels at 180 degrees? It wasn't working eleven months ago. Why is it still not working? Clive Wixley reckons *everything* works in Zimbabwe. Maybe we should be doing charity work there? Though things can't be all that great there, if he's no longer farming there!

What a night! The lodge is located not 100 yards from a railway crossing. At regular intervals freight trains rattle through emitting loud, long, ghostly wails of anguished warning to unwary pedestrians and drivers. Truck drivers trundle across speed bumps installed on both sides of the level crossing.

Then just our luck, an NGO workshop appears at breakfast. Its participants demolish breakfast faster than vultures feeding off a carcass. Eggs, bacon, toast, cereals, all disappear with alacrity. How Zambians love workshops, almost as much as fast food and mainly because of generous per diem allowances and nights away at someone else's expense.

"What's the betting their subject today covers eradicating poverty!" I rant as the last boiled egg vanishes never to reappear.

Today is our main day for purchasing materials for Simooya clinic project. Since there are only three hardware shops in Choma, comparing prices then purchasing materials should hopefully not prove too difficult. Even Milden has hit town first thing, having set off at 04.00 from Lusaka.

Unfortunately however Mr Simasiku, of the still largely unpronounceable name, has an agenda of his own, destined to sabotage all thoughts of quickly accomplishing anything. From the very start he queries everything: amounts, prices, sizes, specifications. In no time we have entered a war zone where blood will surely be spilled before the end of today.

Eventually we say, "Mr Sima . . . can we make one, no, maybe two things clear? We are not enlarging the clinic veranda . . . Nor putting on extra roof trusses . . . Nor blowing the budget on ceiling boards . . . Not that a rural health clinic needs ceiling boards!"

And all this before we even set foot in the first hardware shop, which doesn't stock much of what we want anyways apart from reinforced bars. Next door, yet still part of the same shop, they do however sell Chilanga cement, Zambia's own brand.

"They are selling Zimbabwean cement cheaper down the road," points out Mr Simasiku unhelpfully and by now wearing a dour expression.

"Ah but it is not such good quality," retorts Milden. "Maybe it is because they are putting stones and ash in to fill up the bags."

"Besides, we are needing more than fifty-two pockets," tries Mr Simasiku again. "Because of the extended veranda."

We let this pass and proceed to the timber yard where none of the timber sizes correlate with the estimate. "And we are needing more than it says there," Mr Simasiku tries once more. "For the extra roof trusses to support the extended veranda."

Enough is enough! *Read our lips, Mr Sima . . . we are not extending the veranda! Nor changing the roof trusses! Nor blowing the budget on ceiling boards!* Which announcement shuts him up, at least temporarily.

However nothing can be done about the timber till we measure up at the clinic. We return to the hardware store to purchase reinforced bars from one side of the shop and cement from the other. As we emerge from the dingy shop interior to the dazzling brightness outside, Zambian pieceworkers swarm around us shouting and gesticulating to grab our attention. "Piece work! Piece work!" "Me, Me!" "I am the one!" "I am first!"

Why should we pay more money to load cement already bought from the shop? We insist the men from the shop trundle fifty-two bags of cement out onto the pavement, then load them into the Ministry of Health truck.

*But where has the truck driver gone?*

"He has gone to get the petrol coupon before he can drive the truck," Mr Simasiku informs us.

*Couldn't he have sorted that earlier?*

Clearly not! Leaving Bob to guard the cement and await the return of the driver, I drive off with Mr Simasiku to another hardware store in search of roofing sheets. Mr Simasiku seems extremely nervous with a 'mzungu' woman behind the wheel even to drive such a short distance. And then the shop does not have enough of the larger roofing sheets until Friday. I pay up front for what he has and arrange to collect the balance on Friday.

"But Friday's our last day!" sighs Bob in exasperation, having caught up with us and learnt the bad news. "How do we know he'll have them then?"

"Well if you can do any better . . ." And there we call a lunch break. Leaving Milden and Simasiku to load the roofing sheets on top of the cement, we head back to Kozo Lodge for lunch, except . . . we can't get into our room.

"We will change the lock for you," they promise at reception once the door is finally opened. Then just as we finish a scrambled lunch, a receptionist appears to say, "Sorry, but you will have to change rooms."

In the remaining five minutes we bundle all our bags and baggage together in a heap in the centre of the room and race back to Choma to collect Milden. Of the truck there is no sign, either in Choma or on the road. Even at the 20km peg, there is still no sign and we told them to travel steadily.

"I can't see their dust!" moans Milden as we turn onto the dirt road. "Even they are travelling at some speed! Or maybe they haven't left yet?" But we don't even want to travel down that route.

Mercifully we find them unloading roofing sheets at the clinic. Milden is eager to set to work straight away. However there are no workers on site because he told them he wasn't arriving until tomorrow, so his eagerness must go on hold like a kettle simmering on the hob.

"Also two of my bricklayers are coming," announces Mr Simasiku. "They are coming from Batoka on motorbikes."

"Myself I am preferring Clive Wixley's bricklayer," counters Milden stoutly, perhaps also suffering the effects of the constant agro emanating from Mr Simasiku. *Why, oh why can't he just leave one arrangement as it is?*

Now Mr Simasiku diverts turns his attention to reducing the number of roof trusses. Instead of embedding them into the walls, he wants to rest them on top. *Is he now after releasing spare cash for a veranda perhaps?*

We tell him no, no and no again! The whole clinic structure could well crumble to dust if the entire weight of a galvanised roof is resting on three or four roof trusses, which have not been properly cemented in.

There is *still* more buying to do in town, even though the temperature has rocketed again to forty degrees. Constantly drinking water makes no difference, since our day's water supply long since became tepid and unpalatable. Though the truck will make another delivery to the farm, at least we don't have to drive out there again today. But that does not absolve us from the buying process, nor from Mr Simasiku's increasingly irritating interruptions.

Back to the timber yard, where they promised to make two sample interior doors by the end of today. But these turn out to be absolute rubbish, so we refuse to buy them, though we still need the timber for which we have now measured up. We sit in an airless office while they produce a receipt. Sweat is forming a puddle at the back of my neck and running in rivulets between my breasts. As for down below . . . don't even go there!

And we *still* have to return to the original hardware shop to collect fascia boards. There we find a delivery lorry is blocking the entrance while paid piece workers unload lethal planks of conti-board, swinging them off the back of the lorry with enough gusto to slice off your head in one clean swipe.

"Do you think I could sit down?" I plead weakly, feeling increasingly weary and teary to the point of being unable to tolerate any more from Mr Simasiku.

"What about the mukwa doors?" a voice pipes up. *Now who would that be?*

I groan loudly. "You buy the ruddy doors!" And with that I shut myself inside the vehicle and leave buying mukwa doors to the males of the species. "When you have the price, come back and I'll give you the cash!"

Since this morning I have carried almost £3000 in kwachas in my bumbag. Admittedly it has by now dwindled considerably, so that, left alone, I reflect . . . *will there even be enough for mukwa doors?* Sometime this afternoon we also bought window glass, though I have no clear recollection of doing so, other than that irritating man changed the specification of every single window in the clinic!

Finally we limp back to Kozo Lodge expecting to find we and our bags have been relocated to chalet number four. "Ah, but we have gotten new locks which we are just now going to fit," announces the receptionist.

"But you said we were moving so we packed up all our stuff!" I wail. "All I want is the toilet, a shower and a cup of tea, not someone fiddling around changing the lock on our door!" By now, no excuses, I am shouting.

"Okay, so here is your key." The receptionist hands me one. Probably the key for number five, because five minutes later we are still trying to get in.

"You go back to reception!" I yell at Bob. "Because if I go I will implode!" Which sounds far more dangerous than simply exploding. "Is it too much after a day like today, that you can't . . ." But he's gone, preferring not to wait around for the threatened implosion.

"We're moving to number four," he returns to announce.

So hot, sweaty, dirty, dusty, smelly and thirsty we move all our belongings to chalet number four where mercifully the door opens, but the bathroom door grates on the floor and there is no hot water because no-one thought to turn on the geyser. "If anything else goes wrong today, I swear I will *scream!*'" I say through gritted teeth.

But tonight Bob draws the short straw, one dried up chicken leg because the same vultures that devoured breakfast have now demolished all the chicken. He receives a free scoop of ice-cream in compensation. Initially we paid for two nights here. Tomorrow we must decide whether to stay or find somewhere else. That could depend on several factors: trains, lorries, boiled eggs for breakfast, or whether one of us gets locked in the bathroom overnight!

Sweet dreams? No such luck! In the morning we decamp to a 'mzungu' run lodge nearer to town where all appears a haven of peace and quiet. There is only one problem, the moving process makes us over an hour late for meeting Mr Simasiku who phones gruffly to find out just how long we will be. We find him kicking his heels by the shop where the doors are ready as promised.

"Also we can collect the glass," he says.

"But they said the glass wouldn't be ready until tomorrow," I remind him.

"I have already passed by there and it is ready." Which is in part true. It is ready as in cut, but not ready as in packed for transporting. While waiting around, we sneakily price up ceiling boards, hoping to collect sufficient damning evidence to say later, *'Well, you can forget about . . . '*

"Hang on," says Bob. "I think we might just manage . . ."

"Let's not be too hasty, at least till we know we're on budget." So we keep stum for now about the possibility of installing ceiling boards.

With glass on board, the journey to Simooya is slow. We don't want to present the community with shards of glass instead of windows. Milden is waiting to greet us. He looks refreshed and in honour of finally restarting work on his beloved clinic, he has donned a cowboy hat. Already this morning he has mobilised the workforce to make all of the roof trusses and to apply wood preservative on most of them.

"However we have run out of wood preservative," he tells us. "Also of fascia boards and we have used some of the wood supplied for the framework of the pit toilets to make extra trusses. And we need more cement and thinners . . ."

"Whoa! Hang on a minute!" Cowboy Milden has saddled up and is racing ahead. "All this will surely blow what little contingency there is," we remind him, though omitting to add . . . *and any thoughts whatsoever of ceiling boards!*

"First we must check you have enough essential materials to complete the clinic. Tomorrow we are out of here. An unpainted wall is not too serious, but if you run out cement or timber, that is." Unfortunately this announcement initiates yet another rigmarole concerning the size of roofing sheets required, to which no-one has an answer, not even Mr Simasiku.

"What is the size of the building?" demands Bob, seizing the opportunity to don his builder's hat. Since no-one knows, he measures it using the tried and trusted 'foot' measure . . . his feet measure one foot, so he paces out the length and width of the clinic building in 'feet'. Bob may be no builder, however his maths skills surpass the skills of those present. He works out we have twice as many 3.5m roofing sheets as we need, but only half as many 2.5m sheets. *Just as well then we're not off back to Lusaka today!*

But hang on a minute. I smell a rat, so I spell it out clearly, "The reason we have more large roofing sheets is because *someone* ordered roofing sheets for a clinic with an extended veranda, instead of the clinic being built according to the plan!"

"Aaaah!" A long drawn out sigh escapes from all and sundry gathered around. The madam has sussed it yet again!

"Enough is enough! Time for lunch!" I announce before an implosion threatens once more. *And we thought we were going to have an easier time of it down here in Choma!*

Bob and I escape to the neighbouring village compound where Milden's brother has made a 'village' hut available for our use, leaving Simasiku behind to explain to the community why not enough money remains in the coffers for the essentials, because the wrong size roofing sheets were ordered for a clinic perhaps only he was building!

Our 'executive' village rest lounge is quite something. Armchairs line two long walls, while a motorbike stands propped against a third wall. Against the fourth wall is an array of TV sets, radios and music player all powered by a solar battery festooned with wires leading in all directions. Every single chair is decorated with embroidered or crocheted antimacassars. There is also a coffee table and a dining table and chairs. We sink thankfully into armchairs to enjoy two boiled eggs each, which Kozo Lodge charged almost £6 for earlier this morning. From outside comes the sound of women ululating as they summon the men for their 'nshima' and relish.

We have no intention of lingering this afternoon, other than to settle what essential materials can be purchased tomorrow with the now dwindling contingency allowance. But no, Simasiku is complaining once more. Sometime during their lunch break, he reckons Milden *'stole'* his coke, which he brought with him to drink.

"Ah that man!" Milden reveals on the quiet. "You know a long time ago our two tribes fought a great battle. Since his tribe won, he now thinks he will lose face over a coke!"

Secretly I think there may be more to any bad feeling between the two of them than simply a missing bottle of Coca cola. To calm things down, I give Mr Simasiku some orange squash by way of compensation, while reflecting . . . *only one more day to go!*

By 09.00 on Friday morning Mr Simasiku is on the phone. Where are we? We are bemused, Messrs Chama and Mbai could still learn a thing or two from him about punctuality.

We pick him up outside Joko Hardware, along with the balance of our galvanised roofing sheets, 18 x 3.5m plus 8 x 2.5m. Since we do not have the lorry today, we must transport them in our pickup. We slide them in the back with the flap resting down and a polythene bag instead of a red flag fluttering from the back. With a prayer that we don't encounter a police checkpoint en route, Bob sets off at a cracking pace, considering we have twenty-six iron sheets protruding illegally almost two metres out the back of the pickup. "So far so good!" he jokes as he turns off onto the dirt road at the 20km peg.

His confidence is sadly misplaced. We're no more than three miles along the corrugated dirt road and travelling at 80kph, when disaster strikes. With a clatter and crash the entire load of twenty-six galvanised sheets thunders off the back and lies scattered along a hundred yard stretch creating a shiny galvanised road to nowhere. Even on a little used dirt road they are a hazard. Farmers travel at high speed along this road, not expecting to meet other traffic let alone obstructions. The sheets must be loaded back on as quickly as possible.

While Bob and Mr Simasiku retrieve and reload the iron sheets, I station myself back up the road trying to avert disaster. I stand out in the scorching heat, passing the time by applying the principles of Paulo Coelho whom I'm currently reading . . . listening to my surroundings. A hot wind rustles the dry leaves. Flies sensing tasty meat hone in buzzing angrily. The occasional long tailed bird twitters and stops for a look. But no cars come.

The iron sheets clatter as the men lift them back on the vehicle. But are they any safer? This time they prop them up against the cab of the pickup. I am voted driver, strictly forbidden to exceed 20kph, while Bob and a thunder-faced Mr Simasiku, who clearly feels adopting such a position is beneath his dignity, ride pillion behind holding onto the sheets. Neither of them enjoys the experience. When we reach our destination, Mr Simasiku is glowering at the affront to his dignity, while Bob suffers an acute attack of the wobbles and accuses *me* of driving like a lunatic.

"But I was never out of second gear all the way!" I declare, declining to mention having to negotiate the dreaded dam wall and the very real fear of letting one wheel stray even a couple of inches either side!

All is a hive of activity at the clinic, though there is one small problem . . . "The roof trusses don't line up," announces Bob the builder to everyone's dismay. And yes, some are sticking out further than others, while some are higher up than others. "Place a roof on those and it will be a very uneven roof indeed," he adds.

Milden eyes up this morning's handiwork. "I think we can just knock out a brick here and there and it will be okay," comes his expert response.

For once Mr Simasiku appears reluctant to get involved and stands to one side. Maybe he is he still sore about the coke, or has he finally run out of complaints?

"Milden" continues Bob, "every truss end must be level and the height must be the same all along the top ridge."

"Is that so?" Milden looks bemused at such desires for accuracy. *And we are leaving them this afternoon to drive back to Lusaka and catch a plane to the UK!*

So Bob patiently explains how they must check all the ends are level as well as along the top ridge. Only then can they start putting on the roofing sheets. He even climbs up a ladder to get them started, then paces off into the bush from where he shouts directions until all is finally declared level and ready for roofing. Phew, just as well we have Bob the builder on board!

"In fact we have just now worked out there are not enough palings to complete the job," says Milden. "Nor enough 4" nails. And the creosote . . ."

"Stop Milden!" I hold up my hand as if stopping a runaway cart and horse. "By the time we bought the extra cement, paint brushes, thinners and timber this morning, there is precisely K574 000 left in the kitty."

"Is that so?" Milden finally realises the bottom of the pot is reached.

"How much do you suppose we have spent this week?" I ask him.

"I suppose a little over the K15m budget," he concedes.

"Nearer K21m, almost half as much again as was allowed," I tell him.

"Ah, so we are a little over budget then!" Which is an understatement.

So, it's goodbye from us, and it's goodbye from them. As we drive back over the dam wall, we stop to enjoy the magnificent sight of two black and white fish eagles circling high in the blue heavens and calling plaintively one to the other. "So, will we come back to a completed clinic?" I put to Bob.

He sighs wistfully. In the past few days he has discovered a new side to himself, that of the Bob the builder, who would be more than happy to stay and see the whole roofing process through. Unfortunately that's not possible.

"I only hope so!" he says and drives on, taking care as ever not to let one wheel stray inadvertently either to left or right and thereby put us over the side into the dam, or worse, rolling over and over down into the ravine far below. Now that really would make a dramatic ending to this chaotic week, and with nobody but the fish eagles to witness our untimely demise. Though Mr Simasiku for one might not be sorry to see the back of us!

# CHAPTER TWENTY-SIX: MAKE MINE A PINK ONE . . .
## *Thursday May 28th, 2009*

On days that don't start well in Zambia, particularly when up in Kitwe, it's as well to recall Brenda Naomi Kabwe, one of eight former pupils of Musonda Community School being sponsored by Starfish. Brenda rises at 5am, walks one and a half hours on an empty stomach to reach school at 7.30am. She has five hours of lessons, then with nothing more than frozen sugared ice, walks all the way back again. *Yet Brenda considers herself lucky!*

So maybe guard dogs in the flats over the road barking all night long and only one breakfast instead of two arriving at the flat and that ten minutes late, is really nothing to moan about at all. This trip, because of all the power cuts last time at Kumasamba and also because we need to cut down our travelling times by staying in Kitwe rather than 15km outside, we have returned to Rosewood Flats where owner Grandma Chali has agreed a discounted rate.

"Are you sure it includes breakfast?" On signing in the receptionist produced forms for us to tick our preference: fruit juice, cornflakes, eggs fried, boiled or scrambled, bacon, pork sausage, beef sausage, baked beans, tomato, white or brown bread, jam or marmalade and tea or coffee. That is supposing any of these are available. This particular receptionist has not met us before. Nevertheless, she seems to know exactly who we are. Perhaps she can also guess what we might want for breakfast. Faced with such a bewildering choice for Zambia, we hadn't a clue.

"For sure," she smiled sweetly. But in Zambia such assurance meant nothing. Breakfast may well become chargeable.

Later Mrs Chali's daughter, who manages the flats and who does recognise us, clarifies, "Breakfast is included for people who pay the full rate, not the discounted rate."

"So what you are saying is . . ."

"You are entitled to breakfast."

Which makes as much sense as anything in Zambia. So every evening we fill out a form ordering what we want for breakfast and the time we want it. Next morning it arrives at the flat door courtesy of a chef in spanking whites.

At least it does when the young chef is on duty. When the older chef is on duty, panic reigns in the kitchen. Patricia, former cleaning maid now promoted to housekeeper, is roped in to help the old chef in a panic cooking fry-ups for the occupants of up to twelve flats. Which has happened this morning . . .

Breakfast does arrive, but only one, mine. "Ah, sorry," the old chef shakes his head helplessly. "The slip for the 'baas' must be at the bottom of the pile."

He hurries off to conjure up yet another fry-up. Instead of fuming, we recall Brenda. Brenda wouldn't even know what a cooked breakfast is, let alone whether it is ten minutes late. And in a country where most people start every day with no breakfast at all, we must consider ourselves lucky.

Today Brenda springs readily to mind because we are catching up with the former Musonda pupils, whom Starfish has already sponsored through four years of secondary education, and who now are in year eleven. Since both Damson and Evelyn have left Chep, we are in the hands of Kai. Previously Kai has created the impression her head is in the clouds, not out in the field with the desperate needs of orphans and vulnerable children.

"So Kai, which school is first?" The eight pupils out of the original eleven on the sponsorship programme are spread between four secondary schools. Usually it is a battle to catch all eight in the right school at the right time.

"Today we are only going to one school," announces Kai.

Our hearts sink at the prospect of an aborted trip before we even start. "But what about the others?"

"In fact there is no problem," beams Kai. "Since most teachers in government schools are currently on strike and there are no lessons, I have asked all eight pupils to present themselves at Mitanto School."

We are impressed. Forward planning is not a familiar concept in Zambia. Maybe this is a sign of changing times. Meeting all the pupils in one school will certainly make today's monitoring task easier.

However nothing is ever simple in Zambia. We arrive at Mitanto to find only three pupils waiting inside the deputy head's room. They look at us sheepishly. "So where are the others?" we ask.

"They are not coming."

"Not coming as in not yet here, or not coming as in not at all?" It is as well to get these things clear.

"They are not yet here," says one.

"But maybe because there are no lessons, they are not coming," adds another.

"But this is our only contact day," we turn to Kai. "What can we do?"

"In fact I have contact numbers for the parents and guardians of all of the pupils." Kai is rising in our estimation. "However I have no talk time on my phone."

I pass over our cell-phone so Kai can start phoning, while I contemplate the small miracle of even the most impoverished people in Zambia these days possessing a cell-phone, generally courtesy of a better off relative who wants to keep in touch with all the family.

A series of rapid conversations ensues in Bemba punctuated frequently with 'ays' and 'ahs'. "They are coming," announces Kai. "Three are on their way, while one went to her own school for lessons and afterwards she will come."

"But that makes seven pupils, not eight."

"Of the last one, Michael Bwalya, there is no hope."

We fear the worst. He has died, been abducted, left the programme . . .

"He is guarding the house and cannot come today."

"Surely his mother realises the importance of meeting his sponsors?"

Kai shakes her head. "His mother says she is very sorry, but today she must go to a funeral. There is no-one but Michael to guard the house."

Since funerals in Zambia last the greater part of the day, there is indeed little hope of seeing Michael. As we discuss the current needs of the orphans, the remaining four walk in. Seven out of eight is not bad going. They look bright, confident and we are delighted to see them once more.

"So all is well?" School fees were paid in January; all *should* be well.

The pupils glance covertly at each other. No-one wants to speak first.

"In fact me, I have no school uniform," says Brightness Malama, a pupil from Mukuba High School.

Strange, since he is actually wearing the navy and grey school uniform of Mukuba. We point this out.

"Each day I borrow this uniform from someone else in order to go to school."

Since he is an afternoon pupil, it is just possible he borrows the uniform of a morning pupil, though we cannot be sure. Now Tamara announces,

"Me also, my skirt is split." She shows her much patched and stitched skirt.

"But surely you had new uniforms when your fees were paid?"

Kai explains this was not the case.

"Also we are needing school bags," says Bathsheba, our bright star in the firmament, who originally scored the highest mark in the grade seven exam and who, four years later, is fulfilling all expectations.

"And shoes," adds Tamara Phiri who is wearing flip-flops, not at all suitable school wear.

"In fact it is two and a half years since we last received school shoes," says Bathsheba who slips easily into the role of spokesperson, confirming our belief this girl will go far.

"For me, all my school books are completed. I am even having to write inside the covers . . ."

"Whoa! Hang on a minute!" We halt their litany of requests. We had only allocated £100 this trip for the Musonda pupils. Besides this, there is only a small contingency fund of about £500, which the two on-going building projects will swallow up in no time. Clearly money sent through in January covered no more than school fees. We need to verify their most urgent needs, cover those today, then send through more money from the UK.

Eventually they agree their most urgent needs are school books, shoes and school bags. Purchasing these will overspend the budget, but not by as much as purchasing new uniforms.

We bundle all seven pupils into and onto the twin cab pick-up hired this trip. For them this is a great treat. Firstly there are no lessons. Secondly they get to ride up behind the 'mzungus' car. Everyone they pass will surely recognise they are not mere school kids, but kids of some importance riding up behind a pick-up driven by 'mzungus'.

First stop is Mama Africa, a wholesale outlet in town, which sells almost everything including exercise books and record books. The school books must contain eighty pages and be hard backed. We buy eight packs each of ten books, though the bemused Asian behind the till has clearly never sold eighty books in one go before.

Next we head for Bata shoe shop in the second class trading area where we have had dealings before. Shoes have gone up in price, about £12 for a pair of girls' shoes and nearer £15 for boys'. However, from past experience, we know to haggle for a discount.

The problem is finding enough shoes of the right size in the right style at the right price. Kelvin Mwape, a gleam in his eye, fondles a pair of brown winkle pickers with squared off ends. When persuaded to return them to the shelf, his face falls. Heavy duty school shoes are no match for brown winkle pickers.

Eventually everyone has a pair of shoes complete with shoebox. In Zambia a shoebox has one hundred and one uses. Such a treasure would never simply be discarded.

"They also have school bags." I point to some displayed above the cash-desk.

"I am thinking, they are not the right sort," announces Bathsheba.

"So what is the right sort?"

"They must be strong bags to carry all our books."

"Some days we carry all eight," adds Evans Mulwa, a big boy, for whom carrying eight books should not be a problem.

We agree the Bata bags look insubstantial. "So what sort of bags do you want?"

"We want bags like your bags," Bathsheba indicates our backpacks.

"But these bags are from the UK. I doubt you can get these bags here."

"Maybe in town," suggests Kai, "but they will be expensive."

"So what do you suggest?"

"We can try the African market," she says as if proposing an innocuous trip to Tesco or Waitrose.

My heart sinks. In all our years of coming to Kitwe we have avoided the African market like the plague, perhaps because the plague, or its near equivalent, is rife inside the market. On our very first visit Alick Nyirenda, then Director of Chep, warned us about the risks of cholera from the infected stream running through the centre of the market.

Not forgetting that white people rarely venture in there for fear of getting robbed or attacked. How effective would a guard of Kai plus seven under-nourished teenagers prove under threatening circumstances?

Worse, since the area surrounding the market is also a swarming mass of humanity, it is not safe to leave a vehicle there. Thus a dilemma of gigantic proportions has arisen. Who will stay with the vehicle, and who will brave the terrors of the market?

"Well you're carrying your backpack with everything in it," I say to Bob.

"While you're carrying a handbag stuffed with cash," he reminds me.

In the end I go, while Kelvin Mwape stays with Bob and the vehicle. Nervously I scramble out. Kai, dressed in scarlet top and teetering on 4" heels, leads the way threading between the mass of people followed by myself, Bathsheba, Loveness, Brenda, Tamara, Brightness and Evans. Immediately we are swallowed up more surely than Jonah in the belly of the whale by a heaving mass of humanity.

"Please don't leave me behind," I call faintly after Kai's receding back.

Inside the market is more orderly and less chaotic than it appears from the outside. True stalls are cramped together and pathways narrow and uneven or non-existent, yet the central part is uncovered and filled with stalls selling fruit, vegetables and dried fish. The rank sickly smell of dried kapenta sours the air as we wend our way in single file around the centre. Then Kai plunges once more into narrow uneven passageways between tiny crowded shops and stalls. At times the paths cross black infested streams and open drains and sewers. The noise level is deafening. People shout at one another to make themselves heard. Music blares from radios and CDs. People are hammering and banging on wood and metal as they repair, create and recreate the necessities of life.

Eventually Kai halts by a stall selling bags of every size, shape and colour, even bags like ours. Mainly they are second hand bags in good condition. Some are cheap foreign imports.

"How much are the bags?" I ask the man in charge of the stall.

"They are K85 000," he is quick to respond.

At over £10 per bag the price is outrageous. We may as well have gone into town, if not back to the UK. "We want eight bags, can you give a discount?"

"There is no discount. It is a fixed price."

"Why don't you sell us eight bags for K65 000 each? If you do, your wife will be very happy when you get home this evening," I try.

No deal. Maybe he doesn't have a wife. We head for bag seller number two who wants K75 000 per bag, less than the first one, but still quite a price.

"If you sell us these bags for K65 000 each," I tell him, "you'll be selling bags the rest of the day."

Still no deal.

"Maybe it's my white face," I mutter to Kai. Certainly I am the only white face in the market. "We have this problem when buying building supplies, so Mr Mbai and Mr Chama usually leave us sitting in the car."

"I think that is so," Kai concedes.

"So what is to do?" I certainly don't fancy wending my way alone back to the car.

"I think you must stay here with these pupils, while I find another bag seller and fix the price with him then come back for you."

"Maybe if you get him to write down the price?" I suggest. "Then he can't change it later when he spots my white face."

Kai takes one pupil with her leaving me with the other five. Are five pupils sufficient to safeguard against the perils of the market? God alone knows. I toss up a silent prayer for protection.

Kai is gone ages. The pupils become restive with wanting to wander off in search of other distractions. Eventually Kai returns, brandishing a piece of paper. "They have bags at K50 000, K40 000 and K35 000," she exclaims triumphantly.

We pick our way gingerly around to bag seller number three located in the very depths of the market. The alleyways have become even narrower. At one point we cross a rickety plank over a pitch black and foetid stream. *Cholera, was it Alick warned against?*

There are two bag sellers side by side. Neither seems unduly fazed by a white face in the depths of the market. They have bags of every size, hue, shape and colour. The kids are spoilt for choice. Bathsheba settles on a blue one, but then is captivated by a beige one with teddy bears imprinted on it.

"Me, I like this pink one," announces Tamara.

I point out tactfully that baby pink, powder blue and teddy-bear beige are not the best colours for the dust and dirt of the dry season, nor for the mud and rain of the rainy season. So they search out bags in more suitable khakis, browns and navy. Now the overriding criteria shifts to the number of side pockets and internal pockets each bag contains. They pass bags from one to another, eagerly opening and closing zips and fasteners.

Eventually everyone has a bag, though some come from one bag seller and some from the other so each one must be dealt with separately. Even at the last minute Bathsheba changes her mind yet again, only to find . . . "Oh no, my bag is the same as the bag for Evans!"

"Does that matter?" By now I am eager to return to the car. I have spent long enough in the stifling confines of the market, while Bob has equally spent long enough in a stifling vehicle with only one teenager for company. Someone may even have mugged him.

"But Evans is in the same class as me," says Bathsheba.

"So do you want to change it in case your bags get mixed up?" I ask her.

"No, I can know which one is mine," she assures me.

Now we need receipts.

"You want a receipt?" asks the first bag seller incredulously.

"We need a receipt for the records. You have a receipt book?"

He searches round for anything resembling a receipt book. There is nothing. "Any piece of paper will do," I tell him. "Just write the number of bags and the amount."

This takes some reckoning up, because although the bags started off at various prices, they have magically all become one price, the highest, K50 000. I am too weary to argue and pay the price.

"You want another receipt?" asks the second bag seller clearly under the impression that one receipt is enough for any 'mzungu' in any one day.

"I need a separate receipt for the bags you sold me," I tell him.

"I will see what I can do," he says and disappears for ages. He returns bearing a dog-eared receipt book borrowed from another stallholder. He then painstakingly writes out in full the purchase of bags from his stall, then rips the receipt as he removes it from the book. I tell him not to worry. It is fine.

We retrace our footsteps along narrow alleyways and broken footpaths across drains and streams and sewers, then through the seething mass outside to find Bob and Kelvin mercifully in one piece and still inside the car.

"Where on earth have you been?" demands Bob fretfully. "You've been gone for ages!" Which under the circumstances is fully justified.

"Don't ask!" I groan.

Later he recounts how Kelvin kept him going with endless expressions of gratitude for what Starfish is doing for him and what a big difference his education will make to his life.

When Kelvin finally dried up, they were entertained, *surely that isn't the right word,* by street kids washing themselves in water running from the pipe which drains out of the market, the same black, infected water we crossed over gingerly inside the market. Some street kids were smoking boiled dagga, the cheapest dope there is. They were out of their minds on the stuff. According to Mr Mbai they smoke it to forget the horrors of their existence.

We drive the pupils back to Mitanto High School. Though it is lunchtime and there are no further lessons today, most of them left stuff there to collect. At the school gate we toot to enter. A head pokes out. "You cannot come in," protests the guard more convincingly than if he was guarding Lusaka Prison.

"Why ever not?"

"The teachers are on strike," he says. "If I open the gate to let you in, all the pupils will get out."

Through the space where his head is poking, we can see hundreds of pupils milling around, pushing and shoving at the prospect of an open gate. We've heard of lock-outs during strikes, but lock-ins?

"There was a riot here yesterday," Kai informs us. "The pupils are angry because they have no lessons but are being kept inside the school. Maybe it is safer if we move further along the road."

We drive a hundred yards along the road to let off the seven pupils each clutching a Bata shoe box, a school bag and a pack of ten school books. We take their pictures and shake hands all around.

By now the noise behind the school gate has built to a crescendo. Sensing that some of their fellow pupils are outside while they are still inside, the pupils mount a mass attack on the school gate. Both gatekeeper and gate give way to pressure and a seething mass of chanting and shouting pupils swarms out onto the dirt road. It is time we weren't here. The middle of an African compound is no place for white people when a riot, school kids or not, erupts.

It has been a satisfying if rather eventful morning. Time now for a swim in the pool and lunch. But what about Brenda?

Ah well, Brenda still faces an hour and a half walk to reach her home. There she eats her one meal of the day. Maybe then she does some homework before darkness falls. That is unless her mother needs her to look after younger brothers and sisters, or go to the market in the compound and sell vegetables for a few hours. Then of course she would have to do her homework later by the light of a single candle.

But hey, didn't we say right back at the start of the chapter, Brenda, she's the lucky one, isn't she?

# CHAPTER TWENTY-SEVEN: TAKING THE BUTTERFLY HIGHWAY TO BUILD THE HOUSE WITH NO PLAN!
## *May 19th -> 21st & June 9th -> 12th, 2009*

Any trip to Zambia is fraught with anxiety as to what we will find on our return there. This year it is no less so to Simooya, where last year completion of the rural health clinic was left in the questionably capable hands of Milden with his cowboy hat, Mr Simasiku who was determined to change everything, and a community that had never built anything but mud huts.

Returning in May 2009, Mr Simasiku is currently on leave in Livingstone, while Milden is not joining us until later in the trip, leaving us to face alone the community and its endeavours to complete the clinic. And there it is, looking quite superb, its shiny roof and spanking white paint sparkling against the blue dry season sky. So what were we so nervous about? True, a couple of things need purchasing immediately, wood preservative for treating the timbers and something to attack termites which have taken up residence uninvited both inside the clinic and in one veranda pole.

Four holes for pit toilets have been dug and one already concreted in. And if because of heavy rainfall, the second one caved in, while in the third the brick inner lining collapsed for the same reason, so what! In constructing a fourth hole, they're on the case after all.

"We are wishing to show you the site for the nurse's accommodation," announces the project secretary. "Which we are proposing should be made bigger."

By that he means the nurse's house, which we *never* said we were building, only to find that, since building teachers' housing at Kaputula *still* remains on hold, in fact we *are* building a nurse's house here. Then the two-bedroom house, which later became a three bedroom one, and has now just been enlarged still further. With moveable walls perhaps? Noting our confusion, they offer to take us tomorrow to visit a nurse's house under construction at a place called MFUNGU.

Is there any option? Not really!

On Tuesday we collect Howard from the District Health Office in Choma. But there is one slight problem. Howard has never been to Mfungu. "Though they have told me where it is," he says none too encouragingly.

The turnoff to Mfungu lies 40km out of Choma back towards Lusaka. Immediately across the rail track we turn right onto a seemingly endless red ribbon of dirt road stretching as far as the eye can see into the distant haze of the bush. There is little sign of life along the way so that we wonder if anything lies along this road, let alone a health clinic. At last a crossroads bears a sign to Mfungu School, which looks hopeful.

"Thankfully it's a good road," says Bob. Too soon unfortunately, because the road immediately deteriorates into a bumping, grinding lurch, permitting progress at no more than 10mph till we reach a spanking new clinic with a half built nurse's house next to it. There is no sign of life. Bob sets to and begins pacing out the nurse's house using the ever ready 'foot' measure and proves it to be larger than what is planned at Simooya.

"Do we need one that size?" we ask Howard.

"For reasons of economy, yes," he assures us, "because a larger house will take either a nursing couple or two nurses of the same sex."

"Two for the price of one?" Zambia's version of a BOGOF perhaps?

"But there is even another nurse's house," he offers, "nearby at NDONDI."

So we bump and grind our way along another atrocious track to reach Ndondi clinic where smiling Nurse Musonda hastens out to greet us. "Welcome! Welcome!" she enthuses under the mistaken impression that we are inspectors come to inspect her clinic.

We assure her we merely want to see her house. But first she insists on showing us proudly around her humble clinic before taking us over to her house. The clinic is simple in construction. There is a veranda waiting area, nurse's reception room, treatment room and labour ward for the women who frequently give birth by candlelight, since there is no on-site electricity and the hurricane lamps might explode. Radio and cell-phone are Nurse Musonda's only means of contact with the outside world, as long as there is a signal and no thunderstorms. Even then she can only handle non-urgent cases. Emergencies must wait for a vehicle to come out from

Choma hospital to transport into town both the patient and a relative to look after them. Return transport is not provided.

This may sound horrendous, yet it is 100% better than having no health facilities at all which sadly is still the case in so many parts of rural Zambia. Now the construction of a clinic here at Ndondi, along with the adjacent school has created a community centre in the heart of the bush. Progress indeed! And yes, Nurse Musonda's house, by the 'foot' measure, is the same size as the Mfungu house.

So where does this leave us? With some hard thinking and the need for a community meeting back at Simooya on the morrow.

Wednesday morning dawns cloudy and cold. This year winter has arrived early in Zambia. Today we face a community meeting at Simooya without the benefit of either Milden or Mr Simasiku. However we do have on board a Tonga interpreter from the Choma Health Clinic called Florence whose hair is streaked in lurid shades of lime, lemon and orange. Decidedly fruity! With her is Wilson who is on the building side, which could prove useful. With us, are two small bottles of deadly poison to be used solely for attacking termites in situ.

This is our last visit before Milden joins us in June, so it's important to get things right. The community is out in force, workmen, elders, mothers, babes in arms, toddlers and assorted villagers and committee members. First they want to know what today's agenda is, which proves embarrassing because there is no more an agenda for today's meeting than there is to date any accurate plan for constructing the nurse's house. But such technicalities can always be overcome as we go along . . . as long as no-one asks too many questions!

Bob begins by telling them how we have been raising money in the UK to pay for the materials for the nurse's house. Then I outline what needs doing before we return to commence work in three weeks' time: applying wood preservative to the remaining roof timbers in the clinic, assassinating the termites and completing the pit toilets.

"Will you be providing protective clothing for the application of the termite treatment?" demands one villager.

"When will you build a community school for us?" asks another.

"When will the clinic be operational?" comes from yet another.

"We would like to thank you for the football and the football jerseys which you sent us last year," this last from Milden's brother.

Though we manage to field the first three questions, this last one floors us because it wasn't us! So we tell them, then escape to much singing and clapping and dancing and ululating from the jubilant women along with the promise to return in three weeks' time to begin work on the nurse's house.

Three weeks later Milden flies in from the UK, clearly geared up for a week of intensive effort. And if after yet another gruelling trip up to Kitwe caused by the snail's pace progress at Chilumba and the on-going saga at Kaputula, combined with the long drive down, we feel more like a week's holiday, we put this behind us and knuckle down. Milden has booked an afternoon appointment at the DHO, which there is no avoiding, since we made it clear three weeks ago that it was impossible to build a nurse's house with the wrong plan and no Bill of Quantity, so would they please get something together for our return . . . *which is now!*

Unfortunately Mr Mwani who assisted us before is not around so one of his minions has been delegated to help. "I have here three plans," he says.

But since he can't give us even one let alone all three and the agreement to photocopy any of them is made decidedly reluctantly, we fear progress will grind to a halt. "And the Bill of Quantities?" we remind him.

He rummages round in Mr Mwani's desk and eventually produces one. But is it for the smaller or the larger house? "It is for the larger house," he fibs shamelessly.

All three of us pour over it, yet it is quite clearly for the smaller house, since it is for less materials. "Do you have one for the larger house?" we try.

"Okay, so I will photocopy this Bill of Quantities also, then maybe you can work it out for yourselves. Even you can start marking out the foundations," he offers generously.

"But what if they make them the wrong size?"

"Ah, you must not pour any cement in or build any walls."

*So, no sweat then!* We turn to the thorny issue of transport, which was formerly Simasiku's brief, but Simasiku still has not appeared. It's beginning to look like everyone has gone AWOL down here in Choma. *Is there something they're not telling us?*

"There is a lorry, but no petrol," says our unhelpful helper. "Maybe you can see Agnes." But Agnes is not there. "Maybe you can see the DHO?" But she is closeted in a meeting.

We are rapidly losing patience. The three of us have flown in from the UK bearing funding along with a willingness to build a nurse's house for a clinic with no plan, the wrong B of Q and no prospect of any transport to get building materials out to the project. With steam just about emerging from our ears, we are eventually shown into the office of the DHO.

"Regrettably," she tells us stiffly, "the Ministry of Health is currently experiencing some funding difficulties." *Is she referring to the scandal of the missing K15 billion? She is indeed!* "And unfortunately at the present time all of the petrol stations in town have closed down their credit facilities to us."

And it will take a minor miracle to set this to rights before tomorrow, when we need to start shifting cement in bulk out to the project. Water into petrol perhaps? If Simasiku returns, maybe he will turn out to be the miracle worker we're currently praying for?

In the night I dream it is raining. In June in Zambia, surely that cannot be? Yet it is, cold and cloudy and raining. Aaggh! The world is turning upside down.

While we wait for Milden to arrive in town, we set about drawing up a Bill of Quantity for the nurse's house using three others. We have the original B of Q for the smaller house, the one we were given yesterday for an even smaller house and a Chilumba B of Q drawn up by Mr Mbai, which, if nothing else, might at least give a more accurate idea of prices and amounts. Added to this melting pot is our own limited and indeed questionable building experience.

We have just completed estimates for substructure to superstructure when Milden phones to say we can go to the DHO to see if they will give us a lorry plus fuel. Today we are shown into Mr Scouoni's room and told, "Yes, we have a lorry and fuel, but the driver has not yet arrived."

Eventually the driver appears. "So we can go?" we ask, but it appears first he must get the voucher for the fuel. So we wait again under Mr Scuoni's at times bored and bemused gaze.

"I think you are perhaps not comfortable with us waiting around in your room?" asks Milden sensing his discomfort.

"I am," concedes Mr Scouoni, "though I have other things to do. Are you suggesting I should leave everything to deal only with you?"

Whoops, relations with the DHO take a sudden nosedive. I escape to the loo for a bit of light relief, yet return to find still no driver and still no lorry or petrol. Eventually one hour later we have all three along with a voucher for petrol.

It takes the rest of the morning to load the lorry with cement (*but have we bought enough?*), conforce wire (*but is it the right thickness?*),

270

ant and termite treatment (*but is it the right strength?*) plus brushes, nails and thinners all according to our hastily concocted and possibly totally inaccurate B of Q.

In the afternoon we resume purchasing again.

"That man said you will purchase another 10 litres of fuel for the lorry," announces the lorry driver, presumably meaning Milden, or maybe Scouoni.

"Don't you have enough to get to the farm and back?" we check.

He assures us there is not, so we send him over to the garage to buy 10 litres and 10 litres only. However there is no diesel at the garage. "I will drive slowly so I don't waste fuel," says the driver and promptly drives off at 100kph, which leads us to think . . . *was he trying it on?*

We chase after him as far as the Wixleys' farm where the bulk of the materials will be stored until needed. As we finish offloading, Clive Wixley appears, looking as weather beaten as ever and working his butt off to save his entire mealie crop from the unseasonable rain which has swept across southern Africa, Botswana and Zimbabwe wreaking destruction and catching Choma in the tail end of its path.

"And if the rain continues?"

"Ach man, I could lose my entire crop!"

In spite of the threat of imminent disaster, Clive invites us for a cup of tea at the farm. What a setting! Sitting looking out from the veranda perched on an incline overlooking the shimmering waters of the dam he built himself, it is a scene of total peace and seclusion, though it is all secured by four guard dogs and surrounded by an eight foot high electric fence. What price paradise!

"Theft is a real issue," he tells us. "These guys thieve everything, seed, fertiliser, sacks of harvested corn. Man, I give them seed to grow their own mealies and still they steal from me!"

Clive's wife Elma is a gentle soul who repeats their offer of accommodation for our next trip. The Wixleys built and lived in two basic chalets before the main farmhouse was constructed and these Elma offers for our use next time. As we talk over past times, Milden arrives puffing and panting. While we were drinking tea and admiring the view, he was waiting fuming at the village.

We tell him, "Slow down, Milden, this is Africa, not the UK!"

We drive back to Choma, trying not to hit any of HH's cows on the way. This glimpse of the enviable lifestyle of the Wixleys, who have kept Africa, even if at a price, has proved unsettling. But would we ever consider returning permanently? And if we did, could we still hack it? Maybe with the heightened need for security, theirs is not so enviable a position after all.

The wind howls all Tuesday night and Wednesday dawns dull and dreary. We are wearing sweaters, socks, shoes and even a vest. Yet more rain is forecast. Zambians are taking it hard, standing huddled around or else hurrying to work clad in parkas, blankets, overcoats, even woolly hats, scarves and gloves. Can this be the tropics? At this rate we shall be glad to return to the warmth and sunshine of the UK!

Milden seems confused when we find him at the DHO. First of all we can't have the lorry today, then we can, but only if we put petrol in it.

"But there was no diesel yesterday," I remind him.

"Ah but there will be today," he assures me.

Bob follows the lorry driver to the garage to ensure he puts 15 litres only of diesel in the tank. Meanwhile at the hardware store I negotiate the return of one roll of conforce wire of the wrong thickness because somebody got the calculations wrong. Would that somebody be us? *Oh for our dear friend, Mr Mbai, to do all this calculating for us!*

"The problem is your purchases today do not total the amount of the refund due," the sales person tells me and refuses outright to give me the cash back. "If you want cash you must go to the boss's office."

But unfortunately the boss himself is not there but at the airport and maybe we can go to the airport? I tell him impossible, or words to that effect!

"Then maybe you can buy some more things to the same value?"

But we only want materials from the other side of the shop and the man that side is not at all happy. "So you are asking me to give you doorframes for which you will not be paying me?" he asks incredulously.

By this time Bob has arrived to discover one doorframe is bent. So while he shouts in one ear about exchanging the doorframe, the man from the shop shouts more loudly in the other ear about where his payment will come from. Meanwhile the lorry driver starts moaning there is not enough petrol and Milden shouts over and above everyone about the time it is taking.

Somehow amidst all this brouhaha, we end up with a lorry load of conforce wire, brick force wire, one unbroken door frame, various steel rods and four pots of paint and all without paying for them. Are we finished?

"I cannot give you a receipt until I have yesterday's receipt back," announces the sales person. But that we don't have, so we agree to come back later to settle the receipts.

So, can we go? Not a hope! There are still the remaining doorframes, window frames, latches, locks and stays to collect from a different shop, because the lorry driver claims he knows where they are a better price. But that's better as in more expensive. We are past caring and pay the inflated price. At least the Asian owner does have everything in stock right down to the last window stay.

So, can we go? Ah no, suddenly the lorry driver notices four window frames are of the wrong sort. Not surprising, since our knocked together B of Q hadn't quite got as far as window level. So off come four window frames and on go four different ones, the right ones but naturally the price is different. Yet more adjustments, which, with discounts and knockdown prices and VAT added in, promises to make this an absolute nightmare for the purposes of auditing.

We send Milden and the lorry on ahead telling them we will join them this afternoon. Since we don't meet the lorry driver on the way back, we can only pray that he has returned the original roll of conforce wire to the correct hardware shop so that we will get our receipts.

We arrive to find . . . "We have turned the nurse's house around to face the other way." Apparently it was facing the sun, which is not exactly an ideal position in sunny (sic!) Zambia. An easy enough matter since digging the foundations has only just started. *But why didn't anyone think of it before?*

We carry out a tour of inspection. The trenches are underway and going well. The materials have been properly stored both here and at the farm. Work has recommenced on the pit toilets. Not a lot of point in hanging round then unless, like the male spider, we want to get eaten after the fun is over.

At least on Thursday the sun is shining when Milden arrives at 09.30 for a budget meeting to explain exactly how much has been spent this week and what little is left. But can Milden stay focused long enough to take it all on board.

"I am thinking it will be good to get the electricity supply connected to the clinic . . ." Then, "I have approached the Maidstone Rotary Club on the subject of a running water . . ." Followed by, "On the question of dental services . . . " And finally, "There must of course be toilet facilities for the nurse's accommodation."

"Stop Milden!" I hold up one hand. "The clinic toilets aren't completed yet. Even the clinic itself still needs creosote on the timbers and a veranda pole replacing, not forgetting filling up from beam to roof level."

"And you've only just started digging the foundations for the nurse's house this week!" adds Bob for good measure. "One thing at a time!"

For the moment it's into Choma to purchase any last materials the budget will allow for and to deliver them to the building site. It's a pleasure to drive out to the clinic today. After the dreary weather of the past few days, today's sun has produced a haze of brightly coloured butterflies, which throng the dirt road out to the farm, creating a colourful cloud of yellow, blue and white around the vehicle. I fancifully rename the road the Butterfly Highway.

We arrive ahead of Milden allowing time to inspect the foundations and stroll over to the neighbouring village. But what is all this building work taking place there?

"This is my new house," announces proudly Milden's brother of the long shorts and mobile phone dangling from his waistband. "Though I am using my own local cement," he hastens to add.

We admire his handiwork. "But why six bedrooms?" Naively we assume he has a lot of children.

"That is for my six wives." He hangs his head. "In my youth I was a very foolish man and married too many wives."

Later, while visiting a small cultural museum in Choma, we learn polygamy is still fairly common amongst rural Tonga people. These village marriages are neither officially recognised nor recorded. Milden also reveals that every time his brother brought another wife home, his mother would get mad and shout at him, "Do not bring another wife to this house!"

Friday is our last visit to the clinic. Our time in Choma and indeed in Zambia is almost over. A village meeting is scheduled for 10.00, but will Milden, who has phoned to say he is in town, arrive in time? Indeed we have passed by the farm to drop off a bottle of wine for the Wixleys, inspected the electoral role of all the six thousand neighbouring villagers who will benefit from the clinic, been over to see how the foundations are progressing and shaken hands all around before Milden finally arrives. "So, we can start now?"

"Maybe by 13.00 most people will be here," responds Milden.

We remind Milden, we'd like to reach Lusaka before dark, so he proposes we say just say a few words. So we say a few words reminding the community of what we hope to see on our return.

Then Mr Simasiku, who has miraculously reappeared on the day of our departure, also says a few words leaving the community in no doubt he will resume full control in our absence. He is followed by Milden, who says rather a lot of words alternating emotionally between Tonga and English, because in his great emotion he forgets which language he is using.

"Did you hear him mention a school," I mutter aside to Bob. *Maybe we'll leave that one to someone else!*

And so it's time for goodbyes. Simasiku can barely conceal his relief. Milden remains overwhelmed at what Starfish has done for the community, as does his brother, though fortunately omitting to bring up again the gift of a sheep. Maybe his numerous wives create a heavy demand on his resources. The villagers look apprehensive, perhaps at the thought of all the work that lies ahead. Only the women are jubilant as they clap and dance and ululate us on our way.

"Do you think they can actually build this house?" I ask Bob as we drive away.

"Who knows! We've done what we can with purchasing materials, now it's up to them."

"Hey, slow down!" I call out suddenly.

"Whatever for?" he demands. "I thought you were the one in a hurry to get back to Lusaka?"

"I am, but at this speed, you're massacring all the butterflies!" Which he is because sadly the speed of our passing windscreen is committing a massacre of gigantic proportions on the poor hapless clouds of tiny winged creatures.

"Massacring the butterflies?" Bob repeats incredulously shaking his head. Nevertheless, he slows his speed thus diminishing the massacre somewhat. After all, it pays to get one's priorities right. It may be raining out of season. We may have left a community with barely enough materials to build the wrong nurse's house to the wrong plan entirely, but at least let's not give the butterflies any cause to complain!

## CHAPTER TWENTY-EIGHT: SENT BY GOD, WHAT AGAIN, but did somebody move the goalposts when we weren't looking?
*May 29th & June 2nd 2009*

May 29th is the day scheduled for our 2009 visit to Kaputula. As we bump and grind our way with Kai and Mr Chama along the atrocious road, we ponder together just what we will find there this time. Will the community still be riven by disputes? Will the school have fallen even further into disrepair? Will yet more pupils have left and gone elsewhere? And after last year's emotionally charged meeting at the DEB's office, will Mrs Tembo finally have moved on?

Since Kai is more used to the niceties of the Musonda pupils' programme, she appears somewhat perturbed by what the rest of us are saying. And rightly so, the Kaputula community at one time so unnerved Chileshe, that she refused to go back there!

As ever we plan to surprise them. But first we need to get there. This year the rains finished unseasonably late barely two weeks ago after one of the longest and heaviest rainy seasons in living memory. Conditions have rendered the road so bad that for once Bob can say with conviction . . . "This road surface is getting worse!"

Ridges of still drying mud ride as high as the wheel hubs. Cavernous potholes gape jaws open wide threatening to swallow us whole along with the hired 4x4 vehicle. Humps at times larger than a camel's backside seriously hinder progress. It takes twice the normal travelling time to get there.

Ah Kaputula, how this place tugs at our heartstrings! Bob negotiates the vehicle down the narrow sandy track till finally the now familiar blue and white building hoves into view.

Deputy head teacher Mr Nkoma, for once smiling broadly, emerges to greet us. "In fact now I am the acting head teacher," he announces with

276

aplomb. Indeed he wears a new air of authority along with his smart tie and white shirt and neatly pressed pants.

"And Mrs Tembo?" we ask.

"Ah, she has gone to another school at Chililabombwe."

So, a positive result from that unpleasant meeting in the DEB's office last September. We gaze around at the familiar sight assessing whether anything has changed. At a rough count over one hundred pupils are on site today. Maybe still not up to the full complement of the old days when the school was merely a dilapidated pole and thatch structure, yet certainly an improvement on last year's dwindling attendance.

"And the staffing situation?" Perish the thought Mr Nkoma now sails this unruly ship alone and unmanned on the turbulent sea of Kaputula!

"Myself and two other qualified teachers are here now," he tells us. "Also there is one student teacher who is living in the community. Even Mr Chapuswike has been reinstated as chairman of the PTA."

This is all good news, especially that grey-haired Mr Chapuswike, one of the community's wise old men, is in charge of the PTA. Mr Chapuswike was formerly a government teacher, then acted as night-watchman and occasional interpreter on the building project.

Yet even with good news, one thorny question remains. "Has any maintenance work been done on the school building?"

"As yet, no," says Mr Nkoma. "However the PTA has passed a plan to levy money for this purpose from parents of pupils and also to purchase blocks for making the teachers' houses."

*Which might have impressed us more, had he said the blocks were actually being made on site by the community!*

"But what about those who cannot, or else who refuse to pay the money?"

"Those who cannot afford the levy may pay in kind. However those who refuse to pay, will be taken to the Area Chairman. Even we may take them to the chieftainess."

We stroll over to the kiln constructed for firing twelve thousand bricks for three teachers' houses. Yet no work has been done on it since last year. Mr Chama gives it a desultory kick to test its strength, or indeed its weakness. "Bah, they have not been applying enough heat," is his considered judgment.

So will this supposedly improved situation draw us any nearer to building teachers' houses for Kaputula? Undertaking further building work here could be construed as foolish in the extreme, given the problems encountered in the past. It could also commit us for two or more years if wrangles and disputes were to threaten yet again.

Besides, how can we be sure a new order really reigns here? Might these improvements be not merely evidence of a happy honeymoon period between Mr Nkoma and the community? One swallow does not a summer make, and two new teachers plus a student have not quite turned the school around yet. Nevertheless, still reluctant to call it a day, we agree to meet again on Tuesday of the following week.

Which leaves an entire weekend to fill in Kitwe because, for once, we are not racing 500 miles up and down to Lusaka. Though let's face it, if there's little by way of distractions in Lusaka, there is a whole lot less in the smoke-shrouded pollution filled atmosphere of Kitwe.

Actually weekends in Kitwe are often spent working anyways, so Saturday morning finds us just about the only white faces in Kitwe town centre (sic!) trying to buy thirteen navy blue school jerseys and thirteen blankets for the Kaputula double orphans. However, the one clothing store in town, PEP, turns up nothing in the way of school jerseys and little choice of blankets to suit our budget.

We try phoning Mr Mbai, phone a friend, but he is no help. However an assistant in the shop suggests we try an Indian store along the road. Let's hope they can help, since the only alternative is risking the perils of the African market . . . on a Saturday . . . alone!

Clutching our £200 budget closely, we make our way along the broken-up pavements of Kitwe which on such occasions appear threatening since they are peopled with street kids, thieves and beggars, all of whom, given the slightest opportunity, would doubtless relieve us of Starfish cash.

Into a small store called CITYMAN, where an Asian sits watching every move from the cash desk strategically located by the door. Little hope, we suspect, of a discount here! However they do sell navy school jerseys at a price, almost £10 each! Also they have blankets cheaper than at PEP.

"Can you give us a discount?" I try. "These jerseys and blankets are for orphans in a rural area." No response!

Then they only have ten blankets of one sort, two at slightly more and one at a lot more. "Can we have the one blanket at the same price as the cheaper ones?" I try.

Reluctantly the man behind the desk agrees then, when he hands over the bill, he shrugs and gives us one free blanket. A real heart must beat beneath that steely exterior after all!

This afternoon we have the delights of the annual Kitwe Agricultural Show, which may seem a bit bizarre in both a town and an area renowned for their copper mining industry. However somebody must be farming around here since the whole of Kitwe seems to be on the march, flocking along the main road to reach the Agricultural showground on the outskirts of town.

But first we have to get in. Why is nothing ever simple in Zambia? Though the queue is not extensive, we still have to wend our way along almost a quarter of a mile of pathways twisting and turning between fencing in order to reach the turnstile. Try skipping the queue? You must be joking! "Ah no, you must go this way," we are told. At least we are getting some exercise, since exercise is always in short measure in Kitwe where going for a walk would be unthinkable.

Inside we could be forgiven for asking what on earth we have come for! Our interest in pumps and generators and farm machinery is somewhat limited. There are arenas where not much is happening and a host of fast food outlets selling very Zambian food. Then there are sellers, doubtless Congolese, of a host of cheap plastic knick-knacks round which most of the Zambians in Kitwe, at least those who can afford K10 000 to get in, are crowded.

Surprisingly there is a sprinkling of 'mzungus' inside, roughly in the ratio of 1 to every 1000 Zambians. They are of the diehard, 'we know how to survive in Africa' type, clad in shorts, knee socks and sporting vast bellies fuelled by endless beer and 'barbies'. And that's only the men! The women are clad in clothes at least thirty years outdated or else skimpy tops, shorts and bejewelled flip-flops. It is an experience we would not have missed for anything!

Which still leaves Sunday. So far this trip we have not attended church on one single Sunday. Today is a chance, albeit reluctantly, to remedy this with a three hour marathon at St Michael's, Kitwe, an imposing red-brick relic of the colonial era located to the rear of the vanilla hues of Shoprite and the salmon pink Edinburgh Hotel and adjacent to the throng of the African minibus station.

How to describe a service at St Michael's? Well, it is basically Anglican by nature, though you could be forgiven for thinking that, although the order of service appears familiar, somewhere along the line they lose the plot. Generally in the midst of the exuberant praise and worship section where the all Zambian singing and dancing music group becomes transported into distinctly un-Anglican realms. Or else during the prayers of intercession

279

lasting anything up to twenty minutes and invoking the Almighty with such highly impassioned words rarely heard in the UK. And if not there, then during the sermon promising hellfire and damnation and which invariably lasts up to one hour. They are certainly serious about worship here!

Today Father Oguru is preaching which surprises us since the rector, Canon Zulu, is also there. However Canon Zulu looks somewhat the worse for wear. I realise he was part of a wedding party I saw yesterday having their photos taken in the middle of a traffic roundabout. Since there are few places of beauty in either Lusaka or Kitwe, wedding parties resort to the flowerbeds on traffic islands as providing the colourful backdrop for their wedding photos.

Indeed Canon Zulu explains this was the case when he invites us to join him for a cup of tea after the service in his house. Previously Tanworth Church responded to a request to provide fifty bags of cement for the foundation slab of a daughter church at nearby Chibuluma being funded by the Kitwe church. Canon Zulu said at that time that he may come back to us at a later date, perhaps when they had reached roofing level. *Has this time now arrived?*

Indeed it has, so we pile Canon Zulu, drooping from exhaustion and in no fit state to drive, into the back of our vehicle and head off out to Chibuluma, about ten miles outside Kitwe. Sunday off? You must be joking, here we are working again!

In fact we pass Chibuluma many times since it lies outside Kitwe along the road leading to Kaputula as well as Chilumba. The community consists mainly of retirees from the copper mines and therefore is not at all affluent. We have already noted while passing that the church is now stuck at gable end level staring roofless up at the heavens as if waiting for divine intervention. Now Starfish has arrived!

"Ah you have indeed been sent by God!" exclaims Canon Zulu passionately.

*Who, us?*

"In fact we have been wondering how we are going to afford the roofing, and now God has indeed sent you to us once more!"

And there were we, not at all willing to attend church today! If there are no doubts in his mind, there are doubts like boulders in our own. Then inspiration, truly divine in nature dawns . . . "Perhaps if we farmed out your appeal to some of our Anglican contacts in the UK, they might respond?" I suggest, while earnestly praying they will, because without them, there is nothing Starfish can do.

"Ah, that will be wonderful! I know for sure they will assist us."

While Bob potters about the surrounds taking photos of the unfinished church from every possible angle, I chat to a slowly recovering Canon Zulu. Bob returns to learn that in the clearing of the bush for this project, which he has just been ploughing around in, they removed many big snakes.

"Especially dangerous ones," emphasises a watchman on guard, "even mambas and puff adders." Which is about as dangerous as it can get for spending a weekend off duty!

Nevertheless, the weekend has created space to plan out what we might say to the Kaputula community on Monday. How many times have we planned out what needs to be said to this community?

"If we were to build here again . . . which we're not actually saying we are . . . then there would be no money for wages, no paying every Tom, Dick and Harry to fetch and carry . . . In fact we would not be prepared to pay *anybody* beyond a professional bricklayer, plasterer and carpenter . . . all community labour therefore would be strictly voluntary . . .strictly materials only . . . And we're not actually offering any choice . . . What we're saying is . . . TAKE IT OR LEAVE IT!"

We survey the motley group of people gathered today in one of Kaputula's classrooms. It's a disappointing turnout, not least with the absence yet again of deputy head teacher now supposedly acting head teacher, Mr Nkoma. Apparently he has been summoned to the DEB's office for a meeting re the worsening situation in the teachers' strikes.

Faces blank with shock, those present allow what has just been said to sink in. Heavens, surely the fact that we've built nothing here for over two years makes some point to them! But no . . .

"So, we are wanting to know, who will dig the trenches?"

"And who will chip stones?"

"Who will dig sand and fetch water and make blocks?"

*Did we not make the position clear enough?* Apparently not! So we repeat, "Any future project here would entail voluntary community involvement. Having your teachers living on site would benefit the community, therefore the community should be willing to labour for free. It is what happens on all our other projects."

Have we given them food for thought, or simply served up an indigestible lump? Certainly there will be much to talk about in the fields and around the evening fires before it is finally digested. But there is one final thing, "THERE IS NO NEGOTIATION!"

So do we leave it there? Not quite a final goodbye, but yet another 'au revoir'? Can we honestly not bear to tear ourselves away from this place? Or are we simply reluctant to draw a line under any further involvement here completely?

"In fact, Mr and Mrs Cooke, our plans are already in hand." Mr Chipotyo's face is drawn with pain. He certainly will not to let us slip that easily from his grasp.

"Which are?"

"We have arranged to employ a Mr Lungu of Chati to make eight thousand blocks," he reveals.

"Which the levy will pay for?"

"Indeed, to the tune of K6.5 million. Unless of course . . ." His eyes behind his outsize glasses glint speculatively.

*Is he seriously suggesting Starfish stumps up for this?*

"That's a lot of money," we tell him. "However, if it is the community's wish to proceed by purchasing them, then we will just have to wait and see." Which is all we're prepared to say for now. Over the years the Kaputula community has spoken so many fine words and made and broken so many promises, there is nothing to indicate these ones will be fulfilled.

"Ah, you will see!" Mr Chipotyo's pained expression pleads . . . *how could we doubt his words?*

"They are paying way over the odds," murmurs Mr Mbai to us on the quiet.

"You think so?"

"In fact they would be better employed making the blocks themselves," adds Mr Chama.

Which words we repeat to them a little more kindly, suggesting a number in the region of 8000 blocks, before agreeing that Messrs Mbai and Chama will report to us in the UK. On this report will rest Starfish's decision whether to proceed with the construction of a teacher's house here or not.

Just where the money might come from to build here is another matter. Currently the coffers in the UK are almost empty. A conservative estimate for the money required to roof the nurse's house at Simooya as well as roofing and finishing Chilumba's three classroom block, and not forgetting St Andrew's Church at Chibuluma . . . *ah yes, we have mentioned that one now!* . . places the total in the region of a whopping £18 000. Finding another £4 –5000 for even one teacher's house seems an impossible task. Maybe it would just be kinder to tell them here and now?

Yet something holds us back. For the moment there are school jerseys to hand out to the thirteen double orphans currently attending the school, also four hundred exercise books, one hundred pens and one hundred biros for the children. And since the teachers also have needs, there are four record books and a box of white chalk for them. Their eyes light up in gratitude and joy that someone still cares for them!

The time has come for yet another goodbye. We shan't return to Kaputula this trip. Our time is fully taken up with travelling four hundred miles up and down Zambia between the Chilumba project and the clinic project near Choma. Even, due to the ever increasing costs of travel and accommodation here, whether we shall make it back to Zambia again later this year is uncertain.

I drive off thinking . . . *I hope we will be back.* Yet over the past few weeks and months, a number of worrying factors have combined to make this seem somewhat less certain this time. Chep, our partner organisation, has a new director and there does not seem to be the same willing disposition to continue channelling funding for Starfish projects during our absences overseas.

Then the District Education Officer, on a further visit to her office, has made it clear that control of Kaputula, in common with other community schools, has now passed quite firmly into her hands. As a result control of the planning and building standards for any future building project there now lies within her brief. This means we can no longer walk in there and build what we like. As for funding, in her opinion, this should pass through her office. And that presents an immense and possibly even insurmountable obstacle for Starfish, which to date, has *never* channelled any funding through government departments.

Add to this the reality of our long standing project manager, Mr Mbai, almost certainly going either to the UK or South Africa on study leave for two whole years. With Mr Mbai off the scene, combined with the other complications, we have been forced to accept that things have become a little trickier than before.

*Whoops, did somebody move our goalposts when we weren't looking?*

So, do all these worrying factors spell the end of the line for Kaputula? As ever its fate lies in the hands of a higher authority than ours. And there yet again we must leave it. Today's damp squib of a parting calls to mind the following poem:

*'This is the way the world ends,*
*Not with a bang but a whimper.'* (T S Eliot)

I really hope this will not be the way of it with Kaputula. There really should be more to a swansong than this. A fanfare or gold watch? No, that's expecting a bit much! But certainly emotion, and by the bucket-load, oh yes! So watch this space. After all . . . we haven't as yet said we won't be back!

# CHAPTER TWENTY-NINE: STICKING TO OUR BRIEF
## while a suspected poisoning occurs!
### September 1ˢᵗ –> 18ᵗʰ, 2010

When Starfish first began some eight years ago, it was only intended initially to fund the anti-retroviral treatment for Tresford. That Starfish would build a seven classroom school at Kaputula, construct half a school, chicken sheds and hammer mill shelter at Salem Centre for street kids as well as refurbish their sanitary facilities, project manage the building of Kafubu Baptist Church, roof St Andrew's Church at Chibuluma, complete a clinic plus nurse's house at Simooya and provide Chilumba Orphans' Centre with three classrooms, never entered anyone's mind.

Not forgetting running individual and community sponsorship programmes, as well as providing assistance to needy individuals and struggling communities.

Yet everything runs its course. During 2010 a stark wake-up call forces us to face the unwished for realisation that we won't be able to carry on forever. This further rouses such unwelcome considerations as swapping over to non-building projects, which could be satisfactorily funded from the UK. Yet one thorny question immediately arises . . . if we were forced to call a halt to active participation in building projects, where would we draw the line?

As we prepare to depart for Zambia in September 2010, some six months later than planned, three Starfish projects have reached the roofing stage: the three classroom block at Chilumba Orphans' Centre, the nurse's house at Simooya and St Andrew's Church at Chibuluma (*yes, we really have told you about that now!*) The completion of these three would create a convenient cut-off point. Indeed the committee's briefing before the trip was to place certainly the first two of these in a position to proceed to completion.

Yet Africa doesn't let go that easily. That *still* leaves the unresolved issue of Kaputula, where building work began all those years ago and where arguably it's still not finished. Even allowing for all the problems while building the school and yet more after it opened, could we simply abandon it to its fate? Because incredibly the community *still* expects us to carry on building there.

It's hardly surprising therefore that our emotions on arrival are more turbulent than an aircraft flying through a tropical thunderstorm. Indeed, barely forty-eight hours into Zambia, with a cell-phone which won't charge and a car hire company that's gone bust, combined with the impossibility of getting a night's sleep in Lusaka, I'm ready to board the first plane out. How will I survive six weeks of see-sawing emotions? In desperation I start counting the days . . . three down, only thirty-nine to go!

Yet the phone dilemma does eventually sort itself out in the insalubrious and inaptly named Seven Diamond Shopping Mall, while Rajesh, an Asian garage owner in the second class area of Lusaka, saves our bacon with the hire of an immense 4x4 Prada, albeit at a hefty price.

Soon we are winging our way to Choma, praying we will arrive before dark. This trip we have finally accepted the Wixleys' invitation to stay on their farm. If we still remain uncertain of the road there in daylight, then we would never find it after dark. Lose our way once off the tarmac and we could be lost for a very long time!

We arrive at Chisoboyo Farm at 18.00 just as the sun is sinking in splendour like a fireball balanced on the rim of the horizon, wowing us into stunned silence. We are staying in one of the original chalets constructed by the ex-Zimbabwean Wixleys when they first carved the farm out of virgin bush almost seven years ago. Thirty kilometres out in the bush, their farm stands on the shores of the dam, which they also constructed. In fact everything here represents a gigantic saga of escape from the clutches of Mugabe, followed by survival against the odds in the midst of the African bush.

Yet what exactly is God playing at? Last year's management issues combined with this year's health hiccups, have made it seem that He is slamming the Africa door shut in our faces. Now here we are cast adrift amidst everything we have so loved about Africa. Is this a tease of Almighty proportions, or merely a test of stamina? If our brief also was to examine how things might proceed without our presence, why are all thoughts of getting back on the plane fading along with the sunset. And giving way to the growing realisation that we should survive a week here very well indeed!

Day seven and we are one-sixth of the way through the trip. After a blissful night with nothing but the raucous lullabies of crickets and frogs to rock us to sleep, we are back on the job. Firstly we pass by the clinic project to assess what stage the nurse's house has reached.

Since we have been unable to send funding out to this project from the UK, it stands forlornly at gable end level, exactly where Milden left it earlier this year. However, the villagers are overjoyed to see us, whooping and ululating and dancing in ecstasy because the project is to be restarted. Milden's brother of the six wives is so overjoyed he promises to drop three live chickens by the farm later. Village chicken for dinner? Maybe I will get on that plane after all!

Then it's off to the District Health Office in Choma to meet Mr Simasiku. Before leaving the UK, Milden assured us Mr Simasiku would assist with buying materials, also that the DHO would provide transport for the same out to Simooya. Since we have not previously enjoyed good relations with Mr Simasiku and Choma DHO ran out of money last year, hopes are not over high for enjoying a trouble-free partnership.

However to our surprise Simasiku is there and waiting. There is even a Bill of Quantity for completion of the nurse's house along with the promise of a truck, even fuel after a bit of a quibble. *Come on guys, we are building you a health post, after all!* So it's off to buy fifty pockets of cement for plastering and floor screeding, before sending them out to the clinic.

That evening Elma Wixley's mother has arrived from Zimbabwe for a visit. *Heavens, are people still surviving there?* We listen astounded while she recounts a very different version of life in Zimbabwe to that portrayed by the media. But then she's not still living on a farm there, but in the relative security of a retirement complex in Harare, though to listen to her, people are still living the life there.

Later as we fall asleep in the chalet, there is a small scratching noise. Something is after our emergency rations. A quick flash of the torch reveals nothing. Though in the wee small hours, Bob swears he hears a distinct squeak . . . It appears a tiny squirrel or rat type creature is in residence with us. What else lurks hidden up in the rafters or the thatch is perhaps best not known! Certainly all foodstuffs need locking away at night.

Next day the sky is the endless blue of the dry season, when the jacarandas display their intense lilac blue flowers against the unending blue of the sky. In the bush native mopani and msasa trees are adopting their glorious early spring hues of copper and bronze. However no time for waxing lyrical,

287

there is work to do. Today we have to buy all the materials needed for roofing the nurse's house, then check exactly what materials remain on site at the clinic. Tomorrow, in strict accordance with our brief, we will then buy every last item needed to complete the nurse's house.

Amazingly both Mr Simasiku and a lorry are waiting at Choma garage so that the buying is completed before 11am. But there is still the checking to do out at the clinic. Somehow Milden has had a container of school materials shipped out to the clinic, for a school which no-one is currently building. *Now hang on a minute, surely he doesn't think . . .?*

Inside the container, along with desks and chairs for the non-existent school, are all the materials not yet used on the project. Every last item has to be checked down to the last screw and window stay, then a list drawn up of what is still needed. But no-one can decide whether the windows of the nurse's house need window stays or window slides. Then there are bolts, or maybe not enough bolts and tins of paint, which may not be the right paint, so that it becomes impossible to say what is or isn't needed.

"Also we are needing ceiling boards for the clinic," announces Mr Simasiku true to form.

"We have no budget for ceiling boards," we remind him. However further examination reveals that ceiling boards would ensure both privacy in the doctor's room and security in the storeroom. We add ceiling boards to the list. *Whoops, did that just blow the contingency?*

Back at the farm, three village chickens have arrived and are lodged in a former rabbit run. A friend of the Wixleys from their Zimbabwean days has also arrived. There is so much shared history passed around the dinner table tonight about the good old/bad old days, it gives rise to a distinct feeling of having stepped back in time to all those years ago in Rhodesia.

Perhaps also the wine befuddles our senses, because later we catch a movement up in the rafters of the chalet. Whatever is there will have thin pickings tonight. Elma has loaned us a vast cool box and every last consumable item is safely shut in there.

The next day is our last opportunity to buy the remaining materials for the nurse's house. Yet again Mr Simasiku plus lorry is waiting so that we are done in no time. Except that back at the nurse's house they have not put up enough trusses to support the roof. Well, we can't be in two places at once and they will be on their own for four weeks after tomorrow anyways. So we supervise them while they insert another row of roofing timbers on either side of the roof so that the roofing sheets will not bow or get blown off in a wind.

"I would like to show you the proposed site of the new school," announces Gilbert Palale, project secretary.

*That would be the school we're not building?* Even though Milden thinks we might be, and even that Elma might project manage it. Besides, we have no brief for taking on new projects, and, with all the hiccups of this year, Starfish has lost at least one major funding opportunity. Maybe it would be wiser, and certainly kinder, *not* to trek over a kilometre in blistering sun along a sandy track which appears to lead to nowhere, yet leads to an area the size of a football pitch already cleared and waiting for the school which no-one as yet is building.

Tonight Elma has cooked one village chicken. Sadly its head was bitten off last night by a civet or genet, while the cockerel took fright and flew the coop. The others politely decline the village chicken and opt for Elma's tastier alternative. We feel obliged to try a morsel.

In the morning we must be away early. On the bedside table last night I carefully placed my watch, two rings, cross and chain. Now on the same table lie watch and cross, but only one ring. My five diamond eternity ring, bought by Bob for our twenty-fifth anniversary, has vanished in pitch darkness from a chalet in which we were the only occupants. Apart that is from our small furry friend, but then he wouldn't, he couldn't . . .

We search high and low. Has the ring become snagged in the mosquito net, or caught in the bedding, fallen under the bed? There is no sign. After breakfast we search once more joined by Clive and Elma. Clive is for climbing up into the rafters above the bathroom, but we tell him no. How could a heavy ring have got up there?

With heavy hearts, we depart ringless. It is just a possession, I tell myself over and again on the drive back to Lusaka while trying not to give way to tears. Back in Lusaka I text Elma to ask the maid if she has seen anything, but they have already thought about that.

Mid afternoon the phone rings. It is Elma. Clive has climbed up into the rafters and crawled dusty and dirty right to the back above the bathroom. There in the squirrel rat's nest he found . . . my ring! I can't help myself and burst into tears of relief. Also of surprise, because last night we had our first good view of the creature. The name squirrel rat suits it. It is no bigger than a small mouse but with a furry tail like a squirrel. But how a creature that size manoeuvred a heavy ring in the dark up to its nest, I'll never know!

After a weekend in Lusaka, it's off to familiar pastures, though not without mishap, because the village chicken strikes back with a vengeance all day Sunday. Thus, bound up with Lomotil, we set off on Monday for Kitwe, this time accompanied by a driver. Because of the appalling accident rate in Zambia, a hefty insurance excess, merely for the privilege of driving the hired vehicle ourselves, means it costs exactly the same to employ a driver. So we sit back and let Windas, clad in charcoal grey suit and sporting wrap-around sunglasses and with a blue-tooth perched behind one ear, speed us safely, we pray, up to Kitwe.

We also have the novelty of somewhere different to stay. Having worked our way over a period of eight years through just about every accommodation option in Kitwe and on the way experiencing problems ranging from theft and burglary to outside drinking and soliciting, a search on the internet has unearthed a newly opened lodge which promises none of the above.

However closer acquaintance reveals the cracks already appearing, not least a total failure to rouse any hot water. We are offered a bucket of hot water or else decamping to another room to shower. *Haven't we been down this route before?* Indeed yes, so first thing next morning I furnish the management with a list of thirteen complaints before setting off for a briefing with Chep, our partner organisation.

Starfish currently has only one programme running in conjunction with Chep, the sponsorship of eight ex-Musonda pupils through secondary education. Since they are in their final year, that programme should draw to a natural conclusion in line with the committee brief.

However that still leaves the dilemma of Kaputula, where Chep originally monitored building work during our absences overseas. In the last eighteen months Chep has had a massive turn around in staff, particularly in senior management. This has resulted in a shift in focus, which may not include managing other organisations' building projects or handling their funds. Even though we have no brief to build there again, we need to confirm whether *not* building would be with or without Chep involvement. Confused? *So are we!*

Mr Mbai also is finally set to depart to South Africa. However that still leaves Mr Chama, building supervisor on most of our projects, who is delighted to see us back in Zambia and raring to commence construction of teachers' houses at Kaputula . . . with him replacing Mr Mbai as project manager on this non-starter building project.

"Whoa, hang on!" we say, reining him in like a racehorse under starter's orders. "We don't actually have any brief . . ." His face plummets so low I fear it will drop clean off his shoulders. Yet disappointment is part of life in Zambia, so instead of planning a house, he accompanies us to meet with Faith Lyena and Mr Chalwe of the Faith Orphanage Foundation, which controls the Chilumba Orphans' Centre where the three classroom block is nearing completion.

Before we left UK I chanced on a Tools with a Mission magazine in our local Methodist church. Glancing through, I found a photo of Faith receiving a container of goods in Zambia from TWAM. I have brought it all the way to Zambia to show her the photo.

"Ah yes, that is indeed me!" she grins in delight. "Even I am going there next year, to their headquarters in the UK."

"What to Ipswich?" I ask astounded. "But that's only thirty miles from where we live."

"Is that so? Then I must come and visit you!"

And bring with her photos of the Chilumba Orphans? Has God just opened a chink in the impenetrable wall currently blocking all paths forward? I think he has. Should we no longer be able to come back here, then *Faith can come to us!*

That night back at the lodge they have remedied most of our complaints with amazing rapidity. We order lamb for dinner, a treat rarely available in Zambia. We sit in lone glory in the dining room since other guests clearly prefer eating in their rooms in front of DSTV.

"Aggghhhh! That's disgusting!" I spit the first mouthful back out.

"What have they done to it?" Bob stubbornly swallows some down. But the meat is salty beyond belief and so highly flavoured it could be anything but the succulent lamb we'd anticipated.

We call the chef. Because it is Monday night, the head chef is off duty. The barman cum receptionist clad in apron and chef's hat is masquerading as chef, though clearly with few skills in that field. "You are not liking the seasoning?" he asks incredulous at our lack of taste.

At our request he produces the offending pot of Aromat, which contains monosodium glutamate as well as other nasties designed to enhance (sic!) the flavour of meat. I manage a few more mouthfuls before abandoning it. Bob finishes his and even eats mine also, maybe not such a wise move.

During the night waves of nausea create an illusion of sailing upon a perilous sea. My one, no two saving graces, are that I didn't eat all of the meat and also drank copious amounts of water.

Not so Bob, who flounders throughout the following day at Chilumba, before sinking defeated . . . during the night before the day when we are due to visit Kaputula finally to tell them, that for a whole host of reasons,

Starfish is not in a position to build anything further for them. *Some people really do chose their day to be sick!*

"I swear that chef tried to poison me!" Bob rants deliriously from the depths of his sickbed.

"More likely what upset my stomach last Sunday," I remind him.

"Ha, well how do you know you also weren't poisoned . . . by village chicken?"

What's to do? Today is the only day available for visiting Kaputula. Do I fancy travelling fifty kilometres out into a rural area alone with four Zambian men? Since I would trust my life with at least two of them, our dear friends Mbai and Chama, that is not an issue.

What is an issue is that, as well as looking after money, writing up notes, buying orphans' rations, handing over an album of photos for Kafubu Baptist Church, I will also have charge of Bob's camera . . . and will also have to pass on alone the bad news to Kaputula about not building there. *Anyone care to swap places for the day?*

I text the men to say: PLEASE BE ON TIME. HUSBAND SICK. I WANT TO BE THERE AND BACK BY LUNCHTIME. Along with Windas we pick up Pim from Chep, then Mr Chama who has already priced up grain and fertiliser ready for me to buy it for the orphan carers, then finally Mr Mbai by the Coca Cola Bottling Factory gates.

What will we find at Kaputula this time? We have heard a new head is there. What will he be like? Will he have gained the respect of this difficult community?

Mr Mutale is a neatly dressed and quietly spoken gentleman to whom I take an immediate liking. With him are Mr Chapuswike, still chair of the PTA and Mrs Kauseni also of the PTA as we crowd into the small office where we held so many difficult meetings with Mrs Tembo. Since Mr Mutale's first words express gratitude at our coming to build teachers' houses, then handling this meeting suddenly appears even more difficult than I'd anticipated.

I present him with a whole catalogue of reasons: my health problems, our increasing age, the escalating costs of travelling to Zambia and hiring vehicles, funding issues, supervision and monitoring in our absence, issues of community involvement . . . Already the poor man must feel as if he has been felled by a sledgehammer. But how to dispel the disappointment etched on his face in furrows so deep you could plough them?

"Look, I can't make any promises," I tell him, "but my husband and I will pass by the DEB's office in Kalulushi and see what the position is there." By which I mean that, since they are so keen to remind us that community schools now come under their control, maybe they should fulfil their obligations and actually build the houses themselves.

Since there is not a lot else to say, Mr Mutale shows us what has been achieved since his arrival. A large area has been cleared to make a netball pitch, also a football pitch. Added to the now properly constructed kiln with almost five thousand bricks fired and ready to build the teacher's house we are not building, this should all be most impressive. Things are definitely changing for the better here but . . . *Oh dear, how do we solve this dilemma?*

As the vehicle draws away from Kaputula, I try to envisage this being the last time here. If there is no brief to restart work here, and the odds are so heavily stacked against us anyways, what is the point in keeping on coming back here? To punish or torment them? But try as I might, I cannot imagine this being the last time *ever* that I will be here. Besides, what must Bob feel like, missing out on the whole day?

In agreement with the others we pass by the DEB's office on the way back to make an appointment for Monday. If nothing else, I must abide by my promise to put the situation to the DEB's officer. Then it's back to Bob who by 3pm must be wondering if his lucky day has finally come and I have absconded with four Zambian men.

He is alive just, but running a high temperature and unable to eat which points to an infection rather than death by Aromat! A rough-cast Scottish guy and a boorish South African also staying at the lodge offer their services in the form of medication, a self-test kit for malaria, even to doing anything I might require in the middle of the night. Now there's an offer I might find hard to resist . . . but naturally only should the patient deteriorate further!

Day seventeen dawns and I'm still counting. Yet a subtle and surprising shift has occurred in that I'm no longer sure whether I'm counting days till we leave . . . *or days we have left!*

Certainly there is a renewed purpose in what we are doing and a good reason for getting out of bed in the morning. Which Bob does, announcing he is ready to get back on the job. This is a great relief since today is the main day for photographing the Chilumba orphans and he assures me that, since they all have black faces, my limited photographic skills would not cope with the technicalities of choosing the right exposure. Hmmm! How do I love thee? Not so much when you make comments like that!

The problem as I see it is not so much that they all have black faces, well actually not all of them do. Josephine, the centre manager has remarried a local man and had a baby. Due to some dodgy ancestor way back, the baby is white, well almost. So, no problem photographing baby Wendy who is easy to spot. Not so the others, since Bob's fickle camera jiggles the order they are photographed in as he downloads or edits them. This means yours truly has to scrupulously record every rag and tatter of clothing, hair clip, smile, hand on hip so that they can be correctly identified later.

We also have a presentation to make. Granddaughter Jodie overheard us saying how children in Zambia have so little. She has sent out a shoebox containing a pink blanket, storybook and sweeties for one of the orphans. The youngest orphan called Gwen is chosen to receive the gift, though she is clearly scared stiff by our white faces.

Later that evening I phone UK to tell Jodie about little Gwen who lives out in the bush.

"What, she lives in a *bush?*" Jodie is outraged.

"No Jodie, she lives in *the* bush. It's like the countryside." But Jodie's perception of the countryside amounts to her grandparents' idyll up in Suffolk. I fear Gwen's living conditions are a world away from that.

Saturday is day eighteen out of a total of forty-two days away. If I counted days actually in Zambia, it would be day eighteen out of thirty-nine, a fraction which doesn't cancel down. Whoops, I've just realised it does and we are six-thirteenths of our way through our time in Zambia or three-sevenths of the way through the entire trip. What does that prove, other than our time here is rapidly running out. Indeed that time is running out full stop. Maybe this is a wake-up call of a different kind, the kind which demands petulantly . . . *surely you're not giving in that easily?*

So, on Saturday morning we sit on the veranda by the pool working out exactly how much it *might* cost to build one teacher's house and how with no project manager or partner organisation we *might* go about it.

*No, we do not give in easily!*

Since Bob arguably possesses a greater gift with numbers he works out, using the bill of quantities for the nurse's house at Simooya, exactly how much it would cost. And since I also arguably have a better gift with words, I work out what conditions we might set in place. But would Chep, Mr Chama, the Deb's Office, the Kaputula Community all of whom *might* become involved, agree to all of the conditions . . . or indeed to any of them?

What then to do with the rest of the day? We decide to visit Kumasamba Lodge on the banks of the Kafue River where we have stayed on so many trips to Kitwe. It is far enough out of town to really get away from things for the day. But will the Krugers still be there? They are, and pleased to see us, though sadly our old friend George has retired and gone back to his village.

It is so peaceful there, not a sound or a movement except a silent croc slipping midstream up the fast flowing Kafue. Having greeted the family we retire to our favourite spot on the island in the dam. Afternoon entertainment is provided by the dam's resident croc nick-named Francesca 'begging' for food in the shallows from people on the fishing platform. Maybe she also hopes one of them might fall in, and she could make short work of them also. The Zambians tossing scraps to her seem unaware that she has already demolished the family Alsatian!

After a walk through the bush, we say our goodbyes and head back to Kitwe. The sun sinks in a huge orange ball as if the bush was swallowing it up for the night. As we enter Kitwe, the stark ugliness of the mine chimneys stand silhouetted against it. How many Zambian, or indeed Kitwe sunsets, have we experienced after a day out in the bush? For a fleeting moment I ponder how lucky we are. I mean, how many people experience all we have experienced in one short life?

But then reality kicks in. Goodness, next I'll write how much we are enjoying it! Only till the next community challenge arises, or the next policeman steps out into the road, hand raised, saying, 'You have committed an infringement!'

Or maybe only until Monday, when we face yet another meeting in the DEB's office to try to formulate a plan to build a teacher's house which we have no brief to build and for which there is no support network to make the plan work anyways. Still confused? *So are we!*

# CHAPTER THIRTY: THE SIGN OF THE HOOPOE ...
## and the prospect of a very 'wet' nurse.
### *Sep 19th - > Oct 11th, 2010*

The past six days in Kitwe have solved nothing. We are more confused than ever about Zambia and about where we go from here. Perhaps it's time to come clean. In May of this year I was diagnosed with malignant skin cancer. *What then am I doing in Zambia?* You might well ask!

In addition Bob is waiting to see the same dermatologist, whose attitude towards trips to the tropics is cavalier to the extreme . . . *why keep going back to the very place which caused all your problems?* Which may not strictly be true, yet working underneath the furnace blast of the Zambian sun is without doubt no longer wise for us. Hence the wakeup call mentioned in the previous chapter!

Add to that our project manager, Mr Mbai, is finally off to study in South Africa for two years, while our partner organisation, Chep, continues to show a worrying reluctance to remain involved. Then, with the ever increasing cost of air fares, car hire and accommodation threatening no longer to make trips here viable, you could be forgiven for thinking that the Starfish train has just run headlong into the station buffers.

All these issues were shared with the Starfish committee back in June, resulting in the brief to bring current projects to a stage where, if necessary, they can proceed to completion with or without our active presence.

So far we have stuck remarkably well to this brief. Every last nut, screw and bolt has been bought for the Simooya Project. At Chilumba roofing is already underway. All that remains are finishes such as painting, glazing, doors and plastering, which can be funded by money transferred from the UK. We have even promised further financial assistance from the UK for the completion of St Andrew's Church at Chibuluma and, since most of the funding brought with us has by now been spent, we could just get on a plane back to the UK.

Yet we don't. Because at Simooya we followed a tantalising trail leading to the proposed site for a school which no-one as yet is building. Then at Kaputula the furrows of disappointment etched so deeply on the face of head teacher Mr Mutale have proved so hard to dispel from our minds, we have been unable to let them go. *So where precisely do we go from here?*

The DEB's meeting on Monday September 20<sup>th</sup> for a start. We arrive forearmed with a Bill of Quantities for a teacher's house, but with no brief to start building it, plus a list of conditions should we nevertheless find ourselves tempted to stray down that very route. And if you have any idea what's going on, you're doing better than either of us. Even as we get out of the car at the DEB's office, I mutter to Bob, "What are we doing here?"

To which he responds, "Search me!"

Today is also day twenty and half way through our time in Zambia, though tomorrow actually is half way through the entire trip. Back at the start I wondered how, with seriously damaged skin, I would ever survive. It may have taken a miracle to get this far, but it's going to take an even bigger one to get any further.

With us at the meeting is Mr Chama, still eagerly angling for the position of project manager on this stop-start project, as well as Pim from Chep to state his ED's viewpoint. Mr Mutale, still displaying creases of anxiety on his forehead, has travelled from Kaputula along with PTA chairman Mr Chapuswike and Area Councillor, Mr Amon Kafwali which rather suggests that, with a full presidential election on the cards for next year, the political football is about to be kicked into play yet again.

A new DEB's officer has been appointed since our last meeting here. She has called in Mr Malama, her buildings supervisor plus a gentleman with an unidentifiable name and position, maybe just to even up the sides.

*So why are we here?* Apart from ourselves, everyone else is under the impression that we are, or else can be persuaded into, building a teacher's house at Kaputula. Certainly everyone present, ourselves included, agrees that, for reasons of stability and security, the building of at least one teacher's house is essential.

*Yet who is to do it?* The DEB's officer is quite clear that their building programme is fully committed for the next couple of years with building new classrooms. Constructing teachers' houses remains a long way off.

This kicks the ball into our half of the pitch. So we explain how our personal circumstances have changed dramatically over the past few months and that, while they may see us here today, we are no longer in a position to give such blithe assurances as . . . see you in six months!

Since this goes down like a lead balloon, we decide now is the right moment to make a dramatic revelation. Until now we have kept this under wraps, yet what we are about to reveal is actually what has kept us going back and back to Kaputula against all the odds.

"Actually we have a private donor interested in funding the construction of one house." Suddenly every person in the room is sitting forward on the edges of their chairs. "However, it would mean working to very strict conditions."

*What conditions?* "Firstly to a very restricted budget."

*How strict?* "Something approaching the K35 million, which we know for a fact is what the nurse's house at Simooya has cost us."

"Is there a plan of this house?" Mr Malama asks guardedly.

We hand over the same plan used for the nurse's house, which he scrutinises carefully before announcing, "Impossible, for that price it cannot be done!" He shakes his head gloomily. "What with hiring a truck this side, then the cost of sourcing and transporting materials that side, it would cost at least sixty to eighty million kwachas!"

Which pronouncement is disappointing, yet not the end of the line, since all figures are negotiable in Zambia. So, undismayed, we proceed with our other conditions. "If the DEB's office were to provide a truck with fuel for transport of materials as the DHO in Choma has done . . ."

*Ah, there is no way the DEB's office can do that!*

Still we refuse to be daunted. "Naturally there is the question of monitoring and handling funds when we are not in Zambia, which role we hope Chep would play as before?"

Momentarily off guard, at first I miss what Pim's response is. Only when Bob asks him to repeat it, does the full realisation dawn that Chep is no longer willing to nest Starfish money for our projects. Like a stone falling into a millpond, Pim's words disperse ripples of unease, which spread out into all four corners of the room.

"But there is no problem, because your money can be channelled through our department," proposes the DEB's officer rather too brightly.

Doubtless she means well, yet this has always been a major stumbling block . . . *Starfish money NEVER passes through the hands of government departments!*

It is time to lay our final card on the table, the one which might still, against all the odds, win the game. We raise the thorny issue of community involvement by the provision of building and river sand and the chipping of stones, as well as providing free labour.

"So what then will we receive, will it be money or food?" the community members want to know.

*Excuse me while I scream!* In placing these proposals before today's key players, we have pushed every button and pulled out every knob, yet the starting point still remains tantalisingly beyond reach.

Last night, because we needed to be absolutely sure of where we stood in the face of any opposition, I phoned our generous donor in the UK. I asked her, if indeed we could not find any way forward, where did she then want her money to go?

"I'll leave it up to you," was her response. "If you think it will be better put towards another project, then so be it!"

This morning's meeting has proved that, if we were so unwise as to proceed with a project based upon such shaky foundations, not only would we risk stumbling at the first tremor, warning of a far greater earthquake to follow, but also it would take weeks of negotiations even to clear away the rubble.

*But where to leave things at this moment in time?*

Pim agrees to confirm Chep's position with his ED, while Mr Malama agrees to draw up his own Bill of Quantity using the plan shown to him. Mr Chama merely looks glum as the prospect of becoming project manager sinks ever deeper into the mire, while Mr Mutale looks as if he is carrying the cares of the world on his shoulders. All we can promise him is that, as soon as we get feedback from Chep and Mr Malama, we will get back to him.

For the moment it's off rather belatedly to Salem Centre for street kids to see what is happening there. Starfish does not currently have a programme running there, but that's not to say Mr Mbai hasn't been building again. Indeed he seems determined to leave a small empire behind before departing for South Africa. But this time has he finally overreached himself?

On one side of the Salem compound stands a most grandiose building, a new library though as yet roofless and staring sightless up to the heavens. The building work has been funded by the Beit Trust, which allocated a specific amount for each stage of the building work. Thus Mr Mbai, having somewhat increased the size of the building, is left with a shortfall of £2000 for roofing materials before the Beit Trust will release further funding for the finishes. *Oh, oh, do we know what is coming?*

"So we were wondering if Starfish could help us out of our present difficulties?"

In fact we play for time saying, "Wait and see!" Having failed dismally to set up any strategy for building a teacher's house at Kaputula, we must now revert to our brief and not get led any further astray.

Next it's on the Faith Orphanage Foundation to make a last payment for transport and skilled labour for roofing the three classroom block at Chilumba. But first over lunch, we reach an 'executive' decision, those decisions made while out in Zambia without the benefit of consultation with the UK committee. Since the private donation exactly equals the amount needed to finish off work at Chilumba, we decide to make that available to Faith.

"You're sure we're doing the right thing?" I ask Bob for the umpteenth time as we sit in the peaceful surroundings of Mukwa restaurant and guesthouse. Since we can't afford to stay there, we can at least enjoy eating there occasionally.

"I think so," he says. "At least it rounds everything off nicely."

*So is that what it amounts to, rounding things off nicely?*

"Ah, the Chilumba community will be so pleased that the funding is there to complete all of the building work!" Faith clasps her hands in joy when we reveal this. "They are becoming impatient what with the rains coming and then the new school year starting in January. Even we will be open by then, I'm telling you!"

So we leave Faith with tears of happiness shining in her eyes, maybe for the moment extinguishing the light from one hundred Bunsen burners in the chemistry lab of her dreams, yet nevertheless her joy is a delight to behold.

Even then, to be *absolutely* sure we leave no stone unturned, we collect Mr Malama's proposed Bill of Quantity for a house we know can be built for K35m. Yet his estimate comes to a staggering K60m, finally dashing any last hopes of a breakthrough.

In a few days we are off down to Lusaka. Since all our programmes running up in Kitwe have reached the closing stages, and if we were indeed to start heeding the dermatologist's advice, we may never be back here again. *A sobering thought!*

Over the last few days we say goodbye to Faith whose prayers bear more than a hint that this is the last time we will pray together. Even Dynass *(will you be my mother?)* at the orphans' centre treats me to such a long lingering gaze of farewell that she also perhaps senses she may not see 'her mother' again.

We phone Mr Mutale at Kaputula to say, "Sorry, no go!" then wish Mr

Mbai God speed to South Africa after Christmas, and to dear, faithful Mr Chama, "Oh well, maybe it just wasn't meant to be!"

Even our check-up with the Musonda pupils is super-charged with emotion. Also sensing that they may not see us again and, since they are about to sit their final year exams, they take it in turn each to express their heartfelt gratitude for what Starfish has done in providing them with an education and a future.

*Heavens, pass the hankies somebody, please!*

Then we're off, leaving behind Kitwe's familiar polluted skyline with the mine chimneys belching out smoke and Africans endlessly walking along the roadsides with their potholes and the dust and dirt, the police roadblocks and lorries belching noxious fumes from their exhausts. . . Just as well I'm not driving, because right now I wouldn't see the road for tears!


However, it's not quite goodbye to Zambia, because we still have to travel down to Choma to check all is well with the nurse's house and to be reunited with the missing eternity ring which Elma claims is burning a hole in their safe.

We sit on the Wixleys' veranda drinking tea and soaking in the late afternoon view over the dam, thinking how hard it will be to leave all this behind. This trip we have reconnected with our Africa life of the past, and not solely with the misery and poverty that dogs so much of life here today. So would I swap it for the cold and chill of the coming winter in UK? You bet! So there, I've admitted it, shout it so loudly they can even hear it in distant Zimbabwe . . . *I'm enjoying it!*

We had told them at Simooya to expect us during the first week in October, however we arrive a week earlier. What will we find? Bob is keen to go straight over to the clinic site, even though at this time of the afternoon, there will be no-one there, which of course there isn't. Nor has much work been done. But then in Zambia, there's a lot to be said for the element of surprise. Certainly the roof is on the nurse's house, but . . .

"You can see daylight through it!" I exclaim in disbelief. "And what about the plastering?" Only one room and one wall in another room have been plastered and both of them badly.

"I think we have a few questions to ask tomorrow," announces Bob grimly.

We are disappointed, because we had come to expect more of the Tonga people. Even we have sung their praises as a shining example to the Bemba and Lamba up on the Copperbelt. Clearly, like all our other projects, unless somebody sits on them, either jobs don't get done, or they get done badly.

But is there enough time left to put matters to rights? We have half of this week and the beginning of next week before a final fling in Lusaka, then it's back on the plane. Looking at the roof, we both agree, "There'll be one very wet nurse in here unless something's done about it!"

That night after yet another scrumptious dinner with the Wixleys talking over the old days in both Zim and Zam, we pick our way gingerly by torchlight back over the crinkling leaves littering the grass, praying we don't step on a snake. As we settle down, yet again there is a telltale wrinkle and crackle. Oh yes, our friend the squirrel rat is still there and on the lookout for pickings. However, every last scrap of food is once more in the cool-box, while my jewellery is securely zipped inside a toilet bag inside a locked suitcase. So hard luck mate!

In the morning I lie watching the first orange rays of the sunrise bouncing off the waters in the dam and piercing their way through the cracks of the curtains to shimmer and dance on the chalet walls. Gradually I have realised that I wake in Zambia with a much greater sense of peace. And also with a greater sense of purpose, so I rouse Bob once again with the words, "You know, being here sure gives you a reason to get out of bed in the morning!"

Even if it is to hear excuses, excuses, excuses from the Simooya community until our ears are ringing with excuses . . . They had to screed the floors first, then the first bricklayer wouldn't do the plastering for the K500 000 allowed, the second bricklayer is sick and wants more money anyways, they had to make scaffolding . . .

*Heavens, this is beginning to sound like a four hundred mile distant rerun of Kaputula!*

"Look, we don't want to hear your excuses," we tell them. "You have until early next week, then we're out of here. Who's going to see work is done then? Milden can't come back here before Christmas and Clive is busy with planting."

So the community starts listing things they want: extra materials, money for wages, money for digging out the pit for the nurse's toilet . . .

"Whoa! Stop right there!" we tell today's pitifully small gathering. "Enough is enough! We will buy the extra materials, then seek advice from Mr Simasiku. We will be back tomorrow and by then we want to see the work restarted. We are *very* disappointed!"

Is this enough to get something done? Time will tell, yet suddenly time has begun running out faster than grains of sand through an egg-timer.

That afternoon we meet up with Mr Simasiku in Choma to tell him what is, or rather is *not* going on at Simooya. In turn he informs us the community has not responded to any of his texts, apart from one headman who lied, telling him all work was finished. Since he is tied up for the rest of the day as well as tomorrow, and not much work will be done on the nurse's house over the weekend, we agree to meet up with him on Monday so that we can all travel together to the site.

As for us we are sneaking a few days away on the shores of Lake Kariba, gazing sentimentally out over the distant purple haze of the Matusadonna Hills in Zimbabwe, speculating as whether we really will ever get back there again. *Now there's a thought!*

However, before travelling to Kariba, we pass via the clinic to check that work really is underway again. And it is! Gilbert Palale, project secretary, and another man are digging the hole for the nurse's pit toilet cum washroom, though bizarrely they have dug it right next to the track leading from the house to the clinic itself. Hopefully the path can be diverted, otherwise there will be not only a wet, but also an exceedingly embarrassed nurse!

Inside the nurse's house plasterer number three is about to start work. Yet so far all he has done is move rickety scaffolding, made from hastily nailed together saplings, from one room to another, even though the room he has moved it from isn't as yet finished. Ours not to reason why!

We hand over the materials bought yesterday and, on the advice of Mr Simasiku, inform Gilbert, "There will be money to come for plastering, but nothing more. Nothing for digging or constructing the toilet, nothing for painting or putting in the ceiling boards, which incidentally the DHO has undertaken to do."

And with that we depart for a weekend at Lake Kariba. This time we're staying in a bush camp at an isolated spot called Siansowa, which is conveniently located for getting down and then back to Simooya again next week. There is literally nothing there but a bush camp. Think *'I'm a celebrity, get me out of here!'* And a crocodile farm containing over 100 000 crocs reared for their meat and skins. *Let's hope the wind remains in the right direction!*

Oh, and animals such as zebra, ostrich, impala, reedbuck, warthog which clearly think their right of residence predates ours and wander at will through the camp in the early hours of the morning or as the sun sets in yet more glory, giving rise by now to such openly expressed thoughts as, "I really have no desire to go back to the UK!"

The owner, a small wiry man called Piet, tells us he is a fifth generation white Zambian, which causes us to reflect that our family could equally be considered third generation Africans. Having lived here for eight years, our children were both born here. Our daughter married a Zambian of Zulu and Matabele descent and we have two grandchildren with as much African blood coursing through their veins as white.

So we have another glass of white wine each and sit beneath the velvet canopy of the African night sky reflecting that there really are more stars in the sky in the southern hemisphere and that, "Maybe our hearts really do belong here!"

"*Ah then Alison, you are Zambian by conception!*" exclaimed one of our daughter's Zambian colleagues many moons ago on our return to Zambia.

"*Ah you people, you really are one of us!*" friend Mr Mbai is wont to enthuse.

And, "*These people, they know us and our ways!*" this latter according one of the grade twelve teachers tutoring Mr Banda and co.

Which sentiments are all very complimentary, especially when coming from Zambians themselves. Yet maybe we are no more than members of that lost white tribe which still flits from one African country to another and never quite belongs in any of them, though five generations down the line, they certainly don't belong anywhere else either.

Even the best of idylls must come to an end. We pick up a dour faced Mr Simasiku at the DHO in Choma on Monday along with buildings supervisor, Mr Banda. Not to be confused with either the notorious Mr Banda of Musonda, nor Mr Banda, fictitious physiotherapist at UTH. Though it's quite true . . . *there are a lot of Bandas in Zambia!*

Since Mr Simasiku insists on stopping to buy the lunch he claims he missed after this morning's seminar, then Mr Banda keeps on opening the back windows thus letting in a temperature approaching forty degrees when we have the air-con going full blast, we are not in the best of the moods as we cross the dam wall to discover a bush fire raging and spitting and hissing and crackling ahead of us, its flames reaching hungrily to devour the tops of trees.

"Er . . . do you think it's safe to proceed?" I ask, recalling the forest fire which destroyed the original school at Kaputula just when we threatened to pull the plug on funding there, as well as the fire which conveniently destroyed most of the orchard which the Chilumba community never quite got around to fencing. *Is the same spirit of defiance at work here?*

However the testosterone-fired males inside the vehicle are of one accord and deem it perfectly safe to drive on, even though we risk becoming trapped in the vehicle and may never get out alive. *What a way to go!*

We arrive at Simooya to find little if anything has been done since last Friday. Daylight is still showing through places where the roofing sheets overlap insufficiently and what little plastering has been done is a complete and utter mess. I could weep to think that we have learnt so little from all our projects, in particular from all the frustrations of Kaputula, not to prevent us from ending up in this position again. Yet standing frazzling out in the hot sun, where neither of us should be, the realisation dawns . . . *Clearly we have not!*

But Mr Simasiku is made of sterner stuff. Roaring like a lion, he berates the villagers, calling them some choice names for not using the materials properly, for cutting corners, for lying and cheating and a few more things besides. Yet something more practical needs to be done, since we travel back to Lusaka tomorrow, then back to the UK on Monday next.

"The roofing needs completely re-doing," I tell them.

"Ah but if we were to move the roofing sheets, that will leave even more holes where the roofing nails have been," says one.

"Let's leave it as it is," suggests another, " and see what happens when the rains come and the nurse moves in."

"And gets very wet!" I snap. "Besides, the plastering is not yet finished and what has been done needs redoing."

"That is because the current plasterer is not up to the job," says one.

"Even he is using the wrong sand for the mix," adds Mr Banda who has said very little up until now, yet has inspected everything closely,

Still standing unwisely out in the hot tropical sun, even when wearing copious amounts of factor 50, we devise ways by which this sorry state of affairs can be turned around. From now on Gilbert Palale, project secretary, must report to Mr Simasiku as each stage of the work is completed. Messrs Simasiku and Banda will then come out and inspect the work before the community proceeds to the next stage, which is possibly what the pair of them should have been doing in the first place.

"W . w . what about the list of materials which you promised us?" asks Gilbert sheepishly. The list being a record of all materials bought which will then be copied into the village record book of the project.

"Ha! First I will give it to Mr Simasiku so that he can photocopy it, then next time he can check that all the materials bought have actually been used on the project . . . and not suddenly grown legs and walked elsewhere."

Gilbert's chastened expression reveals he gets the message. However, just to make sure I add, "Besides, if you want someone to build a school for you, you'd better make darned sure you get *this* project right first!"

"By *someone* I don't suppose you mean us?" Bob is quick to respond.

"Er . . . I don't *think* I actually said *us*. . ." Which in Zambia is an *exceedingly* dangerous way to leave matters!

But will the measures we have left in place be sufficient to encourage the community to complete the nurse's house in a fit and proper manner? We can only hope and pray they will, because until the house is completed, the clinic cannot become operational.

But for now our time here is up. All that is left is one last supper with Clive and Elma. Tonight Elma has made a special treat, a South African dish called 'Babote' made from lightly curried mince containing bread squares soaked in egg and milk. What better way to finish!

Except there *is* one even better way of finishing. Some forty kilometres outside Lusaka lies a private game reserve called Chaminuka. It has become a family tradition to spend our last Sunday there before flying out, in order to celebrate all those family birthdays when we're not together with our daughter and family to enjoy them. Chaminuka is a stunningly peaceful place where you can enjoy game drives, boat trips, horse riding, swimming and most importantly a superb lunch.

As we drive back, that huge orange fireball is yet again balanced on the rim of the horizon, marking not just the end of a perfect day, but also the end of an eventful trip. Suddenly it crosses my mind that this trip I haven't caught sight of a hoopoe. The hoopoe is a special bird, beautiful and striking with feathers of black and tan and white and a crest on its head, which it often displays to full advantage. It's also sometimes called the 'sacred' bird. When we've been fortunate to spot one, the presence of God always seems particularly close.

I reflect yet again this trip really might mark the end of it all, the very last African sunset, the very last time in Zambia. The feeling of loss is so painful I almost cry out. So I offer up a silent prayer, if I could just spot one hoopoe, then maybe, maybe . . .

And then there it is! Not immediately, *heavens not even God is that quick!* However, a few hundred yards down the road, "Look, there's a hoopoe, did anyone see it?" I exclaim.

But no-one else in the car did, only me. Yet then I know for certain, God is on the case. We will be back. To finish what we started at Kaputula? To build a school for them at Simooya? To participate in launch ceremonies for both Chilumba and Chibuluma? The sign of the hoopoe has made it clear that we will be back.

Bible teaching states God uniquely equips people for certain tasks. Well, He certainly equipped us to work in Zambia. After all, reading this, now come on, be honest, would you take it on? I rest my case.

And if nothing else, this trip has finally taught us, Africa may well tug at our heartstrings, but it is indeed the place we are privileged to call our second home, the place where our hearts truly belong!

## THE END

# INDEX OF NAMES AND ORGANISATIONS

employed as night-watchman on Kaputula project, also acted as interpreter

**CHEP** – Copperbelt Health Education Project, Kitwe based NGO

**Chileshe Cecilia** – former member of Chep staff

**Chilumba Orphans' Centre** – run by Faith Orphanage Foundation where Starfish has built three classrooms and runs orphan sponsorship programme

**Chipotyo, Mr Mwansa** – foreman on Kaputula building project, also on Building Committee and community liaison with Chep

**'chitenge'** – piece of local material worn by women as wrap around skirt

**Choma** – nearest town to Simooya Clinic Project situated mid-way between Lusaka and Livingstone

**Community Schools** – free schools set up and run by volunteers for orphans and vulnerable children who fall outside the state system of education

**Damson (Chunga)** – former member of Chep staff who co-ordinated Musonda project

**DEB's Office** – District Education Board Office, located in Kalulushi which now has nominal control over community schools

**Dynass (Chituli)** – from Chilumba Orphans' Centre who asked, 'Will you be my mother?'

**ED** – executive director

**Evelyn Lumba** – former member of Chep in charge of Gender and Advocacy

**Faith Lyena** – Director of Faith Orphanage Foundation, also of Chilumba Orphans' Centre

**Faith Orphanage Foundation** – director Faith Lyena, Kitwe based organisation to help OVCs in Chilumba and Solwezi districts

**George** – chef at Kumasamba Lodge, reputedly former High Court judge

**Gibson (Mr)** – head teacher of Kamakonde Community School

**Global Fund** – international fund set up to assist those affected by the HIV Aids epidemic

**Grade seven exam** – exam taken at end of grade seven which allows entry to grades eight and nine and secondary education

**Grade twelve exam** – exam taken at end of secondary education, which qualifies for entry into higher education

**Heart of Africa Mission** – Pentecostal mission located near Kumasamba

**'heffalump'** – nickname of our 4x4 Mitsubishi which suffered breakdown

**Hockley Heath Baptist Church** – funding partner of Kafubu Baptist Church project (see www.hockleyheathbaptist.co.uk)

**Hungry Lion,The** – fast food chain in Zambia

**Ipusukilo Basic School, Kitwe** – government school attended by ex-Musonda pupils sponsored by Starfish

**Ipusukilo Community School, Kitwe** – one of six schools visited

**Isaac Mumba** – member of Chep staff in charge of Health and Safety on Mines

**Jakes, T D** – American preacher often on 'God' channel on Zambian TV

**Joffrey, Mr** – head teacher of Ipusukilo Community School

**Josephine** – centre manager at Chilumba Orphans' Centre

**Kabulangashi** – fish farming project run by Faith Orphanage Foundation

**Kabwe** – town located halfway between Lusaka and Copperbelt, also location of prison where Frederick Phiri was an inmate

**Kabwe, Brenda Naomi** – one of ex Musonda pupils sponsored by Starfish through secondary education

**Kafubu Baptist Church** – rebuilt by Starfish in partnership with Hockley Heath Baptist Church in the UK

**Kai (Dimingo)** – Chep staff liaison with ex-Musonda pupils on secondary school sponsorship scheme

**Kalingalinga** – high density housing township in Lusaka, where Tresford lives

**Kalulushi** – mining town on Copperbelt

**Kamakonde Community School** – near Kitwe, one of six schools visited

**Kamboye, Rebecca** – member of Musonda teaching staff who voluntarily attended grade twelve tuition classes

**Kapenta** – small fish sourced in great quantities from Lake Kariba

**Kaputula Community School** – in Lufwanyama, new school constructed by Starfish

**Kaputula Orphan Carers' Fund (KOC)** – set up to assist struggling families which have taken in orphans in addition to their own children

**Kasanda, Mrs** – member of Musonda teaching staff who received grade twelve tuition

**Kaunda, Dr Kenneth** – first president of Zambia

**Kauseni, Mr and Mrs** – members of Kaputula community who assisted on that project and also instigated Kafubu Baptist Church project

**Kitwe** – Copperbelt town where most of Starfish work is based

**Kruger family:** owners of Kumasamba Lodge

**KTTC** – Kitwe Teacher Training College, government run teacher training centre

**Kumasamba Lodge** – 12kms from Kitwe on banks of Kafue River, provides basic chalet accommodation and meals

**Kushuka, also Bwana Kushuka and Kushuka II** – goats donated to or purchased by us

**Kwacha** – unit of currency in Zambia, approx. K7500 = £1

**Luanshya** – mining town on Copperbelt

**Lufwanyama** – district near Kitwe, location of Kaputula School

**Lulamba Basic School, Kitwe** – government school attended by ex-Musonda pupils sponsored by Starfish

**Lungu, Mutale, Mvuli, Mzimba, Messrs** – government teachers who provided grade twelve tuition for Musonda teachers

**Mbai, Mr Mwape** – project manager of most Kitwe based Starfish projects, also director of Salem Centre for Street Kids

**Mchinka Community School** – near Kitwe, one of six schools visited

**mealies** – sweetcorn or corn on the cob

**Milden Choongo** – Zambian resident in UK, liaison for Simooya Clinic Project

**Mitanto High School** – where Mr Banda sought G12 lessons for teachers, also attended by ex-Musonda pupils on Starfish sponsorship scheme

**Mufulira** – Copperbelt town where we lived 1969 – 1971

**Musonda Community School, Kitwe** – received desks and other materials from Starfish. Sponsored pupils came from here

**Musungaila, Mrs Nakazwe** – former Head of Accounts at Chep

**Mutale, Mr** – new head teacher at Kaputula

**Mwanawasa, Levy** – deceased, former president of Zambia

**Mwewa, Ms Lilian** – member of Musonda teaching staff who received grade twelve tuition

**'mzungu'** – foreigner, generally white person

**NGO** – Non-governmental organisations, aid organisations set up and run without government aid or control, funding generally comes from overseas

**Nkhoma, Mr** – latterly chairman of Kaputula PTA, in favour with Mrs Tembo

**Nkoma, Mr** – deputy head teacher of Kaputula Community School

**'nsaka'** – open grass thatched shelter used for meetings

**'nshima'** - porridge-like food made from ground mealies, staple of Zambian diet, eaten with vegetable or meat relish

**Nyrongo, Mr** – member of Kaputula community and Building Committee who worked on Kaputula project

**OVCs** – orphans and vulnerable children who fall outside the state system of education and for whom community schools cater

**Pastor Bwalia** – liaison for Twatasha Community School

**Pastor Joseph Mwewa (deceased)** – founder of Salem Centre for Street Kids

**Pastor Mweetwa** – pastor in charge of Kafubu Baptist Church

**Phiri, Dr Antoinette** – acting ED of Chep in Alick Nyirenda's absence

**Phiri, Frederick** – former inmate of Kabwe & Lusaka prisons, Starfish provided him with a pair of crutches

**Phiri, Mr Peter** – senior physiotherapist at UTH

**Phiri, Mr Reuben** – Head of Business Studies at Kitwe Business College

**relish** – accompaniment to 'nshima', may be meat, fish or vegetables in sauce

**Rosewood Flats** – self-catering flats located in Kitwe

**Salem Centre for Street Kids** – Kitwe based centre for street kids, also community school which Starfish helped with many projects

**Shoprite** – supermarket chain in Zambia

**Sichamba, Mr Austin** – Area Chairman for Kaputula

**Simasiku, Mr** – pronounced sim-**ah**-see-koo, from Choma DHO who assisted on Simooya clinic project

**Simooya** – village where Milden Choongo grew up, location of clinic project

**Skills Training Centre** – in Kitwe, run by Faith Orphanage Foundation, where older Chilumba orphans receive training in farming, sewing and carpentry

**St Andrew's, Chibuluma** – church under construction near Kitwe, which Starfish has helped with cement and roofing materials

**St Michael's Kitwe** – church we usually attend in Kitwe, also church managing St Andrew's Church project

**Tamara Phiri** – ex-Musonda pupil sponsored by Starfish through secondary education

**Tavern** – beer hall, generally simple one or two roomed brick building

**TBN** – Trinity Broadcasting Network or God channel on Zambian TV

**Tembo, Mrs Annie Mwape** – former head teacher of Kaputula Community School during building project

**Tonga** – tribe prevalent in and around Choma/Simooya area, also language

**Tresford (Mwame)** – first 'starfish' rescued with payment for Aids treatment

**Twatasha Community School, Kitwe** – nursery school, one of six schools visited

**TYFOTAP** – Kitwe based skills training organisation, provided desks for Starfish

**UTH** – University Teaching Hospital, Lusaka
**VSO** – Voluntary Service Overseas
**Wednesday House Group (WHG)** – of St Mary Magdalene, Tanworth in Arden, where Starfish began and became decision making group for Starfish
**Wixleys, Clive & Elma** – ex-Zimbabwean, tenant of tobacco farm close to Simooya project
**ZESCO** – state owned provider of electricity in Zambia
**ZOCS** – Zambia Organisation for Community Schools
**ZCCS** – Zambia Community Schools Secretariat
**ZIBSIP** – Zambia Institute of Business Studies and Industrial Practice

# POSTSCRIPTS

**AUGUSTINE MUMBA:**
Augustine successfully completed his ZIBSIP course in June 2007. Though he expressed a wish to attend university in the UK, he initially headed for Lusaka in search of employment. He was later back in Kitwe making a living doing piece work, writing letters for people living in the compounds.

**CHILUMBA ORPHANS' CENTRE**
Dynass's request for me to 'be her mother' resulted in Starfish setting up an orphan sponsorship scheme in conjunction with the Faith Orphanage Trust, which administers the Chilumba Centre.

To date, some thirty disadvantaged children are sponsored by people in the UK. They receive clothing, shoes and school materials. Dynass became my 'orphan' and so to that extent she got her wish. She is maturing well and is always first to appear when we visit and is very proud of the role she played in bringing help to the community.

In 2008 Starfish commenced building a three classroom block at Chilumba. This is now nearing completion and should be operational in January 2011.

**ST ANDREW'S CHURCH, CHIBULUMA**
Even as this book goes to press, plans are in hand to send a payment through in order for this project to be completed. Hopefully one day we will share a joyful launch day there!

**FREDERICK PHIRI**
Shortly after our visit, Frederick Phiri returned to Kabwe Prison and was released on a Presidential pardon. We later caught up with him at the Good Samaritan Centre in Kabwe, where he was training to become a tailor. After returning to his village, nothing was heard of him for some time.

On our last trip in September 2010, we heard from Benny Bohan that

Frederick Phiri was back in Kabwe for the hearing of his compensation case. Father Bohan did not hold out much hope, since the prison authorities were apparently claiming the accident was Frederick's fault.

Starfish continues, via Father Bohan, to support inmates of Kabwe prison with rations of sugar, powdered milk and cooking oil. We drop supplies off with Father Bohan on our journeys up and down to Kitwe. Due to a lack of insulin, a spoonful of sugar is the only means they have controlling hypos of inmates who are diabetic.

**KAFUBU CHURCH PROJECT:**
After a successful launch, Kafubu church project continues to go from strength to strength. They continue to receive support from time to time from Hockley Heath Baptist Church in the UK.

**KAPUTULA COMMUNITY SCHOOL:**
The school appears to be thriving under the new head Mr Mutale. There are four fully qualified teachers there now and two more promised. To date Starfish has not committed to building there again, but maintains contact through the Kaputula Orphan Carers' Support Programme.

**MUSONDA COMMUNITY SCHOOL:**
Following the dismissal of Mr Banda, a new school was subsequently opened and refurbished by Chep. Starfish desks, tables and chairs were transferred there. When the Zambian government took over the regulation of community schools, both Chep and Starfish involvement with Musonda School ended. Though there has been no further contact with Mr Banda, we understand from pupils still living in Musonda compound that he is still around!

**EX-MUSONDA PUPILS:**
Our commitment to the ex-Musonda pupils being funded through secondary school continues. There are currently eight pupils in grade twelve, their final year, and sitting their final year exams. All eight have aspirations of becoming nurses, teachers, doctors, soldiers, even an electrician. If they do, the dream really will be fulfilled. Once they are in employment, they will help younger children in the family through school.

**SALEM**
Sadly in 2007 the founder of Salem, Pastor Joseph Mwewa, died. Mr Mbai

subsequently took over as Executive Director, but is currently on study leave in South Africa.

The centre is entirely self-supporting and receives no government funding. Its success is due entirely to the wholehearted dedication and commitment of its director, Mr Mbai, and to the devoted members of staff who work there.

Over the years Starfish has provided four classrooms, hammer mill shelter, chicken sheds, toilets and sanitation, fencing and a strong room.

Return visits are always a great pleasure because of the sheer joy and exuberance of staff and pupils alike.

Starfish's latest contribution was to complete the roofing on the new library block.

## SIMOOYA CLINIC PROJECT:
The clinic was completed in 2009 and the nurse's house late in 2010. Both should be operational early in 2011.

## TRESFORD:
Eight years later, Tresford is alive and well. When asked as the longest serving employee of Afya Mzuri to say a few words, he was overjoyed in his praise for what Starfish had done for him. 'I owe my life to Starfish," he said.

His CD4 count is now so high as to make the illness almost non-existent in his body, though it will of course always be there. In fact Starfish no longer pays for his treatment, since the government system of distributing ARVs to clinics has become more reliable.

Tresford still acts as a voluntary counsellor for people learning to live with Aids. Sadly Chilufya never tested and, shortly after this visit, she died.

## CONTRIBUTIONS TO THE WORK OF
# THE TANWORTH STARFISH FUND
### CAN BE MADE TO:
### THE TANWORTH STARFISH FUND
### BELMOOR
### BLACKHEATH ROAD
### WENHASTON
### SUFFOLK
### IP19 9DH

### FOR FUTHER DETAILS CONTACT:
### Moira and Robert Cooke (above address)
### Tel: 01502 478503
### moiracooke@belmoor.plus.com /robert@belmoor.plus.com

**NOTE:** All accounts in this book relate solely to the activities of:
THE TANWORTH STARFISH FUND REG. NO. 1101416
They do not relate to any other charities, registered or otherwise, of a
similar name, whether operating in Zambia or elsewhere.

Lightning Source UK Ltd.
Milton Keynes UK
UKOW020429121011

180130UK00001B/27/P